Renewing a Modern Denomination

Monographs in Baptist History

VOLUME 16

Ours is a day in which not only the gaze of western culture but also increasingly that of Evangelicals is riveted to the present. The past seems to be nowhere in view and hence it is disparagingly dismissed as being of little value for our rapidly changing world. Such historical amnesia is fatal for any culture, but particularly so for Christian communities whose identity is profoundly bound up with their history. The goal of this new series of monographs, Studies in Baptist History, seeks to provide one of these Christian communities, that of evangelical Baptists, with reasons and resources for remembering the past. The editors are deeply convinced that Baptist history contains rich resources of theological reflection, praxis and spirituality that can help Baptists, as well as other Christians, live more Christianly in the present. The monographs in this series will therefore aim at illuminating various aspects of the Baptist tradition and in the process provide Baptists with a usable past.

Renewing a Modern Denomination

A Study of Baptist Institutional Life in the 1990s

Andy Goodliff

FOREWORD BY
Stephen R. Holmes

PICKWICK *Publications* · Eugene, Oregon

RENEWING A MODERN DENOMINATION
A Study of Baptist Institutional Life in the 1990s

Monographs in Baptist History 16

Pickwick Publications
An Imprint of Wipf and Stock Publishers
199 W. 8th Ave., Suite 3
Eugene, OR 97401

www.wipfandstock.com

PAPERBACK ISBN: 978-1-7252-7982-7
HARDCOVER ISBN: 978-1-7252-7981-0
EBOOK ISBN: 978-1-7252-7983-4

Cataloguing-in-Publication data:

Names: Goodliff, Andy, author. | Holmes, Stephen R., foreword.

Title: Renewing a modern denominations : a study of baptist institutional life in the 1990s / by Andy Goodliff; foreword by Stephen R. Holmes.

Description: Eugene, OR: Pickwick Publications, 2021 | Series: Monographs in Baptist History | Includes bibliographical references and index.

Identifiers: ISBN 978-1-7252-7982-7 (paperback) | ISBN 978-1-7252-7981-0 (hardcover) | ISBN 978-1-7252-7983-4 (ebook)

Subjects: LCSH: Baptists—Great Britain—History—20th century | Baptist Union of Great Britain

Classification: BX6276 G66 2021 (print) | BX6276 (ebook)

JANUARY 12, 2021

Contents

Abbreviations

ACCR   Advisory Committee for Church Relations

BCC   British Council of Churches

BMJ   *Baptist Ministers' Journal*

BMS   Baptist Missionary Society

BRF   Baptist Revival Fellowship

BT   *Baptist Times*

BQ   *Baptist Quarterly*

BU   Baptist Union of Great Britain

CCBI   Council of Churches in Britain and Ireland

CTBI   Churches Together in Britain and Ireland

CTE   Churches Together in England

DCRG   Denominational Consultation Review Group

EA   Evangelical Alliance

IJST   *International Journal of Systematic Theology*

JEBS   *Journal of European Baptist Studies*

PRS   *Perspectives in Religious Studies*

RR   *Relating and Resourcing*

TS   *Transforming Superintendency*

URC   United Reformed Church

Foreword

BAPTISTS HAVE NOT ALWAYS been the most self-reflective of Christian traditions. A common rhetorical trope amongst us, indeed, almost glories in our lack of self-reflection: we claim (not altogether without justification) that our life together is a mimetic repetition of the life of the New Testament churches. We assert, alone amongst the historic denominations at least, that we baptise as the apostles baptised, and that we govern our churches as the apostles governed theirs—and if we have disputes about how to order our lives together, they will be solved by a similar practice of discovering, and then imitating, what the apostles did.

I certainly do not want to denigrate this impulse: it is close to the heart of our tradition and, properly put into practice, it is simply right (at least in my view). It creates problems for us however, particularly in two ways. For the first, I reflect on a sermon preached by an elder of my own church, my colleague David Moffitt, just a few days ago in our evening service. Asked to address the topic of a Christian approach to democracy, he began by insisting that the Bible has nothing, nothing at all, to say about democracy. It has much to say about government of course, and from there we might derive some useful ideas that will give us as Baptist Christians something to say about democracy, but the reminder that there are important areas of our lives where there is no Biblical practice to emulate is an important one.

Second, even when there is a Biblical practice to emulate, our basically mimetic approach has often led us to be unreflective about that practice. Because we baptise as the apostles baptised, we too often do not find any need to think about what baptism actually is, or what it accomplishes—older Baptist writers on baptism are surprisingly often simply uninterested in asking what God might be doing, or what might be happening to the candidate, in the rite. On more occasional questions than baptism, this can lead to an insistence on a given practice as Biblical, without any thought at all to what the adoption of the practice might change or lead to in a Baptist community's life.

The intersection of these two problems is perhaps the most dangerous moment for any Baptist community: where there is in fact no Biblical example or guidance, we can too easily seize on a more-or-less plausible attempt to claim this or that way forward as Biblical, and so mandated; when we do so seize on something, we are reflexively conditioned not to query its potential effects on our life together, but to embrace it uncritically, because it is (asserted to be) 'Biblical'.

For a historian, these two limitations are frustrating; for the contemporary Baptist leader, concerned about understanding his or her denominational context, and the limitations and possibilities that it creates, they are in danger of being debilitating—and their intersection is deadly. If we cannot tell our shared story with care and discrimination, we cannot understand what futures might be possible to us; if we cannot tell our shared story with conviction and prophetic insight, we cannot hope to lead our people towards any given future. If we cannot challenge practices that are in fact damaging us, but that are believed to be Biblical, we have no long-term future.

All of which is to say that careful studies of the recent history of any given Baptist denomination, uncovering the tensions and arguments that were being played out behind the rhetoric of appeals to Biblical justifications, and exploring the practical effects of this or that change, are vital to us as Baptists. Not only will they resource in simply invaluable ways the deliberations of those who are called to take the particular community forward; they will also help us all to reflect more carefully on analogous situations in our own Baptist communities.

Andrew Goodliff's study of the Baptist Union of Great Britain in the closing decade of the twentieth century demonstrates all this admirably, and on the basis of careful and meticulous scholarship. Having worked through a mountain of published and unpublished material, he makes a convincing case that almost every debate that touched on denominational change in the period became a contest between those who emphasised mission as the core aim of the Union (with perhaps a more pragmatic lens) and those who emphasised covenant as the core basis of the Union (with perhaps a more theological focus). It would have been easy to represent this debate as missional pragmatism versus theological seriousness, but—as Dr Goodliff is careful to demonstrate—that would be unfair to both sides. Those who emphasised mission were certainly not unserious theologically—Nigel Wright is the most obvious example, but not the only one—and those who emphasised covenant transparently cared deeply for missional success, believing that proper theological renewal was the way to achieve that, as Leonard Champion argued in the key lecture in 1979.

The contest was never vicious—as Dr Goodliff clearly demonstrates, there was a heartening fraternalism (the right word, given the gender of almost everyone involved) between the various players, who never defined themselves against each other, and always shared a commitment to the health of the denomination and to the progress of the gospel in the UK—but the contest was real. Different visions for how the Union should organise itself, and how the denomination should deploy its energy and finances, were at play. Dr Goodliff traces the ways in which these different visions played out in various debates with care, and with empathy to both sides. His work is (thankfully) not polemic; he does not suggest that one side was right and the other wrong. His work is, however, diagnostic, suggesting that the basic problem through the decade was a failure to expose the fundamental decisions at the heart of this or that debate, and so a failure to grapple with fundamental theological questions about what BUGB should be.

I was a member of a BUGB church throughout the period Dr Goodliff considers, training for ministry for most of the first half of it, and an accredited minister, either in pastoral charge, or devoted to theological education, for the second half (not long afterwards I moved to Scotland, and to a different Union). The story that Dr Goodliff tells is, therefore, my story. Not that I was walking then (or now) any denominational corridors of power; I have so far never been present at a BUGB (or Baptist Union of Scotland) Council meeting. My experiential insight is thus limited enough that it offers little evidence concerning Dr Goodliff's thesis, but for what it is worth, the story he tells seems very plausible to me, given my memory of those years.

It happens that my church membership, and my ministerial accreditation, have been within the Baptist Union of Scotland, not BUGB, for the past 15 years, which makes me very loath to comment on how BUGB should organise itself—that is properly the decision for those who are a part of that Union, like Dr Goodliff. I am not, from the sidelines, going to propose a way forward for BUGB; I will however assert that Dr Goodliff's study represents a carefully researched and powerfully analysed account of the recent past of BUGB. It should be read widely within the Union as a source for understanding and so renewal; it should also be read widely beyond BUGB as an insightful account of how faithfully Baptist denominational disputes might play out.

Stephen R. Holmes

Acknowledgments

FROM THEIR EARLIEST DAYS Baptists have spoken of walking together and watching over one another. This book is evidence of that kind of community, which has walked with me and watched over me while this was written, first as a doctoral thesis completed at University of St. Andrews, and then turned into a book.[1]

I would like first to thank Steve Holmes for his supervision and friendship, which has been patient and encouraging. I feel fortunate he was willing to take me on as a student. His commitment and enthusiasm for the task of theology that serves the church is one he has for a long time demonstrated.

I would like to thank also willing friends —Ashley Lovett, Ivan King, Ruth Gouldbourne and Stephen Copson — who took the time to read through the first major draft and in some cases third and fourth drafts too. In addition to these friends, I want to thank my father, Paul, who has always been a willing conversation partner and reader.

My thanks goes to those with whom I had conversations about the period in question and in some cases generously sent me copies of various papers and addresses — David Coffey, Paul Fiddes, Brian Haymes, Keith Jones, Tony Peck, and David Slater. In the case of Brian, he also graciously allowed me to grow my library with various Baptist related texts he had collected over his ministry.

At a crucial point in my studies, I was able to spend a week at a conference at the IBTS Centre in Amsterdam. Here I was fortunate to meet and talk over several evenings with Curtis Freeman. Those conversations helped guide me out of a fog and in the direction of this book. I am very grateful for the time he gave me and the subsequent conversations we have had in Oxford and London since.

1. The title echoes that of Peter Shepherd's study of the John Howard Shakespeare and the Baptist Union in the first part of the twentieth century: *The Making of a Modern Denomination*.

You cannot write a theology PhD without the help of a library. I am grateful then to the libraries at Regent's Park College, Oxford, Spurgeon's College, Luther King House, and the University of St. Andrews. Emma Walsh, Sheila Wood and Emily Burgoyne were especially helpful in giving me access to the vast archive that is held in the Angus Library, at Regent's Park College. Many hours were spent down in the basement reading through the *Baptist Times* and the Minutes of the Baptist Union Council.

Financial support for this PhD has come from the Baptist Union's Further Studies Grant and the Lacey Ashton Trust and I am grateful to both for their generous giving, which helped pay fees, purchase books and travel to conferences.

Early versions of some chapters were presented at the 2014 IBTS conference, held in Amsterdam; the 2016 Baptist Historical Society Summer School, held in Luther King House, Manchester; and the 2017 Hearts and Mind Conference, held at Regent's Park College, Oxford. I would like to thank the organisers, Stuart Blythe, Keith Jones and Anthony Clarke for their willingness to let me present a paper. A small part of one chapter was offered to the first Theology Live day in December 2017, which it was my pleasure to organise with Simon Woodman and Steve Holmes and I look forward to similar days in the future where Baptists can share their research together. Early versions of some chapters have appeared in the *Baptist Quarterly*, *Baptistic Theologies*, *Pacific Journal of Theological Research* and *Gathering Disciples* edited by Myra Blyth and Andy Goodliff (Pickwick, 2017).

A thank you must also go to Belle Vue Baptist Church, Southend-on-Sea where I am privileged to have been the minister since 2010. They have been encouraging of my study and made no fuss as I went on sabbatical in 2018.

Lastly, but most importantly, I'd like to thank my wife Hannah and our three children, Kirsten, Timothy and Kathryn. They've generously put up with me and my ever growing pile of books. Hannah especially has supported me during the years as I've been away at various points or just needed to get on with writing.

Chapter 1

The Road to Renewal

Introduction

THIS BOOK IS A study of the Baptist Union of Great Britain in the 1990s in the context of two streams of thought that emerged in the 1980s.[1] It is also a study of four of the most influential figures of that period. The first is David Coffey, general secretary of the Baptist Union from 1991 to 2006. He brought a clear sense of leadership with purpose to renew and reshape the structures of the Baptist Union in the direction of mission. The second is Nigel Wright, who in 1991 became the leading evangelical Baptist thinker within the union, who presented to Baptists both a challenge to change and a clear proposal for how the union might change. Together Coffey and Wright offered one stream of thought, which I will call *denominational renewal*. The third is Paul Fiddes, the leading Baptist theologian of his generation. As principal of Regent's Park College from 1989 and the chair of the newly inaugurated Doctrine and Worship Committee in 1992, he made several attempts to provide a theological basis for the union with the concept of covenant. The fourth is Brian Haymes, principal of Northern Baptist College and then subsequently, Bristol Baptist College, who collaborated with Fiddes in several books, but was also the chair of the group that produced the report *Transforming Superintendency*, which argued theologically for the necessity of superintendents as pastoral theologians. Together Fiddes and Haymes,

---

1. Churches in membership with the Baptist Union of Great Britain are almost entirely located in England, with around a hundred churches in Wales (generally South Wales) and a small number in Scotland. Both Scotland and Wales have their own national Baptist Unions.

were the key proponents of a second stream of thought, which I will call *theological renewal*. What will become clear is that in giving these names to the different streams, it is not that the first was unconcerned about theology and the second indifferent to the denomination, but it is about emphasis.[2]

These two streams of thought and those associated with them, largely developed independently through the 1980s, before taking a more central place within national discussions of the union, as Coffey, Wright, Fiddes, and Haymes found themselves in key and influential positions. During the 1990s the two streams, their chief thinkers and their views of renew-al—denominational and theological—came into direct conversation as the Baptist Union, under Coffey's leading sought to refashion itself for a new millennium.

This book will seek to tell the story in detail, examine the arguments and give a critical assessment of the decisions taken and not taken by the union up to 2002. What will become clear is that this was a period of great energy, exemplified in the number of reports initiated and published by the union and the far-reaching changes agreed in their wake. Not since the beginning of the twentieth century did the union undergo such transformation.

This is the first detailed study of this period of Baptist history. How-ever we should note three other studies that overlap with some of the same time frame: Ian Randall's *The English Baptists of the 20th Century* provides a helpful narrative of the period against the background of the whole century;[3] Douglas McBain's *Fire Over the Waters* tells the story from an in-sider's perspective up to the mid-1990s, but with the focus on the impact of charismatic renewal among Baptists;[4] and Darrell Jackson's ThD thesis, "The Discourse of 'Belonging' and Baptist Church Membership in Contempo-rary Britain," which looks at the late twentieth century and early twenty-first century from the perspective of understandings of Baptist church member-ship. This includes a look at what he calls the "covenantal discourse" that emerged in the 1980s onward.

The purpose of this study is to examine how one denomination, the Baptists, responded to the issues that all the churches in England and Wales were facing. Among those issues were a decline in church attendance,[5] a

---

2. Alongside these four individuals, other key people involved in the discussions were all men. I have told the story of how in this period women were struggling to be involved in Goodliff, "Women and the Institution."

3. Randall, *English Baptists*.

4. McBain, *Fire Over the Waters*.

5. The literature here is vast, but see Brown, *Death of Christian Britain*; Davie, *Religion in Britain*; and Woodhead and Catto, *Religion and Change in Modern Britain*. For a challenge to that story see Goodhew, *Church Growth in Britain*.

loss of identity in what has been characterized as post-Christendom,[6] and a diverse set of movements within the churches. In terms of the latter, there were growing charismatic and evangelical movements and a changing ecumenical movement.[7] Where the beginning of the twentieth century witnessed the making of the Baptist denomination, the end of the century was asking how might it be renewed for the twenty-first century. What follows is a description and analysis of Baptists that will contribute to the other emerging studies of Christianity in the late twentieth and early twenty-first century.[8]

A Brief History of Baptists

The beginning of churches named Baptist emerged from the context of the English Reformation and in particular the Separatist movement.[9] Prior to being Baptists, they were first Separatists. The Separatists being those who believed the Church of England need further reform. Two groups or streams of Baptist identity emerged in the 1600s, the earliest group were given the name the General Baptists and the later were called the Particular Baptists.[10]

The first Baptist church in England was planted in 1612 with a small congregation led by Thomas Helwys in Spitalfields, London. Helwys and others had returned from Amsterdam where they had been since 1609 due to their Separatists convictions and where they eventually had undergone believer's baptism. Helwys had at this point had been part of a congregation led by John Smyth and it was Smyth first who baptized himself and created the first Baptist church. Smyth and Helwys fell out and Helwys returned to England and the Baptist movement began. Helwys and Smyth were Calvinists who became Arminians, and the best evidence suggests Anabaptist influence on this shift to a more general view of redemption.[11]

The second stream of Particular Baptists emerged independently of the General Baptists in the 1630s. Their origins lie in a congregation that

6. Murray, *Post-Christendom*. Cf. Randall, "Mission in Post-Christendom."

7. See Hocken, *Streams of Renewal*; Bebbington, *Evangelicalism in Modern Britain*; and Hastings, *History of English Christianity*. The relevant sections of the latter are a good guide to ecumenism in England through the twentieth century.

8. See Camroux, *Ecumenism in Retreat*; Voas, "Church of England."

9. See White, *English Separatist Tradition*.

10. For recent one-volume histories of the Baptists see Bebbington, *Baptists Through the Centuries*, Randall, *Communities of Conviction*, and Hayden, *English Baptist History and Heritage*.

11. For an account of the General Baptists see White, *English Baptists of the Seventeenth Century*.

has been named the "Jacob-Lathrop-Jessey church" named after the three successive minsters that led it from a separatist position toward a Baptist one. By 1644 a confession of faith was issued by seven churches in London that were practicing believer's baptism. Unlike the General Baptists, they were "resolutely Calvinist,"[12] believing in particular redemption.[13]

Through the rest of the seventeenth century the two streams of Baptists grew so that by the time they reached the eighteenth century there were 120 General Baptist congregations and 206 Particular Baptist congregations.[14] Although both practiced congregational government, they also had developed associations and forms of translocal ministry, especially among General Baptists in the form of messengers. Despite this growth, during the eighteenth century there was a period of stagnation and decline, partly as a result of theology,[15] until the impact of the emerging evangelical movement renewed Baptist life and growth. The leading figure among the Particular Baptists was Andrew Fuller and among the General Baptists it was Dan Taylor. Fuller's evangelical Calvinism awakened a new evangelistic spirit and with William Carey, the Baptist Missionary Society (BMS) was founded in 1792.[16] Taylor's New Connexion of General Baptists built new structures organized around evangelism and church planting.[17] The Particular Baptists were more independent minded and did not form a union until 1812.

The General and Particular Baptists amalgamated together in 1891 into the Baptist Union of Great Britain and so the institution began to grow.[18] This was not without some dissension. The most famous Baptist of the nineteenth century, Charles Spurgeon, left the membership of the Baptist Union on what he argued was a "downgrade" in evangelical commitment.[19] The basis on which the union was united changed. In 1812, when it was only the Particular Baptists it had united around Calvinistic doctrine. In 1835

12. Bebbington, *Baptists Through the Centuries*, 47.

13. For an account of the history and theology of the early Particular Baptists see Birch, *To Follow the Lambe*.

14. Holmes, *Baptist Theology*, 22.

15. With regards the Particular Baptists, Peter Morden argues that "the theology known as high Calvinism was an extremely significant cause of decline," Morden, "Continuity and Change," 8. Among the General Baptists there were moves toward Unitarianism and this played a part, although Stephen Copson suggests that "the story is more complex than a single cause," Copson, "General Baptists in the Eighteenth Century," 54.

16. On Andrew Fuller see Morden, *Life and Thought of Andrew Fuller*. On the BMS see Stanley, *History of the Baptist Missionary Society*.

17. See Rinaldi, *Tribe of Dan* and Pollard, *Dan Taylor*.

18. See Payne, *Baptist Union* and Briggs, *English Baptists in the Nineteenth Century*.

19. See Hopkins, *Nonconformity's Romantic Generation*, 193–248.

this had moved to "those who agree in the sentiments usually denominated Evangelical." By 1873 there was for the first time a Declaration of Principle which said "that every separate Church has liberty to interpret and administer the laws of Christ." Payne argues that Spurgeon was "deeply troubled" by the union's move away from Calvinism and was not "happy" at the change in the 1873 constitution.[20] From 1883 up to 1887 when he finally resigned from the union, Spurgeon was protesting the perceived "suspect theology among Baptists."[21] In 1887 it came to a climax with a series of "Downgrade" articles, which gave the controversy its infamous name. The union's changing doctrinal basis allowed it to be more inclusive, especially with regards to the General Baptists.[22]

The Baptist Union's chief period of growth was under the leadership of John Howard Shakespeare as general secretary between 1898 and 1924. Peter Shepherd has argued that under Shakespeare we saw the creation of the "modern denomination"[23] that is largely still in place today: a Baptist Union headquarters, a settlement and sustentation scheme,[24] translocal ministry in the form of general superintendents, and an active ecumenical engagement. Shakespeare was deemed to be "the architect of the Baptist Union as we know it,"[25] although in Shepherd's view he was "motivated more by pragmatic concerns than theological ones."[26] The rest of the twentieth century was in some ways a struggle between those who argued for more centralization and those who wanted a more decentralized union, this culminated in the wide ranging discussion and reform that took place through the 1990s that this study will narrate and examine. Ernest Payne was general secretary between 1951 and 1967 and during his tenure, attempts were made to strengthen the union and to see it begin a more ecumenically committed journey.[27] The union had become a member of the World Council of Churches and of the British Council of Churches from their beginnings. One grouping of

---

20. Payne, *Baptist Union*, 132–33.

21. Hopkins, "Downgrade Controversy," 115.

22. For a brief history of the Declaration of Principle and its antecedents see Kidd, *Something to Declare*, 19–24. Cf. Sparkes, *Constitutions of the Baptist Union*, and Payne, *Baptist Union*.

23. Shepherd, *Making of a Modern Denomination*.

24. This scheme was moved toward a nationally accredited ministry through which ministers would be settled in churches and created funds to support—sustain—ministry, where a church might not be able to otherwise afford it.

25. Shepherd, *Making of a Modern Denomination*, xii, citing F. Townley Lord, *Baptist World Fellowship*, 53.

26. Shepherd, *Making of a Modern Denomination*, xv.

27. On Ernest Payne see West, *To Be a Pilgrim*.

conservative evangelical Baptists—the Baptist Revival Fellowship (BRF)[28]—
was a substantial voice against both the perceived power of the union and its
ecumenical openness, and eventually a number of the BRF churches left the
union, following the controversy over an address given by Michael Taylor
on the divinity of Christ at the 1971 assembly of the Baptist Union.[29] This
controversy reawakened an effort among Baptists toward the union holding
a more consciously evangelical faith and played a small part in the creation
of the first stream in the form of a new group called Mainstream in 1979
which I will go on to describe.

How the Baptist Union Operated

The constitution of the Baptist Union in 1979 said that the "Union shall act
by the Assembly, and through the Council."[30] The assembly was an annual
meeting at which delegates from the churches, the associations, colleges, and
all accredited ministers were able to attend. The assembly included an annual general meeting at which the annual report was presented. The council
met two times a year and was made of representatives of the associations,
national officers,[31] and those co-opted. The council discussed the business
of the union through three main committees: the General Purposes and
Finance Committee, the Ministry Main Committee, and the Mission Main
Committee. The other key committee was the Advisory Committee for
Church Relations.[32] The union itself was led by a general secretary and was
comprised of three departments: Administration, Ministry, and Mission.

        This study will argue that 1979 was an important year because it saw
the launch of two new streams which were pushing for renewal, although
with different emphases, that became central to the events in the 1990s. The
key event in the 1990s was the appointment of David Coffey as the new
general secretary in 1991. It was his leadership that lay behind an attempt
to remake a modern denomination for a new century. As a result the 1990s
were a hive of activity within the Baptist Union as it set out to undergo

28. See Hill, *Baptist Revival Fellowship*.

29. Taylor was principal of Northern Baptist College, Manchester, 1969–1985. For
a full account of the controversy see Randall, *English Baptists*, 366–82; Beasley-Murray,
Fearless for Truth, 145–65, and Hill, *Baptist Revival Fellowship*, 99–149.

30. *Baptist Union Directory 1979–80*, 13.

31. One of the national officers was the president of the Baptist Union, which was
an annual position elected by the churches.

32. This committee had been established in 1963 to advise the general secretary, but
did report to council.

reform and renewal. Central to the decade were discussions around a range of questions: who are Baptists? What is the union and how do the associations relate to it? What should be the role of the general superintendents? Should we be ecumenically engaged? In addition there were questions around baptism, ministry, and church planting.[33]

The Key Events of the 1990s

It was apparent from the beginning that Coffey set out to reform the union.[34] Even before taking up his post he and Keith Jones,[35] who had been appointed deputy general secretary, undertook a listening process, visiting all twelve areas of the union.[36] The Listening Day Process, as it was called, was an opportunity for Coffey and Jones to listen to "the Baptist family" and discover the views of those across the union on what the next five years should look like in terms of the role of the Baptist Union. Out of the Process the purpose was to establish a programme for the initial five years Coffey and Jones would be general and deputy secretaries. Alongside that the aim was "to establish a mission statement of the Union."[37] The *Baptist Times* reported the Process as "innovative"[38] demonstrating that the approach of Coffey and Jones was bringing something new to how they understood their roles and what they both later described as taking "very seriously" the way Baptists discern the mind of Christ.[39]

33. On the discussion on baptism see Cross, *Baptism and the Baptists*; on ministry see Goodliff, *Ministry, Sacrament and Representation*; and on church planting see Doel, "Church Planting."

34. In an interview in the Evangelical Alliance bulletin *Idea* in 1990 he said, "I do tend to lead from the front. I'm not a quiet leader," *Idea* (November–December 1990) 11.

35. Jones was deputy general secretary between 1991–1998. In 1998 he took up the post of rector of the International Baptist Theological Seminary. Jones had trained at Northern Baptist College and after one ministry in Barnoldswick, Lancashire, became general secretary of the Yorkshire Baptist Association. Jones described himself as a "radical evangelical," but one with a high view of the ministry of word and sacrament, *BT*, September 19, 1991, 9. See also Whalley, "Life in Christian Service," 1–15. It was Jones who argued for the creation of the Faith & Unity Executive and its Doctrine and Worship Committee.

36. *BT*, March 28, 1991, 16.

37. The Listening Process. Resume of Events so Far. November 1991. Listening Day Box / Angus Library.

38. *BT*, March 28, 1991, 16.

39. Jones, "Towards 2000: Progress to Date."

From these listening days a new agenda was set for the rest of the decade and shaped Coffey's period in office. Later chapters in this study will engage closely with how that agenda unfolded and therefore it is helpful now to provide an overview of the key events that took place within the union from 1991 onward. See appendix 1 for a chronological list.

What emerged out of the Listening Day Process was a document called *Towards 2000*. This was important in terms of agenda setting, especially its Statement of Intent. The Statement of Intent was agreed at the council meeting in March 1992 and it identified four areas which would shape the agenda "on which detailed policy of the Union will be based." The four areas were:

 – To encourage, support, and initiate imaginative and effective strategies in evangelism and other aspects of God's mission.

 – To develop our distinctive Baptist identity.

 – To strengthen our associating by mutual commitment at every level.

 – To promote the greater sharing of people, money, and other resources.[40]

Each area then had a set of aims and objectives. This process set in motion a wide ranging set of reviews, reports, and resources.

In 1995 Coffey and Jones set about a second series of Listening Days.[41] This was an opportunity to revisit the areas of the union, to "report on the progress" of the *Towards 2000* programme and to listen again to the views of associations, ministers, and church leaders. In 2002 Coffey would say that the process had "stalled."[42] Out of the 1995 Listening Days Coffey and Jones reflected on what they heard. First, there was some concern at the amount and speed of change that had been initiated. Coffey and Jones's response was to claim that we are living in a "change of era" and as such change was required. A second concern was that the tone coming from "Didcot"[43] was managerial rather than spiritual. There was a definite shift into a more managerial approach to union life, but Coffey and Jones responded by stressing the importance of listening to God, that they understood their prime task to serve as pastoral leaders, and that they sought to give a focus to worship and prayer in the decision making processes taking place. A third concern was the threat to independency of the church. Coffey and Jones strongly argued for the importance of interdependency and that "it is the neglect of the inter-dependent principle which impoverishes too many fellowships."

40. The Statement of Intent was also affirmed at the 1992 assembly. See *The Baptist Union of Great Britain Annual Report 1992*, 11.

41. Jones, "Towards 2000 Progress to Date," and Coffey, "Listening Day Questions."

42. *BT*, January 3, 2002, 9.

43. Didcot was the location of the union's national headquarters.

The place and role of associations was one they both felt needed reform. A fourth area was around mission and the appropriate resources needed, and fifth was a concern for ministers, both local pastors and superintendents with regard to what is asked of them.

Following the 1995 Listening Days, Coffey and Jones asked the council to hold a denominational conference in 1996, only the third type of event of the century.[44] The denominational consultation was the focus event of the decade, although it was not conceived before 1995. Reflecting in 2006, as he was stepping down as general secretary, Coffey said to the council that the consultation was "born in a climate of despair"[45] indicating "that the next steps were not clear. This was demonstrated by not being able to appoint a new head of the mission department. The purpose of the consultation was fourfold. It sought to address the financial situation, either to deal with a falling income from the Home Mission appeal or to find ways to increase giving.[46] It wanted to respond to what was called the "frustration factor." Coffey and Jones identified that there was deep frustration within the union coming from all directions—local churches and ministers, associations, colleges, and Baptist House staff were all frustrated in different ways with each other. The consultation was an opportunity to name these frustrations and find a way forward. A third reason was to address the "ferment factor." Coffey and Jones saw the discussion of the future of the union had produced wide-ranging contributions, but it had the potential to pull the union apart. They wanted to see the ferment being pushed in the direction of "denominational reform." The fourth factor was the most important, the "mission factor." Coffey and Jones wanted the whole consultation to be a "missiological prism" that was not about doing more evangelism or church planting, but to begin with a "fresh vision of the Missionary God."

Throughout the decade there were noises of dissent with regards the process. An example of which took place at the 1996 Baptist Assembly, a few months prior to the denominational consultation, the Broad Alliance of Radical Baptists organized a seminar called "The Baptist Union: A Time for Dissent?" Four speakers were invited to address the question: Ted Hale, Alison Ruth Goodwin, Ruth Bottoms, and Paul Fiddes. It was Hale, described by the *Baptist Times* as a "notable scourge of the Union,"[47] who was most

44. Coffey, "Denominational Consultation." Previous Denominational Conferences had taken place in 1961 and 1970.

45. Coffey, "Comments from the General Secretary," 3.

46. Finance was and continued to be an ongoing problem. In 1992 ten jobs were made redundant at Baptist House because of a lack of finance. See *BT*, October 1, 1992, 2.

47. *BT*, May 16, 1996, 2.

critical. In his address he argued that the Coffey and Jones were "leading the denomination into navel gazing" and were "claiming authoritative leadership."[48] He accused them also of a "substantial propaganda exercise" and of his concern that the BU Council of "having a life of its own." He concluded, "We do not need leaders who ensure that we all contribute to the same central bureaucracy so that its aims are fulfilled." The criticism was an old one around the union being too centralized and seeking to act beyond its remit. In a written submission to the consultation he says his "firm conviction is that the so-called denominational consultation is not the result of a grass roots movement leading a call for change by the churches of the Union."[49] He argues against the agenda, the theology, and the authority that the council was giving to itself. Hale would go on to be critical of the process through the letters page of the *Baptist Times*.[50]

The Denominational Consultation

Taking place between 6–8 September 1996, the denominational consultation gathered nearly three hundred delegates,[51] with the intention that this broader grouping of Baptists would grasp and shape and direct the vision. Among those three hundred delegates were those who belonged or identified with the two streams of renewal I will describe. From the first stream those involved in Mainstream were Paul Beasley-Murray, Douglas McBain, Peter Grange, Michael Bochenski, Rob Warner, among others.[52] From the second stream Paul Fiddes, Brian Haymes, Roger Hayden, and Richard Kidd were also all present. Ahead of the consultation, individuals, churches, associations, colleges, and other groups were invited to write to the general secretaries and offer their response to the question "What kind of Baptist Union for the 21st Century?" These were all collated and analyzed and a

48. Ted Hale, "Address for BARB Meeting—BU Assembly Fringe 1996." It can be found in *Responses. Denominational Consultation*.

49. Ted Hale, "Dissenting Contribution to the Denominational 'Debate' about a future shape for The Baptist Union," dated May 22, 1996. It can be found *Responses: Denominational Consultation*.

50. Ted Hale, *BT*, February 27, 1997, 11; *BT*, May 22, 1997, 13; *BT*, April 16, 1998, 13; *BT*, April 23, 1998, 16; *BT*, June 11, 1998, 13; *BT*, December 31, 1998, 4; *BT*, February 11, 1999, 13; *BT*, April 8, 1999, 6.

51. "The Consultation was basically an extraordinary meeting of the Baptist Union Council with invited guests. We asked Associations to submit names of suggested guests who might be included," Coffey, "Post 2000—What Kind of Union?," 7. In 2006 Coffey said that many of the guests were those on the fringes of Baptist life.

52. Others included Lynn Green, Stephen Ibbotson, John James, Jane Thorington-Hassell, Roy Searle, Brian Nicholls, Glen Marshall, Viv Lassetter.

summary of responses were sent to all delegates, in addition to *Something to Declare: A Study of the Declaration of Principle*[53] and a set of Bible studies called *Beginning with God*.[54] During the consultation worship was led by the Mennonite Ellie Kreider, who was Tutor in Worship at Regent's Park College, Oxford. Tom Houston, Minister-at-Large for Lausanne Committee for World Evangelization,[55] and Brian Haymes were asked to address the consultation.[56] The rest of the time was spent in small groups through seven sessions. At the end of the third day a statement was agreed to go the Baptist Union Council.[57]

Houston's address focused on the sociocultural context of mission. It centered on the experience of globalization and how this affected institutions. Houston argues that globalization is accompanied by a pluralism of truth, to which the response is either ecumenism or fundamentalism; ecumenism looking to build relationships and fundamentalism a retreat into a closed life. Houston warns of both tensions being present in the local church and the denomination. He goes on to claim that globalization also affects structures. The old structures are being replaced and this is true within the church, with denominations being rejected for new alliances, partnerships, networks or learning organizations. With this also comes leadership, leadership that seeks to find consensus rather than making commands. Houston suggests that Baptists need to be clear what kind of leadership they want. He concludes that there is a need to work out how to be both local and global, which requires flexibility. He ends with saying that he believes that the Baptist Union "could itself become a learning organization, and help all our churches to do the same in their own contexts."[58]

Haymes's address was titled "Towards a Classic Baptist Ecclesiology." He contrasts the difference and tension between the church as movement and as institution. There is a need for both—"every organism needs some form and organization to flourish"[59] and yet there is the danger of the passion to fade and the organization to remain. Haymes suggests that this had

53. This was jointly written by the principals of the English Baptist colleges—Paul Fiddes, Brian Haymes, Richard Kidd, and Michael Quicke.

54. This had been prepared by the Baptist Union's Doctrine and Worship Committee.

55. Houston was an accredited Baptist minister until 1983. He had pastored a church in Scotland and in Kenya, before working for the Bible Society, World Vision, and then from 1989 the Lausanne Committee.

56. It could be argued that Houston represented stream 1, while Haymes represented stream 2.

57. This was shared via the *BT* the following week.

58. Houston, "Overview of the Context for Mission in Society," 5.

59. Haymes, "Towards a Classic Baptist Ecclesiology," 2.

meant that Baptists have always been pragmatic, looking for "the appropriate forms of life that best express the part we have in the mission of God."[60]
He identifies six "recurring emphases" that are part of a classic Baptist ecclesiology: the church as a fellowship of believers; Jesus Christ as the head of
the church; the authority of Scripture; ministry is the gift and calling of God;
associating; and religious liberty. His comments on associating are the most
extended. He says Baptists have from the beginning practiced associating,
and in this no forms have ever been "fixed or final," so, he asks, what is
appropriate today? He highlights that new networks are appearing, this is
both good as Christians work together, but with it comes a danger, that of,
"partisanship and fragmentation in the body of Christ."[61]

The statement that the consultation agreed offered advice around
associating, the union's method of working, finances, justice, leadership,
ministry, mission, and the proposal of a new alliance.[62] It failed to include
anything on ecumenism, although this was added later. The issue of associating was the top priority, with an almost unanimous majority voting for new
ways of associating, for much smaller areas and for increased personnel. In
terms of the union's method of working many wanted to see a more personal method of communicating, with greater listening to the churches, with
a small central office and a smaller deliberative and representative council.
In the area of leadership, strong pastoral and prophetic leadership by the
general secretary, superintendents, and ministers was encouraged, with a
high number also suggesting that the general secretary and superintendents
be released from administration to enable this to happen. In the area of
mission, there was strong call for the union and BMS to have a much closer
relationship, with some suggesting that BMS becomes the "mission arm of
a Federation of British Baptists." Also in terms of mission there was a view
that the mission department should be replaced by regional teams or that
it should be focused on becoming a "training, coordinating resource, with
a prophetic research/development role." Finally, the consultation statement
advised that the union become an alliance, with "light flexible structures,
fewer tiers (that is, the abolishment of Areas) and that superintendents
should be appointed and paid for locally."

Following the consultation the next few years contain a complex story
of the council receiving, debating, and making decisions. As Coffey and
Jones remarked, "We find that keeping people up to date with the progress
of what is happening is a challenging task as the scene is changing all the

60. Haymes, "Towards a Classic Baptist Ecclesiology," 2.

61. Haymes, "Towards a Classic Baptist Ecclesiology," 4.

62. "Denominational Consultation," BT insert, October 3, 1996.

time."[63] At the council in November 1996 the important report *Transforming Superintendency* was presented, but it was not debated until the council in March 1997, by which time the Denominational Consultation Review Group (DCRG) had been established with the task of ensuring "a continuing responsibility for the process and to monitor progress on 'outcomes' of the Consultation."[64] Members of the DCRG were agreed by the council's General Purposes and Finance Committee and it met for the first time in February 1997. They continued to meet and report at each council meeting until March 1999. *Transforming Superintendency* was debated in March 1997, but its proposals were now heard in the wider process of Denominational Consultation. At the same council meeting, it was agreed to recast the Mission Department in the direction of "research and training" and to commission a Task Group on Associating.

Mission had been central to the denominational consultation.[65] The union though had been without a Head of Mission for the Mission Department since Derek Tidball stepped down in 1995 to become principal of London Bible College. One of the suggestions from the denominational consultation advice was to change the mission department into one that was centered on research and training in mission. The Mission Executive brought a proposal, which the DCRG commended, for the new department. The Mission Department as it had been was centered around specialist subject areas (evangelism, social affairs, youth, education), the new department was founded on the importance of "research, evaluation, training and development in holistic mission." By the November 1997 council the DCRG reported again to council, offering a "Guide Interim Statement." In summary, the DCRG said that the process was "moving towards a Union of Baptist communities of faith bound together in covenant for mission to the world, based on mutual trust."[66] The key words here are covenant and mis-

---

63. Coffey, "Guard the Vision."

64. Minutes, Baptist Union Council, November 1996, 14. The members of the group were Tony Peck (convenor), Rosemarie Gotobed, Terry Green, Rachel Haig, Stan Jones, Jane Thorington-Hassell, and Gillian Wood. Peck had been secretary of Yorkshire Baptist Association since 1991 and would in 1998 become a tutor at Bristol Baptist College, and then in 2004 go on to be appointed general secretary of the European Baptist Federation.

65. At one point in January 1997 Coffey was exploring the possibility of the union creating a new body he called the English Baptist Mission. In his thinking this would have sat alongside the union, but may eventually have replaced it. There were those in November and December 1996 inviting Coffey to offer a lead and this was his "big idea." It did not go any further. See Coffey, "The Way Ahead: General Secretary's Report to the SMT 3 January 1997," in Denominational Consultation papers.

66. DCRG Report to BU Council—November, Minutes, Baptist Union Council.

sion, which will be explored in later chapters. At the same council meeting
a report on trans-local leadership was presented. In its report to the March
1997 council, the DCRG had said it agreed that "the issue of leadership is
crucial to all discussions in all areas of our denominational life today." The
Trans-local Leadership report was meant to assist those discussions, but due
to time, it was basically a summary of biblical and recent Baptist reflections.

The March 1998 council was a key meeting, in which the report on
core values was agreed and the report on associating—*Relating and Resourcing*—was discussed alongside that of *Transforming Superintendency*. The
core values report was in some ways intended to be a more minor report
demonstrating the consultation advice that the union be committed to diversity and equality in terms of class, gender, and ethnic justice.[67] In the
report from DCRG in November 1997 it records that there was "confusion"
as whether the task group was asked to offer general core values for Baptists
today or those which were more specific with regard to biblical justice. The
core values report stated that

> our core values must . . . flow from and reflect the nature of God
> as revealed in Jesus Christ . . . These values should determine the
> nature and purpose of the Church . . . We follow Jesus not simple
> as individuals. As Baptists we emphasise the significance of the
> gathered church.[68]

The core values were then listed as being a prophetic community; an
inclusive community; a sacrificial community; a missionary community;
and a worshiping community. The report concluded that this is not all that
could be said and that this was not an attempt to rewrite the Declaration of
Principle, and that the aim, following the Sermon on the Mount was to be
"descriptive rather than prescriptive or programmatic."[69] Peck believed that
it was important "in the process of change in the Union to have a document
on Core Values which we will go on finding challenging, and to a certain

---

November 1997, 33.

67. The group that wrote this report was chaired by former general secretary Bernard Green. Other members included Anne Wilkinson-Hayes, Hilary Wilmer, John
Claydon, Andy Bruce, Stephen Greasley, and Chris André-Watson. The group did not
have any of the key voices from stream 1 or stream 2.

68. *Five Core Values*. Report of the Core Values Task Group for the March 1998 BU
Council, 2.

69. *Five Core Values*, 2.

extent disturbing."[70] The council agreed the report "unanimously" and it was published later that year as *Five Core Values for a Gospel People.*[71]

DCRG called *Relating and Resourcing* a "pivotal document" and should act "as a filter through would other Reports and initiatives might be viewed and acted upon." It had superseded the *Transforming Superintendency* report. This highlighted that the reform of associating was the top priority of the consultation.

Between April and July 1998, a series of focus days took place in the twelve areas of the union. This was another attempt at listening, but the denominational consultation process and the reports *Relating and Resourcing* and *Transforming Superintendency* were clearly now the focus of discussion. The outcomes of these days fed into a special council meeting in September 1998.

The September 1998 council saw several resolutions agreed arising from the *Relating and Resourcing* report.

1. Churches are encouraged to make a new start with regard to associating, by identifying both Baptist and other traditions to build mutually supportive relationships, clusters, and networks.
2. At the same time to see the continuing value of larger structures in regional and national forms acting as sources of missionary vision and challenge for discerning the mind of Christ, and as providing resources, support, and the means for remaining connected to one another at wider levels.
3. The reform of the council.
4. A final resolution committed the existing associations to "undergo substantive reform."

At the November 1998 council further decisions were made:

1. The creation of a National Pastoral Team and a National Mission Forum.
2. The primary purpose of associations was defined as the fulfilling of Christian mission through its member churches.
3. That associations should be recast as regional associations, approximately fourteen to sixteen in number.
4. In every association a leadership team would be formed comprising a variety of ministries, led by a senior regional minister, with the team

70. Letter to David Coffey from Tony Peck dated August 21, 1997. DCRG Papers.

71. Myra Blyth called it a "best seller" because of the number of copies sold. Blyth, *Pilgrim People*, 6.

responsible for leading the churches in mission, through pastoral care, general oversight and promoting and encouraging clustering.

On 13 March 1999, the National Baptist Leaders' Day was held at Wembley.[72] The day was an opportunity to explain the purpose of reform, a picture of reform, a plan for reform and how to participate in reform. There were addresses from David Coffey, Lynn Green, Brian Haymes, Tony Peck, and Nigel Wright. The plan for reform was described as being centered on the renewal of the local church, the renewal of relationships, the renewal of ministry and the renewal of mission. With each of these four areas of renewal, a key document was associated—*Five Core Values, Relating and Resourcing, Transforming Superintendency,* and *Research and Training in Mission.*

Following the day a series of Wembley Questions appeared in the *Baptist Times* in the autumn. The questions had been raised on the day but there had not been time to give answers. Coffey argued for the spiritual foundations of the reform process, noting the *Beginning with God* booklet and the more recent *Five Core Values.*[73] Wright argued that the proposed changes to associations were about simplifying structures so that they might be able to resource churches. At the same time with larger regional associations, he recognized the importance of the proposed clusters and networks that the churches might benefit from mutual relationships.[74] Coffey stressed that the reforms did not affect the independence of the local church, but were about "refresh[ing] existing patterns of interdependency."[75] Other topics covered in the series were on the concept of clustering,[76] finance,[77] mission,[78] ministry,[79] ecumenism,[80] justice and ethics,[81] leadership,[82] and on the timetable and implementation.[83]

At the 2001 assembly there was a special covenant service, which had also been shared with all Baptists in the form of a booklet called *Covenant 21.* Coffey reflected that *Covenant 21* and *Five Core Values* "were perhaps

72. This had been planned from 1997. See *Baptist Leader* 16 (Spring 1997).
73. *BT*, September 23, 1999, 11.
74. *BT*, September 23, 1999, 11, 13.
75. *BT*, September 30, 1999, 11.
76. *BT*, September 30, 1999, 11.
77. *BT*, October 7, 1999, 11.
78. *BT*, October 28, 1999, 12.
79. *BT*, November 4, 1999, 4.
80. *BT*, November 11, 1999, 11.
81. *BT*, November 18, 1999, 7.
82. *BT*, November 25, 1999, 4.
83. *BT*, December 2, 1999, 13.

the first moment in the journey of reform when local churches caught the vision of what we were seeking to do."[84] He said that *Covenant 21* should be understood as a "spiritual expression to the restructuring of the Union."[85] *Covenant 21* was therefore the last final public act that gathered the journey of renewal together as "a sign of this new beginning in our Union."[86]

On January 1, 2002, the new structures of the Baptist Union were initiated. Out went twenty-nine county associations and in came twelve (later thirteen) regional associations.[87] Out went twelve general superintendents, officers of the union who had oversight of twelve (geographical) areas and in came thirteen regional ministry teams led by a team leader for each regional association. These regional ministry teams were now appointed and paid for by their respective region. Alongside these structural changes was a union that viewed itself through a missionary lens following a missionary God, relating and resourcing missionary congregations. The *Baptist Times* editorial called it "the completion of an historic process,"[88] at the same time recognizing that there were reforms still to potentially follow.

Coffey wrote at this beginning that from 1996 the number of baptisms had increased, church planting had increased, church attendance had increased, and that growth in "tough places" was also taking place.[89] Having told the story of renewal, Coffey went on to reflect that as well as being about a renewal of structures, it had also been about spiritual renewal: "We are not merely talking about organizational restructuring, but about hearts on fire with a love for Jesus and a care for his world." While there had been criticism of Coffey and the union for its embrace of a management style, Coffey, with his Keswick background, always stressed the need for spiritual renewal. He argued that the new beginning "deserves a good launch" and that this would be a "decade of experimentation." He said that with these structures the key word will be "trust" from churches, colleges, and associations. He commended the importance of clustering at a local level among churches. He concluded, "My hope and dream is that Baptists will realise that we are being given the kind of opportunity that comes along once in a lifetime to make a new beginning."

84. *BT*, January 3, 2002, 9.

85. *BT*, January 4, 2001, 1.

86. Coffey, "Covenant 21."

87. In 2006, the South East Baptist Partnership became the South East Baptist Association.

88. *BT*, January 3, 2002, 5.

89. *BT*, January 3, 2002, 9. See appendix 3 for figures.

David Coffey: Developing a Mission Mentality

As is clear from the account above at the center of the story was David Coffey. He was in the "hotseat."[90] (The other three people mentioned at the beginning of the chapter will be introduced in the next chapter.)

Coffey, born in 1941, was the son of a Baptist minister, Arthur Coffey. Arthur was involved in bringing Billy Graham to the UK for the first time in 1946 and it was at a Billy Graham rally in 1954 that David made his first commitment to Christ.[91] He felt a call to ministry in 1959 while attending Keswick as a teenager and eventually went to train at Spurgeon's College in 1963.[92] After college he ministered in Leicester and North Cheam and then from 1980 at Upton Vale, Torquay.[93] During his time at North Cheam, Coffey was connected into many of the emerging developments around the Church Growth Movement and charismatic renewal as well as staying connected to Spurgeon's.[94] He attended the first British Church Growth Conference and also conferences organized by David Pawson on charismatic renewal.[95]

Coffey's name became well-known through his association with Mainstream and through being a member of the union's council from 1979.[96] Coffey's profile increased through his appointment as the Baptist Union's president in 1986 followed by becoming the Baptist Union's Secretary for Evangelism in 1988.[97] His year as president and then his relatively short tenure as the Secretary for Evangelism reflected twin emphases of his period as general secretary. The theme of his year as president was bridge-building. In his presidential address Coffey saw four concerns: schism and division within the local church; misunderstanding and caricature between the various traditions within the denomination; an ecumenism too small, that is, it was not reaching out to other evangelicals and those in the "house church" movement; and a concern for evangelism to the world.[98] As general secretary

90. *BT*, May 9, 1991, 7.

91. Coffey, foreword to *Mission in the New Millennium*, 5.

92. Coffey was the first general secretary who had trained at Spurgeon's.

93. He was minister at churches in Whestone, Leicester (1967–1972), North Cheam, Sutton (1972–1980), and Upton Vale, Torquay (1980–1988).

94. He joined the College Council in 1975 and was president of the College Conference in 1983.

95. See Coffey, "Mainstream 20th Anniversary Edition," 3. Cf. McBain, *Fire Over the Waters*, 108.

96. Coffey was secretary of Mainstream from its beginning in 1979 to 1984.

97. Tom Rogers had been appointed Secretary of Evangelism in 1985 but died in 1987 from cancer.

98. Coffey, *Build That Bridge*, 1–2.

he sought to be a bridge within the union ecumenically (especially to other evangelical groupings) and to encourage the union to be mission-minded, which of course was reflected in his time as Secretary for Evangelism.[99]

His nomination and appointment as general secretary alongside that of Keith Jones as deputy general secretary was greeted with high expectation. They were called a "dream ticket." Morris West,[100] who had chaired the nominating committee said,

> As general secretary there was a need for someone with proven
> gifts of leadership, someone possessed of deep spirituality, an
> openness of mind and heart to Christians of other denomina-
> tions and a commitment to mission. The committee believes
> David Coffey possesses such gifts.[101]

Like his predecessor, Bernard Green,[102] Coffey was a local pastor. Previous general secretaries Ernest Payne and David Russell had been scholars. Payne, a college tutor, and Russell, a college principal.[103] With Green, and then Coffey, the union appointed pastors with proven experience and national recognition.

Coffey, more intentionally than his more recent predecessors, saw the role of general secretary as an opportunity for leadership. While this required building bridges between different views within the union, this did not hinder his attempt to lead and pull the Baptist Union toward a new future. Although in 2006 he would say: "I think if I have had any intellectual battle to face in my term as General Secretary it is getting Baptists to agree on this issue of leadership."[104] Coffey benefited in part from some of

99. "My three years in the Mission Department were an outstanding preparation for my present ministry. It created the unshakeable conviction that the renewal of the church in missionary purpose is more than a programme in evangelism and social action," *BT*, April 28, 1994, 7.

100. W. Morris West had been a central figure within the union for a long time, chairing both the search committee that appointed Bernard Green and Douglas Sparkes, as well as the committee that nominated David Coffey and Keith Jones. He was principal of Bristol Baptist College between 1971–1987. He joined the council first in 1958 and would remain a member until 1999. See "The Revd Dr Morris West," in West, *Baptists Together*, 2–13.

101. *BT*, March 15, 1990, 3.

102. For a brief account of Green, see the (online) *Baptist Times* obituary written by Douglas Sparkes, http://www.baptist.org.uk/Articles/369911/The_Revd_Bernard.aspx.

103. See West, *To Be a Pilgrim*, for an account of Ernest Payne's life, and see Rusling, "David Syme Russell: A Life of Service," and Clements, "Profile: David Russell," for reflections on Russell.

104. Interview with Clive Burnard in April 2006. See Burnard, "Transformational Servant Leadership," appendix 4, v.

the turbulence, the "ferment," in the union between the 1960s to the 1980s having being left behind. The 1960s began a period of theological tension, partly over Baptist involvement in ecumenism,[105] and this came to a fore following the 1971 Baptist Assembly and an address by Michael Taylor, in which it was felt he questioned the divinity of Christ.[106] This cast a shadow over David Russell's tenure as general secretary as he sought to deal with the fallout.[107] Into the 1980s, Bernard Green as general secretary found himself dealing with the growing impact of the house church movement,[108] the charismatic movement and the ecumenical inter-church process.[109] Speaking ahead of his period in office, Green said, "It concerns me that in recent years we have too often been polarised and divided—we have each tried to corner the truth into our own narrow compartments."[110] By the 1990s, the union had jointly moved its headquarters with BMS to Didcot[111] and had voted to join the new ecumenical instruments the Council of Churches in Britain and Ireland (CCBI) and Churches Together in England (CTE) and the group most advocating change, Mainstream, had moved into positions to make change happen. Furthermore the charismatic movement had become more mainstream and relations with the house church movement had settled down.[112]

Coffey was a charismatic and evangelical leader and in this he differed from his immediate predecessors and also embodied the resurgence of evangelical and charismatic Christianity that had begun in the 1980s, through the leadership of the likes of Clive Calver at the Evangelical Alliance (EA),[113] and with it the rise of Spring Harvest, March for Jesus, and into

105. This came from largely from the Baptist Revival Fellowship, which at one point had a membership of over 1,000, of whom 440 were ministers, Randall, *English Baptists*, 326. For more see Hill, *Baptist Revival Fellowship*.

106. On this see Hill, *Baptist Revival Fellowship*; Randall, *English Baptists*, 365–82.

107. Russell said "that on occasion the General Secretary's chair has felt like the saddle of a bucking bronco," Russell, *In Journeyings Often*, 15.

108. On that see Millward, "Chalk and Cheese?," 436–39.

109. Randall, *English Baptists*, 444–51.

110. *BT*, October 8, 1981, 1, 16.

111. A joint headquarters for BU and BMS had been first suggested as early as the 1930s. For the story of this move see Sparkes, *Offices of the Baptist Union of Great Britain*.

112. Terry Virgo, leader of New Frontiers, where the most tensions had been between Baptists and the house church movement, had a much better relationship with Coffey than with Green. Virgo had been mentored for a while by Arthur Coffey. See Virgo, *No Well Worn Paths*, 23.

113. Coffey was on the EA Council of Management alongside other Baptists like Robert Amess, Derek Tidball, and Rob Warner.

the 1990s the Alpha course.[114] He was the first general secretary who was a member of the EA, a speaker at Keswick[115] and at Spring Harvest. In this he had good credentials in the evangelical world, as well as being comfortable within charismatic worship, with which many Baptist churches identified. Brian Stanley has described Coffey as a "conservative evangelical,"[116] which in the particular version was becoming the mainstream of evangelicalism: open to charismatic renewal and the ecumenical movements, concerned with mission, evangelism, and embodying an activist spirit.[117] However, it should also be said that Coffey's reading habits and spirituality went beyond a narrow conservative evangelicalism.[118]

He approached his time as general secretary with a strong sense of purpose to initiate and oversee the reform of the Baptist Union in a more intentionally missional direction: "I personally knew there was even a bigger task of leadership which was to envision where the Union needed to be for the twenty-first century, this meant we needed to care for the existing structures while casting a vision for a new way of being."[119] From the beginning of his appointment in 1991 right through to his final year as general secretary in 2006, Coffey was someone encouraging and challenging Baptists in Britain to put mission at the center. His chief passion he said in 1991 was "to ensure that the denomination develops a mission mentality, rather than a maintenance one."[120] In the same interview he also speaks of having a "strong interest in worship."[121] This is an indication that the renewal he hoped would be realized would be both structural and spiritual. "There is no better way to lead the local church into renewal of its mission than

114. For one assessment of evangelicalism in this period see Warner, *Reinventing English Evangelicalism.*

115. He spoke at Keswick in 1991, 1993, and 1996. See Rowlandson, *Life at the Keswick Convention,* 181–82.

116. Stanley, *Global Diffusion of Evangelicalism,* 45.

117. It was embodied in the entrepreneurialism of Calver and the theology of John Stott. On Stott see Chapman, *Godly Ambition.*

118. "He still continues to read widely and deeply," *Spurgeon's College Record,* 96 (Autumn 1990) 1. The *Baptist Leader* gives a flavor of Coffey's choice of reading. It included books by David Bosch, Eugene Peterson, Stephen Covey, Kennon Callahan, Walter Brueggemann, Lyle Schaller, Nick Pollard, Eddie Gibbs, and Philip Yancey.

119. Burnard, "Transformational Servant Leadership," appendix 4, ix.

120. *BT,* May 9, 1991, 7. In a similar way, Nigel Wright said, "Baptist identity needs to be transposed into the key of mission, by which I mean evangelism, social action and the struggle for justice," *BT,* February 27, 1992, 8.

121. From 1990–1995 Coffey was chair of Baptist World Alliance Baptist Worship Study Commission.

by the way of worship."[122] This is reflected also in the way he spoke about the need for "deepening of our spiritual relationship with our Lord" which would "give birth to the new missionary church for the 21st century."[123] Coffey's understanding of renewal was shaped by the work of the American Methodist Howard Snyder, who argued that there were "five dimensions to renewal": personal, corporate, conceptual, structural, and missiological.[124] Synder said that if renewal was to be genuine it required both the personal and corporate, and if it was to be long lasting it needed to be conceptual and structural. Coffey's vision for Baptists was that the ten-year plan toward 2000 would see Baptists renewed in each of the five ways. By 1992 Coffey was speaking of the necessity of "radical reform" in the union's structures "in order to make its mission more effective."[125] In 1998, in the midst of the intense discussion reforms taking place he would say, "What is required for the true missiological reformation of the Church at the end of the 20th century, is not a modest tinkering but a radical re-invention."[126]

Coffey believed that "we are facing a critical turning point in the history of the Union." Reform was necessary because of what he saw were huge changes taking place in the world, in which the church was being slow to respond and with it a steady decline in church attendance.[127] In the 1994 Union Annual report Coffey drew attention to the work of Lyle Schaller, who had argued that growing denominations should be less about regulation and more on resourcing "organised around support for mission."[128] Looking ahead to the denominational consultation he said, commenting on the November 1995 council:

> We registered the comments of the respected missiologist David Bosch: "We have truly entered into an epoch fundamentally at variance with anything we have experienced to date."[129]

122. Coffey, "Journey Thus Far," 6.

123. *BT*, April 28, 1994, 7.

124. See *Baptist Union of Great Britain Annual Report 1991*, 11–12. Cf. *BT*, September 23, 1999, 11.

125. *BT*, March 5, 1992, 8.

126. Coffey, "Mainstream 20th Anniversary Edition," 6.

127. See appendix 3 for Baptist numbers.

128. *Baptist Union of Great Britain Annual Report 1994*, 10, citing Schaller, *21 Bridges to the 21st Century*. Schaller was an American church consultant.

129. Coffey, "Denominational Consultation," citing Bosch, *Believing in the Future*, 1.

In this Coffey saw the work of God: "I respond by saying that this shaking of our Union and its structures is God's hand upon us to make us a people who are better equipped for Mission!"[130]

Coffey's constantly spoke of mission, which he defined in 1992 as meaning "church planting and evangelism, social action and prophetic protest, a world mission commitment and a Kingdom of God awareness of international affairs and environmental concerns."[131] However, arguably it was evangelism that drove Coffey and especially as churchgoing was declining.[132] So in the same article that he gave the definition of mission above he also said, "The first priority for our churches is evangelism and other aspects of God's mission." In 1994 he recommended Walter Brueggemann's *Biblical Perspectives on Evangelism*.[133] At the end of 1999 he was recommending Nick Pollard's *Beyond the Fringe: Reaching People Outside the Church*[134] and in March 2000 he addressed the council on "thoughtful evangelism."[135]

Having provided something of the events of the 1990s, the next two chapters will step back and describe the emergence of the two streams in the 1980s and the different sources that they were working with. This will then be followed by a critical reengagement with the events of the 1990s through the lens of mission and identity, ecumenism, superintendency, and associating.

130. Coffey, "In the Unshakeable Kingdom."

131. Coffey, "Towards 2000," 8.

132. In 2006 in his Dr. George Beasley-Murray Memorial Lecture he said, "I discern that the English Church overall is in deep trouble with persistent decline, serious denominational disintegration and social marginalization," Coffey, "Missionary Union," 94.

133. Coffey, "Outsider, the Insider and the Young."

134. Coffey, "Beyond the Fringe."

135. *BT*, March 30, 2000, 7, 12.

Chapter 2

Streams of Renewal

At the Baptist Assembly in 1979 two streams were initiated. The first was called Mainstream and it held its first fringe gathering. The second began in a lecture delivered by Leonard Champion to the Baptist Historical Society from which a small group would subsequently gather. The first was intentional and organized. The second was responsive to a call from Champion. Both streams were concerned with renewal. Mainstream was largely focused on the renewal of the denomination, its churches, and its structures. The second stream was mainly focused on theological renewal that would undergird and nourish Baptist life. This chapter will describe and compare how these two streams began and developed through the 1980s and the places in which they interacted.

Stream 1: Denominational Renewal—Mainstream

In October 1978, a press release was issued from Mainstream: Baptists for Life and Growth. Mainstream was described as those "standing in the mainstream of Christian life in general and Baptist life in particular." They were committed to encouraging and supporting "every venture that will lead to further life and growth." A fringe meeting at the 1979 Baptist Union Assembly and a residential conference in January 1980 were mentioned, alongside the promise of a newsletter and other publications.

The origins of Mainstream can be traced to the previous year through an intervention by Douglas McBain, (then minister at Lewin Road Baptist Church in South London), supported by Paul Beasley-Murray, (then minister at Altrincham Baptist Church, Manchester) at the 1977 Baptist Union Assembly during the session on the annual report of the Baptist Union.

McBain was concerned by a line in the report that mentioned continuing decline in Baptist membership and baptism without any response to reverse it.[1] The forcefulness of their intervention, not a normal experience at the assembly, resulted in the assembly delegates asking that the BU Council set up a commission "to examine the causes of numerical and spiritual decline in the denomination."[2] The result of which was the BU report *Signs of Hope*.[3] Following the assembly McBain wrote a series of three articles for the *Baptist Times*, which analyzed what he understood were the reasons for decline and also some "grounds for hope."[4] He expanded on these thoughts with one final article published in the *Fraternal*,[5] "Survival or Growth?" In this article he identified an emerging new evangelicalism that trusted in Scripture, saw the need for social involvement, was open to the charismatic movement and to ecumenism, and sought to combine heart and head.[6] It was this kind of evangelicalism which Mainstream would embody and which would come to dominate Baptist life into the 1990s. The article ends with some comments that would be significant for later discussions. He argues for a decentralized Baptist Union, with the central organization existing as a "service agency" and a "catalyst for fresh ideas" and a superintendency that would include "skilled itinerants to assist in evangelism and also stimulating church growth."[7]

McBain and Beasley-Murray, who had not known each other prior to that assembly, continued to talk and in February 1978 they met at the home of Raymond Brown, at Spurgeon's College (where Brown was then principal) and at this point Mainstream as an idea was born.[8] A second meeting with a wider group took place during the 1978 Baptist Union Assembly in

1. The report said, "After a relatively small decline in membership last year it is disappointing to note the much greater decline this year. In line with membership figures the number of children, young people and baptisms have decreased . . . respectively. Falling birth-rate apart, these figures reflect this country's continuing drift from Christian influences over the last two generations," *Baptist Union Annual Report 1976*, 11. See appendix 3 for statistics of Baptist church membership from 1968–2002.

2. McBain, *Fire Over the Waters*, 83. Cf. *BT*, April 28, 1977.

3. *Signs of Hope*. It was presented to Baptist Union Council in March 1979.

4. *BT*, May 5, 1977, 2; *BT*, May 12, 1977, 5; *BT*, May 19, 1977.

5. The *Fraternal* was the name of the journal of the Baptist Ministers' Fellowship, it was renamed the *Baptist Ministers' Journal* in 1992.

6. McBain, "Survival or Growth?," 14.

7. McBain, "Survival or Growth?," 16, 18.

8. McBain records he received a number of letters from ministers in support of his action at assembly, including from Derek Tidball, McBain, *Fire Over the Waters*, 83.

April,[9] followed by another meeting in Gorsley in September,[10] from which Mainstream was up and running and the October press release was issued. It was at the September meeting that the name Mainstream was chosen, suggested by McBain.[11] The first newsletter appeared in March 1979 and the official public launch took place at the 1979 Baptist Union Assembly in April. This saw between six hundred and seven hundred people attend, reflecting either curiosity or an appetite for something new. A *Baptist Times* article on the launch was positive and mentions that Brown "hoped" Mainstream would contribute to the denomination in the same way that evangelicals had among the Anglicans.[12]

The minutes from the January 1979 planning meeting indicate that eighteen people were present, with thirteen apologies.[13] The minutes report that Brown had contacted the BRF to inform them about Mainstream indicating that they were not in competition.[14] Brown had also spoken to David Russell, the then Baptist Union general secretary, explaining the vision of Mainstream. Brown emerges as the most important figure in these very early days, by virtue of his position within the union as principal of Spurgeon's College.[15] He gave Mainstream credibility, along later with Barrie White, principal of Regent's Park College, in the wider Baptist constituency.[16] The minutes also report that while a doctrinal basis for Mainstream was discussed, it was thought it would be better to "align ourselves wholeheartedly" with the Baptist Union's Declaration of Principle. That meeting also agreed

9. Those in attendance with McBain, Beasley-Murray, and Brown were Peter Grange, Clifford Roseweir, and Patrick Goodland, see Goodland, "Mainstream Reflections," 16.

10. Patrick Goodland was minister at Gorsley Baptist Chapel from 1976 to 1994.

11. Ramsbottom, "Mainstream Memories."

12. *BT*, May 3, 1979, 4.

13. The eighteen present included Beasley-Murray, Brown, Goodland, Grange, Stephen Ibbotson, Lewis Misselbrook, and Nigel Wright. Apologies were received from David Coffey, David Pawson, Jim Graham, Tom Houston, Michael Quicke, among others.

14. Although by this point the influence of the BRF in the wider Baptist Union had waned. See Hill, *Baptist Revival Fellowship*.

15. Brown was a church historian by training, although he also wrote a number of popular commentaries.

16. In a tribute to Brown, when he stepped down as principal of Spurgeon's College, David Coffey wrote, "I venture to suggest that history will judge that Raymond Brown's early advocacy of Mainstream in the later 1970s was one of the important contributions to the increasing confidence in Baptist structures that have emerged in recent years . . . Ray's open identification with Mainstream was particularly courageous as a vital factor in establishing its credibility within the denomination," *Spurgeon's College Record* 82 (Summer 1986) 5.

the aims of Mainstream, which were then shared in the first newsletter. They are very close to the October press release, focusing on "every venture that will lead to further life and growth within the Baptist Union" and a "whole-hearted commitment to the gospel as expressed in the Union's declaration of Principle"[17] and to the "life and work of the denomination." Mainstream was begun by those who were committed evangelicals, but they deliberately did not use the word evangelical in order "to be inclusive."[18] The structure of Mainstream was agreed to have a small executive and larger council. The first appointments to the executive were agreed as Raymond Brown as president, Patrick Goodland as chairman, Clifford Roseweir as secretary,[19] Peter Grange as treasurer,[20] joined also by McBain and Beasley-Murray. The executive was joined by Jack Ramsbottom[21] as conference secretary in 1979 and in January 1980 by Barrie White.[22]

At the first Mainstream Conference in January 1980, the speakers were Barrie White, Tom Houston, and Lewis Misselbrook, with a celebration led by McBain and a communion service by Brown.[23] Beasley-Murray also spoke on "Grass roots growth." This reflected the different emphases of Mainstream. Raymond Brown was the traditional conservative evangelical,[24] Houston and Beasley-Murray reflected evangelicals who supported the insights of the Church Growth Movement and McBain represented the charismatic evangelicals. White represented a broader evangelicalism, what David Bebbington has called a "centrist school."[25] The strength of Mainstream was its ability to unite evangelicals together with a positive attitude to being

17. Paul Beasley-Murray says the wording of this phrase "had shades of the Christological debate in the early 1970s," Beasley-Murray, *This Is My Story*, 93. This debate was formally closed by a 1972 resolution at the assembly which interpreted article one of the Declaration of Principle as stating firmly "the fundamental tenet of the Christian faith that Jesus Christ is Lord and Saviour, truly God and truly man." The controversy was still very much in the background and consciousness of the union, especially those who were more conservative evangelicals.

18. Beasley-Murray, *This Is My Story*, 93.

19. By December 1979, the secretary became David Coffey, following Roseweir's resignation due to ill health. Coffey had been "persuaded" by Raymond Brown, see Coffey, "Much Loved throughout Our Churches," 5.

20. Grange had trained for ministry alongside Beasley-Murray at Northern Baptist College.

21. Ramsbottom was minster at Kidlington Baptist Church. His wife was PA to White at Regent's Park College, Clarke and Fiddes, *Dissenting Spirit*, 159.

22. McBain, *Fire Over the Waters*, 109.

23. For a report on the conference see *BT*, February 7, 1980, 13.

24. Brown was a regular speaker at the Keswick convention.

25. Bebbington, *Evangelicalism in Modern Britain*, 251.

Baptist. This was certainly the case with White's involvement. McBain says this was a "significant addition . . . indicating the potential breath of Mainstream and showing that it was no mere extremist fringe."[26] This signifies that Mainstream was not merely another BRF, for White was certainly not a conservative evangelical.[27] They were self-consciously evangelical and at the same time they understood themselves not as a protest group against the denomination, but a progressive group, wanting to renew the union.[28] Denominational renewal was its focus. This new evangelicalism was open to the charismatic movement, activist and innovative in contrast with an older more conservative evangelicalism that was concerned with doctrinal questions.[29] It was an evangelicalism that Mainstream recognized as being the mainstream of Baptist life,[30] and as the 1980s went on, they believed needed to be more representative within the union's structures. There was perhaps a deliberate desire to avoid becoming like the BRF which had been the largest evangelical presence between 1930–1970. The BRF became a protest group and made little change. Phil Hill concludes that the BRF's leadership were "insufficiently engaged in denominational life so that its policies were by turns incompetent, naïve and arrogant, despite the Fellowship's spiritual vigour, vision for mission, and high ideal of Baptist renewal."[31] Mainstream, in name and in practice, would go on to realize many more of its goals, and as a result to a larger extent changed the BU into its likeness.[32]

26. McBain, *Fire Over the Waters*, 109.

27. He would call himself a "simple bible believing Christian"; see Fiddes, "Rev Dr Barrington White," 67. Fiddes in private conversation suggested that White's involvement was partly to do with his recognition it was important to position the college as being evangelically friendly. Of Regent's, White said, "The Regent's tradition has always been committed to a thoughtful and reflective evangelicalism which holds fast to the Gospel and proclaims its fullness," White, "Beginning of an Exciting New Era," 3. Rex Mason said of White, "The people in our Churches trust him and appreciate his role as a 'bridge-builder' across all kinds of divide. This has led to greater trust in the College and its special role in training ministers in a true evangelical tradition," Mason, "End of an Outstanding Principalship," 2.

28. "Is Mainstream Evangelical? Yes, certainly. The life and growth we desire for denomination will, we believe, come from a more wholehearted affirmation and implementation of convictions commonly called evangelical," *Mainstream Newsletter* 10 (April 1982) 1.

29. Rob Warner describes this split within wider English Evangelicalism in *Reinventing English Evangelicalism*.

30. For example Nigel Wright argues that "being evangelical is of the essence of being Baptist," Wright, "Agenda for Baptist Christians," 2.

31. Hill, *Baptist Revival Fellowship*, 157.

32. During the 1990s it was the view of some ministers that Mainstream was taking over the union, see letter from Ted Hale to Keith Jones, February 1, 1997.

If Raymond Brown was the one who gave Mainstream credibility at the beginning, it was McBain and Beasley-Murray who were the early shapers of its focus. McBain saw Mainstream as a place in which the charismatic renewal might find a home among Baptists, that it might become normal in Baptist life. Beasley-Murray was a keen advocate of church growth theory. They both wanted to change the default position of the union that remained suspicious of both charismatic renewal and church growth theory.[33] They had their supporters. McBain especially gathered a group of ministers around him, including Nigel Wright.[34]

McBain had trained at London Bible College, before undertaking ministries at Stoke Newington and Wishaw, Scotland, and then in 1968 he went to Streatham in South London. While at Wishaw, McBain experienced the Holy Spirit[35] and found a friendship with Tom Smail.[36] From this he became a leading figure in the charismatic renewal movement among Baptists, alongside the likes of David Pawson.[37] McBain was involved in the background of the Taylor controversy organizing an event in which Pawson spoke on "How Much of a God Is Jesus" and later as part of the group which wrote the assembly resolution that Cyril Black put to assembly.[38] Without McBain there would have been no Mainstream, but he was to some degree a controversial figure in the early years, arising from his advocacy of charismatic renewal, his explicit criticism of the denomination, and his move in 1982 into itinerant ministry.[39] He was concerned that Mainstream did not become just another evangelical grouping, but that it sought to renew the denomination. For McBain this meant not being afraid to speak out. However by 1989 he became general superintendent of the Metropolitan

Denominational Consultation Papers.

33. The *BT* records a second intervention by the two men, this time at a BU council meeting in March 1981 in a discussion over the union's finances. See *BT*, March 19, 1981, 1, 16.

34. See Beaumont, "Growing Together in Committed Covenant Relationships," 2–4, and the earlier article, Wright, "Gleanings from the North West," 4–6.

35. McBain, *Fire Over the Waters*, 38.

36. Tom Smail went on to be involved in the Fountain Trust and become one of the most able expositors of careful theology of charismatic renewal. See, e.g., Smail, *Reflected Glory*, and Wright, *Charismatic Renewal* (with Smail and Walker).

37. McBain describes Pawson in the 1970s as "the one high-profile Baptist in renewal," *Fire Over the Waters*, 51. Pawson was a member of the Baptist Revival Fellowship. McBain had written a series of articles in the *Baptist Times* in June and July 1975 on charismatic renewal.

38. Randall, *English Baptists*, 371n24, 379.

39. He moved from being minister of Lewin Road in 1982 to head up Manna Ministries, a new parachurch organization he created.

Area and in 1998 president of the union, and like others in Mainstream, became less outspoken.[40]

In 1981 McBain wrote *No Gentle Breeze: Baptist Churchmanship and the Winds of Change* as part of occasional Mainstream publications. Where others in Mainstream were cautious, McBain was not. *No Gentle Breeze* argues for change and its target at various points is the institution of the Baptist Union. In the introduction he says: "There is always an inbuilt resistance to change in any denominational establishment, including our own. We must not underestimate that."[41] Later he is more strident:

> Let it be said as explicitly as possible we have the denomination we deserve . . . Now it is vital that our Council, its Executive and its Committees become more of a catalyst for change than a talk shop about history . . . The fundamental question which they must face is as to whether it is possible for the present institution to move reformingly with sufficient speed and conviction to keep a hold upon the new life which is emerging, whilst not losing touch with the continuum of our tradition. I am forced to one conclusion regarding the prospects for Baptist life in Britain. It is that whatever timetable for change God may have adopted for other Christians, His time for us is now. If we do not take it then we sign a death warrant for our institutions.[42]

A decade later, Nigel Wright's *Challenge to Change* would pick up many of the same themes.

Paul Beasley-Murray[43] was minister at Altrincham Baptist Church in Manchester when he read C. Peter Wagner's *Your Church Can Grow* and was introduced to the concept of Church Growth.[44] In 1981 he published with Alan Wilkinson, *Turning the Tide: An Assessment of Baptist Church Growth*

---

40. Although in 1999 he was still happy to challenge, as his call to evangelism at the end of the November Baptist Union Council meeting demonstrated. See Minutes, Baptist Union Council, November 1999, 25–26. See also *BT*, November 25, 1999, 1.

41. McBain, *No Gentle Breeze*, 5–6.

42. McBain, *No Gentle Breeze*, 17. After it was published McBain also wrote four articles picking up the themes again for the *Baptist Times*.

43. Paul Beasley-Murray is the son of George Beasley-Murray, one of the most important New Testament scholars among Baptists in the twentieth century. George had been principal of Spurgeon's College from 1958–1973 and like others played a significant role with the union in the 1960s and early 1970s, before moving to the United States to become Professor of New Testament at Southern Baptist Theological Seminary. See Beasley-Murray, *Fearless for Truth*.

44. For a brief account of Church Growth in the UK see Tidball, "Presidential Address: Church Growth," 1–3.

in England.[45] He would write later that he believed that the BU should adopt church growth insights.[46] He was disappointed that while several Baptists had pioneered the Church Growth Movement in England,[47] they had done so without any support from the Baptist Union. The report *Signs of Hope* had given a section to the Church Growth Movement and had suggested that churches "should give serious thought to what this movement has to say."[48] However, the follow up document, *A Call to Commitment*, prepared by David Russell, gave it one brief passing mention.[49] The early issues of the *Mainstream Newsletter*, which Beasley-Murray edited, featured many articles on church growth, either stories of churches or from church growth theorists.[50] In 1986 Beasley-Murray became principal of Spurgeon's College, a position he held until 1992, after which he returned to ministry in the local church.[51] While principal he oversaw the introduction of new courses, in particular an Evangelism and Church Planting course in partnership with the Oasis Trust.[52] His involvement in Mainstream became less by the 1990s[53] and in 1994 he set up the Richard Baxter Institute for Ministry, reflecting his concern for the practice of ministry.

In 1992 Beasley-Murray, at the request of the union,[54] published *Radical Believers*, which was both an introduction to "the Baptist way of being church" and also an argument for how being Baptist might look into the future. Like Nigel Wright's *Challenge to Change*, which will be discussed below, it stands as another Mainstream contribution to the growing conversation around Baptist identity that had been taking place in the mid-1980s and continued into the 1990s. A foreword by Coffey called it "a timely book and deserves the widest circulation." Beasley-Murray describes himself as

45. See now Beasley-Murray, *This Is My Story*, 79–97, for his account of his time as minister of Altrincham.

46. Beasley-Murray, "Evangelism—a National Priority," 20.

47. Alongside Beasley-Murray, there were Derek Tidball, who was the first chairman of the British Church Growth Association, started in 1981, Tom Houston and Roy Pointer, who were both Baptist ministers working for the Bible Society. The latter published *How Do Churches Grow?* (1984).

48. *Signs of Hope*, 37–42, 47.

49. *A Call to Commitment*, 18.

50. See articles by White, McRae, Thompson, Tidball, and Pointer.

51. For Beasley-Murray's account of his time as principal of Spurgeon's, see *This Is My Story*, 98–127.

52. See Randall, *School of Prophets*, 38.

53. There is a sense that the new direction Mainstream took in the 1990s toward charismatic renewal was not one which Beasley-Murray was comfortable with, see Beasley-Murray, *This Is My Story*, 94.

54. Beasley-Murray, *This Is My Story*, 106.

"a Baptist by conviction." He defines and commends Baptist membership in terms of covenant.[55] He emphasizes the importance of interdependence to the extent that he claims that "a church which fails to live in fellowship with others is a gross mismutation."[56] He describes the Baptist Union as "in the first place . . . a mission agency."[57] He argues that its origins were from a concern for mission and this remains true today. He contends that the assembly should be "less inspirational and more deliberative."[58] With regards to associations, he acknowledges they need renewal. They are not an "optional extra," but need to become "meaningful" again.[59] Beasley-Murray's proposal is that what is needed in associations is leadership, not helped, he says, by the key role within associations being called a "secretary."[60] He does see leadership being offered by superintendents, working with others in a team, although he sees that they are generally appointed more for "their pastoral than their evangelistic qualities."[61] He believes what is needed and most important is that "a lead is given in mission and ministry to the churches and pastors of the associations." He disagrees with those, like Nigel Wright, who argues in *Challenge to Change* for Baptist bishops. Beasley-Murray says the most important reason for this is that it has "unhelpful associations" with other understandings of bishops among Anglicans and Roman Catholics. In terms of ecumenism, he argues that it was right that Baptists joined the new ecumenical instruments in 1990. He affirms the centrality of mission among Baptists, and especially evangelism, but argues that it must include social action. He argues for a "wide range of strategies" for effective evangelism, and highlights in particular the church growth movement.[62]

55. This section on covenant appears to have learned something from Fiddes, *Bound to Love* which is included in the bibliography. *Bound to Love* will be discussed in more detail when we look at the second stream of renewal.

56. Beasley-Murray, *Radical Believers*, 73.

57. Beasley-Murray, *Radical Believers*, 75.

58. Beasley-Murray had first argued this in an article in the *Fraternal*: "Assembly—a Deliberative Body?" This article was written following the assembly in which he and McBain had intervened and reflected his frustration that the assembly was not open to or at least did not encourage deliberation.

59. Beasley-Murray, *Radical Believers*, 78.

60. The importance of leadership has been a central theme of Beasley-Murray's contribution to church. See Beasley-Murray, *Dynamic Leadership* and *A Call to Excellence*.

61. Beasley-Murray, *Radical Believers*, 96.

62. Beasley-Murray, *Radical Believers*, 105.

Mainstream in the 1980s

Despite the presence of those across the spectrum of evangelicals within the BU, Mainstream was not devoid of issues and tensions through its first decade. There were some who felt it was too charismatic. In 1981 Jim Graham led a workshop on worship,[63] which some felt was overtly charismatic in tone and content, which led Beasley-Murray to contend that Mainstream was not "the Fountain Trust in another guise."[64] The tension increased the following year when McBain led the closing communion service. The speakers that year had included Bernard Green and Bill Hancock, both union officers,[65] which meant one response saw it as "a glorified BU Assembly."[66] However, in his sermon, McBain spoke of the union as "the hybrid family we all to love to hate."[67] He concluded by saying:

> [Caleb] would say to a Baptist Union that if that union is concerned about self-protection, even self-perpetuation at any cost, at the defence of the status quo, to the slightest ripple of change, why a poor little soul raising their hand in a hymn at a Baptist assembly requiring all the courage of time and eternity to do so, if that sort of thing is really going to shake our confidence, well, our union is not worth a lot.[68]

This was seen as an attack on the union. One letter to the Mainstream Executive called McBain's language "intemperate, unconstructive and somewhat rabble-raising."[69] The *Baptist Times* review saw it as a tension within Mainstream between what it called "the priestly and the prophetic":[70] those wanting to support the union and those who were advocating change. In the following *Newsletter* the executive wrote to stress that Mainstream was evangelical, open to the charismatic and "truly Baptist."[71] When the

---

63. Graham had been minister of Gold Hill Baptist Church, Chalfont St. Peter since 1968. Graham was undoubtedly a charismatic as his 1982 book *The Giant Awakes* demonstrates.

64. Beasley-Murray, "Mainstream—the Fountain Trust in Another Guise?," 1.

65. Bernard Green was general secretary-designate; he would take office from April. The Mainstream conference took place in January. Bill Hancock was area superintendent for the South Eastern Area and in 1985 become secretary of the Ministry Department.

66. "Swanwick Conference Post Bag 1982." Barrie White papers.

67. *BT*, January 28, 1982, 7.

68. *BT*, January 28, 1982, 7.

69. "Swanwick Conference Post Bag 1982," Barrie White papers.

70. *BT*, January 28, 1982, 7.

71. Mainstream Executive, editorial, *Mainstream Newsletter* 10 (April 1982) 1.

Mainstream Executive met in March 1982 there were "frank discussions." What is indicated is that while for some the conference as a whole had failed to provide "enough of a challenge to the Denomination neither had the conference been as radical or inspirational as it should have been."[72] Coffey is recorded as pointing to the positive contribution Mainstream had already provided in terms of presence on council, the mood within Baptist life and the evangelical wing being taken more seriously. In his later reflections, McBain says he had been frustrated and particularly, he writes, that Mainstream "under the careful and guarded leadership of Ray Brown was likely to become just another evangelical grouping in the Baptist Union."[73] Derek Tidball's analysis is that the issue was "as much about strategy and personality as theology,"[74] which suggests that the description of McBain was fairly accurate. Brown would write to White in 1985 to express his "unhappiness with the way Mainstream appears to be going."[75] His concern, reflecting earlier tensions, being an "attempt to push the thing from the warmly evangelical centre firmly into the charismatic wing." Part of his reason was that the April 1985 edition of the *Mainstream Newsletter* had included what he saw was an uncritical account of John Wimber's theology.[76]

The relationship between the BU and Mainstream was generally good. The Mainstream Executive had meetings with the union's officers and the Superintendents Board, although the union at times did not like the criticism Mainstream sometimes gave. In April 1983 Campbell gave a negative assessment of the union's assembly,[77] which generated a letter to Coffey that was critical of most of the Mainstream Executive for their lack of attendance at assembly and the tone of Campbell's words as "only stressing divisions which need healing."[78] Equally there was concern from Green about McBain's itinerant "apostolic" ministry and how that related to the ministry of general superintendents. There was a suspicion that McBain was seeking to undermine or bypass the union's recognized ministry.[79]

72. Minutes of Mainstream Executive, March 22–23, 1982, 2. Barrie White papers.

73. McBain, *Fire Over the Waters*, 112.

74. Tidball, "Mainstream," 213.

75. Letter from Raymond Brown to Barrie White, dated April 22, 1985. Barrie White papers.

76. *Mainstream Newsletter* 19 (April 1985). Wimber was a American church leader, and important figure within the charismatic movement. He advocated what he called *Power Evangelism*.

77. Campbell, "Scratching the Surface," 1.

78. Letter to David Coffey from (I think) Barbara Askew (administrative assistant) and assembly organizer, dated April 29, 1983.

79. See McBain's account in *Fire Over the Waters*, 116–17.

Brian Haymes has called Mainstream the "politically most active"[80] of all the various renewal groups within the denomination. This is something Mainstream was up front about. In 1989 part of their new agenda was to seek "the appointment of men and women to positions of denominational responsibility who are mission-minded and forward thinking" and a "renewal and deepening of evangelical faith and life among Baptist churches."[81] This was already apparent very early in the life of Mainstream. In 1981, one of the aims of the Mainstream Executive was to "represent the mainstream of the denomination" and this would be evident they believed when "the General Secretary and many of the Area Supers are in active sympathy with us."[82] They go on to say that their "immediate goals" were "checking through that evangelicals are nominated to the BU Council" and "to go for more representation at G. P. and F. and B. U. Council as well."[83] Mainstream recognized they needed to be located where decisions were made. From 1979 to 1994 they increased their presence on the council and in key union positions (see appendix 2). In fifteen years, Mainstream had occupied nationally significant roles within the union and in particular that of general secretary. This was intentional. At various points in the minutes of the executive it speaks of needing to "fill posts"[84] and that "it is important that evangelicals be nominated for these posts."[85]

In the 1980s Mainstream were concerned that the denomination was not evangelical enough, which reflected, in part, that while it actively participated in the World Council of Churches (WCC) and British Council Churches (BCC), it was less involved in wider evangelical bodies like the EA.[86] The Mainstream Executive became a member of the EA in 1986. Several of the Mainstream Executive through the 1980s and 1990s would be part of EA's own council—Beasley-Murray, Coffey, Grange, McBain, Tidball, Warner, and Wright.

Mainstream's evangelicalism gave emphasis to their concern for evangelism and church growth. This they believed needed to have a higher

---

80. Haymes, "Still Blessing the Tie that Binds," 92n4.

81. "Mainstream in the Future," *Mainstream Newsletter* 32 (April 1989) 1.

82. Mainstream Questionnaire Response. No date, but likely March/April 1981. Paul Beasley-Murray papers.

83. Mainstream Questionnaire Response. G.P.F. stood for General Purposes and Finance Executive and was the most important committee of the council while it existed. In the 2000s it was eventually replaced by the introduction of the Trustees' Board.

84. Minutes, Mainstream Executive, November 1985.

85. Minutes, Mainstream Executive, March 1990.

86. Mainstream Executive and Advisory Council, "The Aims of Mainstream," *Mainstream Newsletter* 21 (January 1986) 2.

priority among Baptist churches. Within Mainstream there was a broad affirmation of the principles of the Church Growth Movement, some advocating it fervently.[87] Mainstream's diagnosis was that the denomination was too "staid"[88] and needed renewal. The executive did not shy from stating that "we are sometimes very unhappy about the state our Baptist Union is in and about some of the things it does and does not do."[89] Its frustration was one expressed from within the denomination and not outside it. Mainstream were not interested in seeking to break away from the union, but to transform and renew it from within. The Mainstream structures were as such light and they saw themselves as a "forum" to share ideas, a "workshop" to share stories, and a "gadfly," that is, they were willing to challenge Baptist life and its structures to change.[90] Reflecting an evangelical emphasis on vision and leadership, some argued for "strong, clear, spiritual and evangelistic leadership from the Baptist Union";[91] the insinuating suggestion being that this had not been offered. They hoped for a general secretary who would act like "a leader marshalling and encouraging the troops as Mountbatten did in Burma."[92] The practice of the four general secretaries that followed Shakespeare—Aubrey, Payne, Russell, and Green—was not to be this kind of leader. The appointment of Coffey was a significant return to a leader like Shakespeare. He was the strong, visionary, evangelical leader Mainstream had been waiting for. It was not only the general secretary, they saw the need for general superintendents to be "'vision men' more than 'maintenance men.'"[93] This desire for stronger, more visionary leadership was partly a response to the growing House Church Movement with its "apostolic" leadership, with which some Baptist churches were drawn too. Mainstream was sympathetic to these new churches[94] in a way in which the wider union was more defensive.

Mainstream's concern was not just with structures of the union, but also with the life of local Baptist congregations. The *Mainstream Newsletters* through the 1980s discussed issues like worship, elders, church meetings, and church membership. This demonstrated their desire to renew the

---

87. Most notably Paul Beasley-Murray and Derek Tidball.

88. White, "Denominational Enquiry and the Local Church," 3.

89. *Mainstream Newsletter* 10 (April 1982) 1.

90. *Mainstream Newsletter* 10 (April 1982) 1.

91. Thompson, "An Open Letter to Dr. David Russell," 2.

92. Thompson, "An Open Letter to Dr. David Russell," 3.

93. Thompson, "An Open Letter to Dr. David Russell," 3.

94. For example, Wright, "Challenge of the 'House Church Movement'" and his *Radical Kingdom*.

denomination—its institutions, its churches, its attitudes to evangelism and to charismatic renewal.

Nigel Wright

Through the 1980s Nigel Wright established himself as a key Mainstream theological thinker.[95] In 1982, there is a line in the minutes of the Mainstream Executive that says, "Nigel Wright to be encouraged to write more,"[96] indicating perhaps that in Wright they recognized a skilled communicator and thinker. Wright was minister of Ansdell, Lytham St Annes from 1973–1986. He had been part of Mainstream from its beginning, but did not join the executive until 1985. Mainstream gave him "a platform from which to address a wider world."[97] Wright's commitment to theology is seen in his decision to resign his pastorate and study for an MTh at the University of Glasgow in 1986. This involved primarily a reading of Karl Barth's *Church Dogmatics*.[98] In 1987 he became Tutor in Christian Doctrine at Spurgeon's College and he began doctoral studies at King's College London under Colin Gunton, completing a thesis on John Howard Yoder and Jürgen Moltmann in 1994.[99] From 1986 to 1996, Wright wrote a number of books that established him as an authority on charismatic renewal and evangelicalism.[100] He was for a period part of the editorial group for the *Renewal* magazine and was associated with the Gospel and Culture group run by Andrew Walker.[101]

By 1990 Wright was arguing for "extensive change" and reform, especially with regard to what he called the "largely Edwardian structures of the Union."[102] He argued for five points to shape this reforming agenda:

95. For one reflection on Wright see Randall, "Part of a Movement." See also Goodliff, "Nigel Wright's Radical Baptist Theology."

96. Minutes, Mainstream Executive, January 18, 1982. Barrie White papers.

97. Wright, "My Life with Mainstream," 34.

98. Wright, "Pilgrimage in Renewal," 30.

99. It was published in 2000 as *Disavowing Constantine: Mission, Church and the Social Order in the Theologies of John Howard Yoder and Jürgen Moltmann*.

100. Wright, *Radical Kingdom*; *Fair Face of Evil*; Wright with Smail and Walker, *Charismatic Renewal*; and Wright, *Radical Evangelical*.

101. The Gospel and Culture network was the joining together of the C. S. Lewis Centre for the Study of Religion and Modern Culture led by Andrew Walker and the Gospel and Culture network led by Lesslie Newbigin. It ran between 1995–1997, during that period it published a series of books.

102. Wright, "Agenda for Baptist Christians," 2.

1. The union needs to see itself unambiguously and self-consciously as an evangelical and evangelistic organization.

2. The union needs to cultivate a new spirit of warmth and of personal affirmation.

3. The union needs to reform its structures and engage in a sustained period of decentralization.

4. The union needs to reappraise the theology which undergirds it and to see itself more clearly as a resource agency established to enhance the life of the churches and the associations.

5. The union should concern itself with the production of high quality publications which express the principles and values for which we stand.

Three of these points are significant—the need for the union to identify itself more closely with evangelicalism; the need for reform and decentralization, which for Wright meant giving more weight to the powers of associations; and the need for a theology grounded in the local church and so the union should be understood as a "resource agency." These three points highlight the nature of the debate that would take place within the union over the following decade.

Wright developed this article into a book-length manifesto that was *Challenge to Change* and it was published in the same year Coffey became general secretary. In this he argued for a theology of change around five principles of renewal, reformation, restoration, revival, and reconstruction. This amounted to a greater openness to the work of the Holy Spirit and a return to the Scriptures in order to counter a traditionalism that Wright believed inhibited Baptists from change. In Wright's view "radical Baptist thinking has accommodated itself to the establishment"[103] and so was failing to be true to its beginnings as a reformation and restorationist church. These five principles, he says, would affect Baptist worship, structures, government, evangelism, mood, and lifestyle. In general he wanted Baptists to let go of a Victorian culture that was out of date.[104] Worship should shift from "the solemn to the celebratory"; the structures should shift from "the organisational to the organic, or from the institutional to the charismatic"; church government should shift from "constitution to consensus"; evangelism should shift from "programme to power evangelism"; the dominant mood should shift from "formal to the informal"; and lifestyle should shift

103. Wright, *Challenge to Change*, 35.

104. While his 1990 article spoke of Edwardian structures, in *Challenge to Change*, Wright pushes the problem back a generation to the Victorian era; see *Challenge to Change*, 52.

from "the conformist to the Christian." Wright presented a damning critique of traditional Baptist churchmanship.

At the center of the book's argument are three chapters that called for a renewal of the local church and the church meeting; a renewal of associating; and a renewal of the union. In each one Wright detected an institutionalism that was the source of their ills. In terms of associating, Wright argued that the Baptist "bias towards the local" needed to be balanced alongside "a new vision of the catholic and ecumenical."[105] He said that associations were prone to "distorting institutionalism,"[106] so relationships between churches were subservient to the association, with the result that relationships between churches were rarely meaningful. Wright locates some of the problems in doctrinal differences between Baptist churches, that is, there was not a basis of theological agreement and furthermore there were of course differences over churches' reception of the charismatic movement.[107] Wright views the networks among Restorationist churches as providing an example of what associating could look like.[108] Wright presents two steps to renewing association, the first is the commitment of those in ministry to "friendship and mutual accountability."[109] This makes possible the more important, but more difficult to realize, "coming together of churches in a form of mutual support and accountability."[110] He offered three ways to achieve meaningful associations: churches in a region or existing association resolve to forge links together; go beyond existing association areas and forge links wherever Baptist churches find others of like-mind; and develop forms of association between Baptist and non-Baptist churches, in particularly newer churches, where there is much in common.

Wright's discussion on the renewal of the union is headed "Reforming the Powers That Be," which reveals his general attitude to institutions, that he makes plain at the start of the chapter. In this chapter Wright is at his boldest. In this section he repeats his earlier criticisms from his earlier article, but extends his reasoning and how the union might be reformed. Wright is unconvinced by the theological position that the union is the "association of associations,"[111] because it cannot meet the relational test, an as-

---

105. Wright, *Challenge to Change*, 135.

106. Wright, *Challenge to Change*, 141.

107. Wright, *Challenge to Change*, 141–42.

108. Wright, *Challenge to Change*, 144.

109. Wright, *Challenge to Change*, 145.

110. Wright, *Challenge to Change*, 146.

111. Wright, *Challenge to Change*, 163. *The Report of the Commission on the Associations 1964* suggests that the union should be understood as the "associations

sociation of the associations can only be "bureaucratic" and "institutional."
Wright argued that "corporate Baptist life" is strongest, theologically, at the
concept of association, and as a result should be focused here.[112] He advocated a "policy of decentralisation,"[113] which would see a shift from union to
association, in terms of financial oversight and the appointments of general
superintendents. The union should be seen as a resource agency, in comparison with the relationship that the BMS has with associations and local
churches. The union would become a means of helping connect associations
together in terms of national gatherings,[114] communication, literature, legal,
and technical advice and the scope to identify ministry and mission needs
on a wider scope. At the heart of Wright's vision is to "return the Union
to the people."[115]

Having made his argument for renewal, from the local to the national,
Wright makes an argument for the creation of Baptist bishops. What leads
him to make this case is based on the New Testament, his own experience
and the example of the restoration movement. Wright's argument is for a
functional episcopacy, not a hierarchical one. The argument for translocal
ministry of course is not a novel one for Baptists, which has been present
in different forms since the seventeenth century. Wright's concern is that
translocal ministry among Baptists in terms of general superintendency is
not sufficiently mission-orientated. This is because he claimed the areas of
superintendency were too large and because they were employees of the
union and so were too institutionally minded. Wright's argument is that
the ministry of bishops is one in which evangelism and mission should take
priority. Pastoral care is important, but should not be the chief concern. Determining the role of translocal ministry became a chief point of discussion
later in the union and Wright played a key role in articulating a way forward.

In the final chapter of *Challenge to Change*, Wright sees that denominational renewal must be accompanied by "theological renewal to guide
and accompany the process of change."[116] Theology must be for all, that is
"in service of the church"[117] and therefore it needed to be accessible and pas-

---

associating," 26.

112. Wright, *Challenge to Change*, 165.

113. Wright, *Challenge to Change*, 163.

114. With this he argues that the assembly should be abolished as a legislative body,
with those powers residing in a reformed Baptist Union Council, weighted more repre-
sentatively to those from associations.

115. Wright, *Challenge to Change*, 170.

116. Wright, *Challenge to Change*, 240.

117. Wright, "Theology in Service of the Church."

sionate in expression. Wright does not expand any more, but the indication is that *Challenge to Change* is a good example of the kind of theology he thought needed.

In 2002 Wright became president of the Baptist Union. Reflecting on his appointment he recognized the journey he had made since *Challenge to Change*. Back in the 1980s and early 1990s he had been happy to "'critique' from the edges."[118] By 2002 he says he had "become something of a denominationalist."[119] He thought the union had become "one worth staying in," which he puts down to the impact of David Coffey and others.[120] Although this change may reflect that much of the argument he made in *Challenge to Change* would be enacted in the new structures of the union.

Rob Warner

In the 1990s Mainstream entered a new phase of its life. Much of this can be traced to the involvement of Rob Warner and a new generation of Baptist evangelicals. Wright remained the key figure who was part of the first and second generation.[121] Rob Warner trained for ministry at Regent's Park College, Oxford between 1983–1986, having been brought up as a nominal Anglican.[122] While at university he felt a call to ministry and almost trained for the Anglican ministry until a conviction about believer's baptism, ministry, and church-state relations meant he withdrew. He was employed in Christian publishing, and joined initially the Icthus Fellowship, before becoming a member at Bromley Baptist Church. It was from there that he went to train at Regent's. In his final year there he wrote his first book, *Rediscovering the Spirit*. His first church was Buckhurst Hill, Essex, before moving to Herne Hill, London, in 1990 and then to Queens Road, Wimbledon, in 1995. In 1998 he planted a new church in Wimbledon called Kairos—Church from Scratch, where he stayed until 2004. He joined the Mainstream Executive in 1988 and became editor of the newsletter in 1991. He was already a consulting editor and contributor for the *Renewal* magazine. In 1993 he joined the Evangelical Alliance Council and later would become a director. Through the 1990s he was heavily involved in Spring Harvest, the Evangelical Alliance and Alpha as well as authoring ten books. In terms of Baptist involvement, he was a member of the Task Group on Associating that produced

118. Wright, "From Poacher to President," 18.

119. Wright, "From Poacher to President," 18.

120. Wright, "Becoming a Denomination Worth Joining," 18.

121. A third phase of its life began in 2001, with a new magazine called *Talk* and another generation of leaders. Nigel Wright would remain a key figure.

122. Much of what follows comes from *BT*, October 29, 1994, 9.

Relating and Resourcing and part of the Roundtable on Membership that produced *Joined Up Thinking: Membership*.

In 2004 Warner began doctoral studies at King's College London and by 2007 was a Lecturer in Sociology of Religion and Practical Theology at the University of Wales, Lampeter. His PhD thesis was published as *Reinventing English Evangelicalism, 1966–2001*. During his research, he moved away from his involvement in evangelical life. He wrote, "Sustained reflexivity and critical detachment with growing alienation as multiform implausibilities and intrinsic intellectual deficiencies, theological and sociological, became acutely apparent in various schools of pan-evangelicalism."[123] By 2009 Warner described himself as "one who has made a long journey away from and back into Anglicanism."[124]

Warner's chief contribution to Baptist life was his involvement in Mainstream. In November 1992 Warner used his editorial to raise the possibility of a new network for "evangelicals active in renewal."[125] It would be shaped by a commitment to Word and Spirit, be focused on evangelism, renewal, church growth, and church planting and it would seek to provide mutual support and accountability. In February 1993 he set out in a paper the case for a "Charismatic Baptist Network."[126] He saw the space for an explicitly charismatic and unapologetically Baptist network within the Baptist Union. This would enable charismatic Baptist churches to link together as well as possibly other baptistic fellowships. The guiding principles would be the same as he had set out in the editorial. He suggests that this new network could operate within Mainstream, as a separate movement or as replacing Mainstream. The network would be affiliated to the EA and "operate" within the Baptist Union. Regional consultation days took place in 1993 to consider Warner's vision. The result of the consultation days saw Mainstream move to a regional network centered on mission and accountability. By the beginning of 1995 Mainstream was renamed as a "Word and Spirit Network."[127] Warner from 1995–1998 was cochair of Mainstream with Glen Marshall.[128] There was a shift here to a more structured existence

123. Warner, *Reinventing English Evangelicalism*, 32. In his review, Andrew Atherstone says that "Warner's research becomes entangled with his own personal disillusionment," Atherstone, "*Reinventing English Evangelicalism*," 204.

124. Warner, "Transformations of English Evangelicalism," 215.

125. Warner, "Baptists in Renewal," 1.

126. Warner, "Charter for the Charismatic Baptist Network." Paul Beasley-Murray papers.

127. As indicated by the change of name to the magazine from May 1995 onward.

128. Marshall had trained at London Bible College, and then was an assistant pastor with Paul Beasley-Murray at Altrincham (1984–1987) and then was minister in

of Mainstream. It carried some of the features of what would otherwise have been found in Baptist associational life. At the same time through its annual conference and regular magazine it took opportunities to engage with the discussions taking place in the union both constructively and critically.

Warner's reflections in 1998 on the first twenty years of Mainstream are a good summary of its impact.[129] Warner understood the origins of Mainstream as a concern for doctrine and a concern for mission. The name Mainstream was, he suggested, a doctrinal assertion that Baptists were and should continue to be a biblically orthodox, evangelical, group of churches, that were not fundamentalist, but not liberal either. More than a concern for doctrine, Mainstream from the beginning was "missiological," its purpose was seeing Baptist churches grow by conversion and so a belief that the gospel remained relevant and powerful.

Joined to these "two foundational principles," Warner also identified "two underlying influences." The first was "charismatic renewal," which in Warner's view was about a "recovery of rounded and balanced, biblical spiritually" that acknowledged the work of the Holy Spirit imparting both "fruit and gifts to the church." This certainly became more prevalent within Mainstream over time, at first from the conscious involvement of McBain, but wider by the late 1980s and into 1990s, acknowledged, as Warner says, by the move to become a Word and Spirit Network in 1994. The second underlying influence was "church growth teaching," here referencing the particular contribution of Beasley-Murray. Mainstream was a place in which church growth teaching had an airing and later some among it were championing power evangelism, seeker services, saturation church planting and Alpha. In other words it was open to and encouraged the application of new evangelistic techniques as they came on the scene. At the same time, Warner saw that each new technique would be found to have its limitations, alongside its strengths.

Warner's third observation of Mainstream, to accompany its foundational principles and underlining influences, were three concerns it had. The first, to provide a reason for those who were otherwise considering leaving the Baptist Union to stay, by demonstrating a growing evangelical presence at the heart of Baptist life. The second, to provide an alternative to those who were attracted by the new churches, that the best bits of the Restorationist churches, in particular charismatic worship, could be found in Baptist churches. The third concern was a clear desire to see the union

Barnsley and Wakefield, before becoming a tutor at Northern Baptist College in 2004. He is currently co-principal at Northern.

129. Warner, "Mainstream—a Troublesome Irritant?," 28–31.

become more consciously evangelical through the appointment of persons to national roles—general secretary, superintendents, and presidents.

Warner's reading of Mainstream's history is an accurate rendering of this reforming stream. It recognizes that Mainstream's focus was for denominational and congregational renewal that would lead to growth.

Stream 2: Theological Renewal—"Champion" Group

The day before Mainstream was launched in the afterhours at the Baptist Assembly in 1979, Leonard Champion gave the annual Baptist Historical Society Lecture. His lecture, "Evangelical Calvinism and the Structures of Baptist Church Life,"[130] led to a second stream of thinking, focused on what I have termed, theological renewal. This second stream did not set up a new body like Mainstream. It was more ad hoc, yet its participants would become equally influential within the denomination during the 1990s.

Champion was an influential figure in Baptist life through much of the 1950s to 1970s.[131] He was principal of Bristol Baptist College (1953–1972), and had been president of the Baptist Union in 1964. He was involved in many of the important Baptist Union Council reports on ministry, ecumenism, and associating that had been produced during the 1960s.[132] He had also represented the union in the World Council of Churches and the British Council of Churches.[133] In 1961 he had been asked to address the denominational conference and he gave a statement on "The State of the Denomination." One of things he said on that occasion was that Baptists were in danger of a "theological slum."[134] In his view, Baptists were being "neglectful" with regard to the work of theology and what was needed was "a prolonged process of positive, evangelical thinking, teaching and writing" and a "more manifest theological cohesion."[135] The rest of that decade produced a flurry of theological reports, which in many ways only served to highlight the tensions within the union.

130. Champion, "Evangelical Calvinism and the Structures of Baptist Church Life."

131. Hayden, "Stillness and the Dancing"; Hayden, "Leonard George Champion 1907–1997"; *BT*, December 18/25, 1997, 12.

132. He was a member of groups that wrote *The Meaning and Practice of Ordination* (1957), *The Doctrine of Ministry* (1961), *The Report of the Commission on the Associations* (1964), and *Baptists and Unity* (1967).

133. He was a member of the Faith & Order Committee, WCC (1954–1971) and chair of the Mission and Unity Department, BCC (1967–1969).

134. Champion later denied he used this exact phrase, see Hayden, "Stillness and the Dancing," 1.

135. Champion, "Statement of the Denomination," 25–26.

Champion's lecture sought to be a timely word into the situation of changes taking place within the Baptist Union and in wider society. He understood the task of historical studies to be an opportunity to "offer a measure of illumination and guidance" on the present.[136] He argued that the half-century between 1775 and 1825 was a helpful place to look. It was during these years that a new evangelical Calvinism emerged which gave new life among Baptists.[137] It was this period that saw the beginnings of the BMS, the union itself and a number of the Baptist colleges. Champion's argument is that in these fifty years "a renewed theology led to a rediscovery of mission and the creation of organisations for the fulfilment of mission."[138] What happened then, he claimed, shaped Baptist theology and life up to the present, but he asked whether "different patterns" might now be needed. If they are required, Champion argued that what must be learned from the history is threefold. First, "proper structures of church life need a coherent theology,"[139] that is, it was theology, a widely shared theology, which made possible a new emphasis on mission and structures.[140] The theology of Evangelical Calvinism was one, says Champion, that was "increasingly congenial to the majority of Baptists" in the early nineteenth century. It laid the ground for the later amalgamation of Particular and General Baptists in 1891.[141] The new theology now needed was "an urgent task" said Champion, perhaps recognizing it was easy to talk growth and reforming structures without giving attention to a theology beneath them.[142] It was a renewed theological imagination that changed the fortunes of Baptists in the late eighteenth century; growth and structures flowed from there. Champion called on a younger generation to take up this challenge.[143] Second, Champion suggested that we revisit the theology of evangelical Calvinism, not to simply repeat it, but to explore whether it has a new relevance today. He points to the examples of the emphasis on the sovereignty of God, the divine activity of grace through Christ by the Spirit as salvific, and the language

136. Champion, "Evangelical Calvinism," 196.

137. He finds support for his view in the similar arguments by J. Ivimey, W. R. Ward, Clyde Binfield, and Michael Watts.

138. Champion, "Evangelical Calvinism," 197.

139. Champion, "Evangelical Calvinism," 206.

140. In a later article Champion says this need for theology is "not a plea for more academic theology," Champion, "Baptist Church Life in the Twentieth Century," 12. It is a theology grounded in and for the church.

141. Champion, "Evangelical Calvinism," 201.

142. In the background here is the Baptist Union report *Signs of Hope*.

143. Champion was already in his seventies when he gave this lecture and so saw this as an opportunity to pass on the baton to a new generation.

of obligation and responsibility. How might these doctrines be restated in a fresh way in order to capture the vision and commitment of Baptists again?[144] Champion's third suggestion was to see that any new structures are a means of demonstrating that mission is a "corporate activity."[145] New structures must bring people together. This was the achievement of the evangelical Calvinism of the eighteenth century and something similar was needed again in an increasingly fractured union.[146]

A Call to Mind

Champion's lecture was an inspiration to a group of younger Baptist ministers, who came together to seek to provide something of that which Champion was articulating. Roger Hayden and Brian Haymes were present at the lecture and Hayden took the initiative to call a group together. Hayden and Haymes knew Keith Clements through Bristol Baptist College;[147] Paul Fiddes was already being seen as a promising theological mind and as such an obvious choice; and Richard Kidd was a local minister in North London alongside Hayden. "Sufficiently challenged" by Champion's clarion call, these five Baptist ministers met six times during 1979 and 1980 before publishing in 1981 *A Call to Mind: Baptist Essays Towards a Theology of Commitment*.[148] Champion himself attended part of the first meeting, although the book that resulted is the work of the five ministers alone.[149] All five were academics to some degree and so took the task of theology seriously.[150]

Paul Fiddes had completed at DPhil in Old Testament at Oxford in 1975, having already been research fellow at Regent's Park College since

---

144. In this argument to revisit evangelical Calvinism, we might see Champion's dismissal of the theology that emerged in the 1960s onward, with the likes of John Robinson's *Honest to God*.

145. Champion, "Evangelical Calvinism," 207.

146. Issues of ecumenism and Christology had witnessed some churches (those associated with the Baptist Revival Fellowship) leaving the union in the early 1970s.

147. See Clements, *Look Back in Hope*, 118.

148. It was available by the Baptist Union Assembly in April and was published in name only by the Baptist Union, funded instead by "a group of friends who have made a substantial contribution to the cost of this publication."

149. Preface to Fiddes, *Call to Mind*, 3–4.

150. This is noted by the fact that three served in Baptist colleges. All five would hold doctorates. Fiddes and Haymes gaining theirs in 1976, Kidd in 1984, Clements in 1989, and Hayden in 1991. Fiddes, in particular, is the leading Baptist theologian of his generation, demonstrated by the University of Oxford awarding him the title Professor of Systematic Theology in 2002.

1972. In 1972 he was ordained, but uniquely this was to an academic role.[151] He became Tutor in Christian Doctrine in 1975, spending a year in 1976 at the University of Tübingen, where he studied with Jürgen Moltmann and Eberhard Jüngel.[152] In 1979–1980, the same period that *A Call to Mind* was being written, he gave the Whitley Lectures, which would later be published as *The Creative Suffering of God*.[153] He would become principal of Regent's Park in 1989, the same year he also published *Past Event and Present Salvation*. In a positive review of this book, Nigel Wright described Fiddes as an "accomplished theologian."[154]

Brian Haymes trained at Bristol and was ordained in 1965, and was ministering in his third church by 1979.[155] He became a tutor at Northern Baptist College, Manchester in 1981 and then in 1985 principal at Northern, before becoming principal of Bristol Baptist College in 1994. Haymes had completed his doctorate while he was minister of South Street Baptist Church, Exeter in 1976 on the knowledge of God.[156]

Roger Hayden had been ordained in 1961 and moved in 1981 to be minister of Abbey Baptist Church, Reading, his fourth church. Hayden was a Baptist historian and had edited the records of Broadmead Baptist Church, Bristol, and a collection of Baptist Union reports.[157] He became general superintendent of the Western Area in 1986, a position he held until retirement in 2000.

Keith Clements had been ordained in 1967 and by 1977 was tutor at Bristol Baptist College.[158] In 1980 he had completed an Oxford bachelor of divinity on the theology of Ronald Gregor Smith.[159] During the 1980s he would become known for his work on Dietrich Bonhoeffer and from 1990 onward he held positions first in the newly formed Council of Churches

151. Fiddes has never held a pastoral office in a local church. See "Introduction" in Clarke, *For the Sake of the Church*, 1.

152. Fiddes, *Creative Suffering of God*, vii.

153. Fiddes, *Creative Suffering of God*, vii.

154. Wright, "Book Review: *Past Event and Present Salvation*," 13.

155. For an overview of Haymes's theology see Goodliff, "Brian Haymes: Doing Theology for the Church."

156. Haymes, *Concept of the Knowledge of God*. In 1973 he had completed an MA, with a thesis on the theology of H. H. Farmer.

157. Hayden, *Records of a Church of Christ in Bristol 1640–1687*; Hayden, *Baptist Union Documents 1948–1977*. For a brief obituary see https://www.baptist.org.uk/Articles/463095/_A_great.aspx.

158. He had been part-time Lay Training Organizer at the college since 1972. For an account of Clements's life see his autobiography, Clements, *Look Back in Hope*. See also Goodliff, "Keith Clements: A Baptist Ecumenist."

159. Later published as Clements, *Theology of Roger Gregor Smith*.

for Britain and Ireland and then as general secretary of the Conference of European Churches. Clements also became editor of the *Baptist Quarterly* in 1980, a position he held until 1985.

Richard Kidd was ordained in 1976, having trained at Spurgeon's, and from 1981–1983 was recipient of the BU Scholarship while doing doctoral studies at Oxford.[160] He would become tutor at Northern Baptist College in 1986 and then in 1994 he was appointed principal (when Haymes moved to Bristol). From 1994 to 1998 he was the editor of the *British Journal of Theological Education*.

In comparison with Mainstream this was a more academic grouping and this reflects that ultimately their influence within the union was felt most keenly in the colleges rather than in the various forms of local, association, or national life. In 1982 both Hayden and Haymes were co-opted members of council. Fiddes would join council in 1989 on his appointment as principal at Regent's Park College,[161] Clements in 1990[162] and Kidd from 1994 on his appointment as principal at Northern.

The essays in *A Call to Mind* are a summons to Baptists to think and not engage in "a thoughtless treadmill of activity."[163] Fiddes et al. all express concern that Baptists were working with an implicit theology that was "scarcely adequate" to contemporary challenges.[164] The title *A Call to Mind* echoes *A Call to Commitment*[165] which was the follow-up report to *Signs of Hope*. The criticism is that *A Call to Commitment* was simply a call to activity without theology.[166] Clements writes the first chapter on "Facing Secularism" and is troubled by what he describes as "mission has become essentially church development rather than the transformation of society."[167] He sees this in the approach of the Church Growth Movement. In this understanding of mission religious faith is accepted as a private option and so an acceptance

160. Kidd had a completed an MTh at King's College London in 1979 on "The Significance of Jesus Christ in the Theology of Jürgen Moltmann." His DPhil was completed in 1987 on "Human Fallenness: A Comparative Study in the Theologies of Paul Tillich and Karl Rahner."

161. Significantly, in terms of the decisions made, he was not a member of council in 1998.

162. Clements's time as a council member was short. He ceased to be a member by 1994.

163. Introduction to Fiddes, *Call to Mind*, 5.

164. Introduction to Fiddes, *Call to Mind*, 6.

165. *A Call to Commitment*. This had been prepared by the then-general secretary, David Russell.

166. Introduction to Fiddes, *Call to Mind*, 6.

167. Clements, "Facing Secularism," 12.

of a secular agenda. For Clements the only way forward in facing secularism is "a recovery of theology" and in particular "the doctrine of God."[168] Instead of starting with the church, as in *Signs of Hope*, we begin with God. For Clements God is at work in the world, and we should seek to "[apprehend] God in the total realm of the secular experience."[169] If we are to recover the "centrality of God," Clements argues that five ingredients are important: get a better grasp of the Christian tradition; together with the tradition, reclaim a vision of God who "acts in human, worldly history"; discover a natural theology in the sense of God's otherness in the world; develop an understanding of revelation in which God is impinging on all human existence and experience; and fifth to have humility in our apprehension of God. Clements concludes that to rediscover this centrality of God will cause us to see God in the secular, God as the whole world's Creator, Redeemer, and Sanctifier.[170]

Richard Kidd's chapter, "Called to Be," is a challenge to a constant activism that is unconcerned to ask questions of what it is to *be* Christian. He is critical of the Church Growth Movement for their copying of the methods from the secular business world.[171] He is also critical of denominational reports and papers which seem always to be "concerned with matters of ecclesiology."[172] Kidd goes on to explore what an emphasis on being might mean for our understanding of faith, action, and discipleship. In terms of the latter he takes up the concept of pilgrimage and pushes for a church vision that avoids being parochial and as such takes "ecumenical and international concerns at least as seriously as it does matters of local congregational growth."[173]

Fiddes's chapter, "The Signs of Hope," begins with the *Signs of Hope* report and observes that it is theologically thin: that is, hope is used merely in the meaning Baptists should be encouraged.[174] Fiddes sees an opportunity to think theologically about hope, engaging with Moltmann and others.[175] He does not criticise *Signs of Hope*, instead he builds on it in theological terms. It is perhaps deliberate that this is the central chapter of *A Call to*

168. Clements, "Facing Secularism," 12.

169. Clements, "Facing Secularism," 12.

170. Behind Clements's contribution is the work of Ronald Gregor Smith, which was the focus of his Oxford BD. See Clements, *Look Back in Hope*, 116–19.

171. Kidd, "Call to Be," 24.

172. Kidd, "Call to Be," 25.

173. Kidd, "Call to Be," 30.

174. Fiddes, "Signs of Hope," 33.

175. An interest in Moltmann was shared by Fiddes, Kidd, and Clements. Clements had written "Moltmann and the Congregation."

Mind for it is certainly the most theological. Fiddes considers hope as an eschatological concept: hope in the promises of God and new creation, in which "rather than the future being mere projection of the present it is the power which changes the present."[176] This eschatological hope positions itself against a church of the status quo and at the same time a church of social optimism. Instead the God of hope is the God who does something new, signified in the resurrection of Jesus.

Hayden's chapter, "The Faith and Other Faiths," takes seriously the pluralist context of Britain. In his view Baptists have demonstrated a "timidity rather than boldness" in their thinking.[177] The historic Baptist emphasis on evangelism, present in *Signs of Hope* and *A Call to Commitment*, mean Baptists cannot avoid engaging with questions of other faiths.[178] Hayden thinks this is for the good and encourages Baptists, whose forebears argued for tolerance and freedom, to engage in "a loving, free interchange of insights."[179] This would be a "welcome sign of hope."

Haymes begins his chapter, "On Being the Church," by stressing the importance of theology: "Theological reflection . . . is a fundamental need of our denomination."[180] In his view the lack of theology among Baptists has contributed to a "decline in our effectiveness."[181] Haymes's concern is for what he calls "unhelpful and misleading theological influences that shape the life of many a local congregation." Like in other chapters he is critical of Church Growth thinking where it concentrates "on the growing size of local congregations." Instead congregations should be shaped by risk "into the transforming mission of God in the world."[182] Haymes wants to ensure a distinction between church and kingdom. The church, he says, should feature worship, proclamation, Christ-like, suffering love, and the work of reconciliation.

The wider claim of *A Call to Mind* is to see Baptists recognize the increasing secularism of British society and not focus solely or predominantly on internal matters. The authors argue that to overly focus on church growth was to not face up to the more demanding challenge of articulating the gospel in late modernity. Also present in this stream of theological

176. Fiddes, "Signs of Hope," 34.

177. Hayden, "Faith and Other Faiths," 53.

178. Here we note that it was until the mid-1980s that there emerged a Baptist grouping, which was called Joppa, dedicated to these issues.

179. Hayden, "Faith and Other Faiths," 54.

180. Haymes, "On Being the Church," 55.

181. Haymes, "On Being the Church," 55.

182. Haymes, "On Being the Church," 62.

thinking, although undeveloped, is a political theology, a theology that is not just centered on the church, but also society. A final argument within the chapters is that of an open theological enquiry, which is conscious of the debate that arose over Michael Taylor's 1971 address to the Baptist Assembly. While the response of Mainstream was to emphasize that Baptists are evangelicals, the second stream looked to and encouraged more space for a broader theology.

Barrie White, Fiddes's senior colleague at Regent's, and member of the Mainstream Executive, championed *A Call to Mind* in the *Baptist Times*. He called it an "important book" and suggested that "Baptists badly need such theological tracts for times as this."[183] White's hope was that the group, and others, would produce more of the same kind of work, but with some more direct "application" that can be taken up by churches.

Bound to Love

In the second book, *Bound to Love*, the theme of covenant was taken up, having been briefly mentioned in Haymes's chapter in *A Call to Mind*.[184] If *A Call to Mind* was focused on the need for theological reflection, *Bound to Love* argues that the concept of covenant provides the theological basis on which Baptist life and structures can be understood.[185] The context for the book is the rising impact of the Restoration Movement in the late 1970s and early 1980s and its accompanying notion of spiritual authority exercised through elders and apostles, which was seen as a threat by some to Baptist ecclesiology.[186] The focus on covenant was a means of theological retrieval for it had been a key concept for Baptists throughout the seventeenth century. The language of covenant is rooted in the Bible. In the Old Testament, there are several covenants that God makes with Noah, Abraham, the people of Israel at Sinai, and with David. While these covenants are always made at

183. *BT*, December 31, 1981, 2. It was also reviewed by the Methodist Rupert Davies in the *Epworth Review* 10 (1983) 95.

184. "It is God who calls us to be his people, the God who makes and keeps covenant . . . When we gather as local congregations, Associations or in Denominational Assembly we meet as those whom God has gathered together in communion with Christ," Haymes, "On Being the Church," 67.

185. Alec Gilmore's brief review is positive, although he thinks they should have started with the concept of covenant and seen where it led, rather than trying to use it to deal with a set of problems the group identified, *BT*, April 18, 1985, 28.

186. Fiddes had earlier written *Charismatic Renewal: A Baptist View* and *A Leading Question*, where he emphasized the authority of the church meeting and carefully outlined a biblical doctrine of ministry, which was critical without being dismissive of the category of "elder."

God's initiative, some like the Sinai covenant, emphasis a human responsibility to ensure the continuity of the covenant. Fiddes claims Baptists have tended toward this notion of covenant with their stress on personal faith and obedience.[187] He also wants to recognize that "no expression of God's covenant in human words can ever be final."[188] For Fiddes, the covenant relationship is prior to how the covenant might be expressed. This, says Fiddes, means that to speak of covenant is not to speak of something static, but dynamic: "God's people are always on a pilgrimage to discover what it means to be called into relationship with God."[189] Hayden's chapter traces the history of covenant and confession among Baptists. He comments that the Baptist Union owes its structures to Shakespeare and it "has ever since been in search of a theology which will authenticate the organised national life of Baptist churches."[190] Later he goes on to suggest that "perhaps we should see the Declaration of Principle as being comparable to the 'covenant document' in the local church in a previous century."[191] Both these comments are ones that were taken up and developed in the 1990s. For Hayden, covenant theology offers Baptists a means of being rooted in their tradition and yet without being fixed so as to be "incapable of fulfilling our pilgrim role as the people of God."[192] Kidd's contribution is to see covenant not primarily as a document, but an experience of God's covenant love in Jesus. Kidd argues that "the authority of God in covenant love is immediate and personal; the authority of any written document, including the scriptures, is inevitably circumscribed by its derivative and impersonal form."[193] Important for Kidd to emphasize is the work of the Holy Spirit. It is the Spirit's guidance and interpretation in the church community that gives authority to the Bible.[194] The Spirit makes God's covenant love in Jesus present. It is the Spirit that enables the covenant community to discern and test their reading of the Scriptures.[195] Kidd, like Fiddes and Hayden, uses the language of the church as "pilgrims together on the open road of discipleship."[196] A theology of covenant is bound with a pilgrim-shaped ecclesiology. Clements's

187. Fiddes, "Covenant—Old and New," 15.

188. Fiddes, "Covenant—Old and New," 16.

189. Fiddes, "Covenant—Old and New," 16.

190. Hayden, "Baptists, Covenants and Confessions," 30.

191. Hayden, "Baptists, Covenants and Confessions," 35.

192. Hayden, "Baptists, Covenants and Confessions," 36.

193. Kidd, "Documents of Covenant Love," 39.

194. Kidd, "Documents of Covenant Love," 39–40.

195. Kidd, "Documents of Covenant Love," 44.

196. Kidd, "Documents of Covenant Love," 49.

concern is with what he sees as a belief in "community" as its own end; fellowship becomes the goal of the church, rather than conformity with Christ.[197] Clements's use of covenant is centered in the action of Christ; it is the death and resurrection of Christ that institutes the church. The church is not about fellowship or government, but about being open to the word of Christ. Clements asserts an understanding of the church as a covenant community in Christ that challenges a view of community in therapeutic or in authoritarian terms. The final chapter from Haymes draws attention to the "tension" between the notions of universal and particular covenants, which leads into a discussion of mission in a multi-faith context.[198] He concludes that this tension should shape our practice of mission and evangelism and asks Baptists two questions. The first is why Baptists have been reluctant to engage with the BCC's interfaith work, and the second is whether the tension in covenant has any impact on the policies of the BMS.

Alistair Campbell wrote a brief review in the *Mainstream Newsletter* which called *Bound to Love* overall "disappointing" but commended the chapters by Fiddes, Hayden, and Clements.[199] Campbell called it disappointing on the basis that it does not offer any suggestions for how covenant might be recovered again at as the basis of Baptist life. This suggests he accepts the theology. He also criticized them for what he consider generalizing about the restorationist and charismatic movements.

In the later work of the second stream, covenant became the controlling motif that shaped their account of Baptist theology and in particular ecclesiology. It might be noted that while Champion looked to the late eighteenth century for the theology needed, the theological thinkers in this group go further back to the seventeenth century.

Continuing Contributions

The second stream offered an alternative vision to Mainstream. It was a much smaller grouping—it did not seek to establish a movement—however into the 1990s and beyond others became involved to continue the work. In 1996 a third book was completed on baptism: *Reflections on the Water*. Fiddes, Haymes, Kidd, and Hayden all contributed, and Christopher Ellis and Hazel Sherman joined the group.[200]

197. Clements, "Covenant and Community," 60.

198. Haymes, "Covenant and the Church's Mission," 63.

199. Campbell, "Review: *Bound to Love*," 14–15.

200. Clements had left the group due to the pressures of his role as Coordinating Secretary for International Affairs for the Council of Churches from Britain and Ireland. In private conversation, Haymes recalled that Nigel Wright had also been invited,

By 1996 Fiddes, Haymes, and Kidd were principals of three of the English Baptist colleges and, joined by Michael Quicke,[201] principal of Spurgeon's College, they published *Something to Declare*, a study of the Declaration of Principle and in 1997 *On the Way of Trust*. While the second stream produced no manifesto type equivalent to Wright's *Challenge to Change*, both *Something to Declare* and *On the Way of Trust* provide a good account of their vision for the union's future. These two booklets were deliberate contributions to the denominational consultation that Coffey had initiated. *Something to Declare* was published in the months leading up to this and every delegate was given a copy. *On the Way of Trust* was published a year later in the context of where the conversation was going post the consultation. A final book by the principals was published in 2000 called *Doing Theology in a Baptist Way*, chapter 2 of which tells the story of the second stream. Between 1999 and 2008, Fiddes and the other college principals[202] organized a biannual summer consultation of Baptist ministers doing theology in context. The impact of the second stream was not largely felt among local church ministers, but it did have some influence in the council of the Baptist Union[203] and, because of the positions of those involved, in the Baptist colleges and those training there. Reflecting on this second stream in 1999, Fiddes, Haymes, Kidd, and Quicke acknowledged that their work had been "small contributory waves within the immensely broader tide of our denominational history, but it remains pleasing to think that our studies did indeed form a useful contribution to the story which as yet unfolds."[204]

During this period Paul Fiddes would write two more important contributions to Baptist life. A commentary on a Baptist Union Council report on charismatic renewal and a study of ministry and leadership in

but had not joined. I mention this to demonstrate that the two streams were not antithetical to one another. Haymes and Wright shared an interest in Anabaptist thought and practice and were both members of the Anabaptist Network when it began in 1992.

201. Quicke had overlapped with Fiddes while training for ministry at Regent's Park College, Oxford, but he had also been at Cambridge at the same time as Paul Beasley-Murray and was his best man at Beasley-Murray's wedding, Beasley-Murray, *This Is My Story*, 57.

202. In 2000 Haymes returned to pastoral ministry at Bloomsbury Central Baptist and the new Bristol principal was Christopher Ellis. In 2000 Quicke was appointed as C. W. Koller Professor of Preaching and Communication at Northern Seminary, Lombard, Illinois, and the new Spurgeon's principal was Nigel Wright.

203. Here significantly was the establishment of the Doctrine and Worship Committee within the structures of the Baptist Union in 1992 as it gave a means of addressing the council of the Baptist Union through a number of reports. Fiddes, Haymes, and Kidd were all on this committee, alongside others, including Wright.

204. Fiddes et al., "Doing Theology Together," 16.

the church. In 1978 a report on charismatic renewal was received by the council,[205] to which Fiddes was asked to write a commentary. The report itself was guardedly positive toward the benefits of charismatic renewal and Fiddes's commentary strikes a similar tone.[206] In the *Mainstream Newsletter*, Alistair Campbell wrote an open letter to Fiddes, which while critical of the report, is generally positive toward what Fiddes argues.[207] *A Leading Question?* originated as lectures given by Fiddes at a Baptist ministers' summer school in 1983.[208] The context of the book is again the obvious influence of the charismatic movement and that of the ecumenical movement, to which Fiddes also adds the influence of society. The book explores the place of leadership and gifts, leadership and team ministry, and leadership and authority. Much of what Fiddes writes here found its way into the later Doctrine and Worship Committee reports, *The Nature of the Assembly and the Council* and *Forms of Ministry among Baptists*.[209]

Clements, while not writing specifically for Baptists, had two books published in the 1980s by Bristol Baptist College, which are examples of the kind of theological renewal the group were advocating. In both books Dietrich Bonhoeffer was the conversation partner. The first, *A Patriotism For Today* was a timely engagement, in light of the Falklands Conflict, on the Christian's relationship to their country of origin: a question that was pressing for Bonhoeffer himself. At the heart of Clements's argument is the importance of ecumenism. He writes that "British Christians clearly need to break out of parochialism and insularity, into a deeper realization of belonging to one holy, catholic apostolic church of all times and place"[210] and "Britain therefore needs the internationalism of the ecumenical movement, through which churches and peoples represent themselves to each other."[211] The second book, *What Freedom?* was a collection of essays that engaged with the meaning of freedom in the context of the fall of communism in Eastern Europe, racism in America and apartheid in South Africa, and the

205. Members of the working group that produced the report were Donald McKenzie, Edmund Heddle, Geoffrey Rusling, John Briggs, Donald Black, Hugh Logan, and David Russell.

206. Fiddes, *Charismatic Renewal: A Baptist View*. It was published as part of a series edited by Alec Gilmore. Other titles in the series were on authority, the church, the ministry, children, and freedom.

207. Campbell, "Open Letter," 3–5.

208. Fiddes, *Leading Question*.

209. *The Nature of the Assembly and the Council of the Baptist Union of Great; Forms of Ministry among Baptists: Towards an Understanding of Spiritual Leadership*.

210. Clements, *Patriotism for Today*, 154.

211. Clements, *Patriotism for Today*, 162–63.

English Free Churches.[212] Where much of the theological reflection among Baptists had some tendency to be introspective and concerned too much with the structures and growth of Baptist life, Clements was pushing in another direction of a political theology engaged with the world.

In 1986 Brian Haymes published *A Question of Identity: Reflections on Baptist Principles and Practice*, which had originally been delivered as a set of lectures to the Yorkshire Baptist Ministers' Fellowship in February of that year.[213] Ian Randall, looking back in 2005, called it "a 'tract for the times,' initiating wide-ranging discussion."[214] In the following year Mainstream held a consultation on Baptist Identity[215] and published *A Perspective on Baptist Identity*. Seven contributors, from what David Slater calls a "more conservative and evangelical perspective,"[216] engaged with points from Haymes's work and offer a response.

A Question of Identity

In *A Question of Identity* Haymes argued for a renewed sense of Baptist identity.[217] Reflecting nearly thirty years later on why he wrote *A Question of Identity*, Haymes says the ecumenical context meant he was asking what it meant to be Baptist and remain Baptist. He was also asking what held Baptists together in the face of changes taking place.[218] In the booklet he highlighted three. Denominational identity and loyalty are lessened he argues by new divisions that cut across all denominations, that is, how charismatic or evangelical have become the key means of determining loyalty rather than a

212. Clements, *What Freedom?*

213. Keith Jones was secretary of the Yorkshire Baptist Association, 1980–1990. He would later edit another booklet, *Fellowship in the Gospel*, that emerged from the association's Doctrine and Theology Group, whose members included John Nicholson, Iain Collins, David Morris, Anthony Peck, Susan Thompson, and Haddon Willmer. This booklet, a series of six studies, emerged from the discussion that followed *A Question of Identity*.

214. Randall, *English Baptists*, 466. In a *Baptist Times* report, it says it sold 500 copies and a reprint was on its way, *BT*, October 23, 1986, 6. It would lead Bernard Green at the November 1986 council to begin a discussion about Baptist identity, Minutes, Baptist Union Council, November 11–12, 1986. The language of "tract for the times" is one used by Nigel Wright in his preface to *Challenge to Change* with regards his own hope for his book.

215. This was an invitation only study conference that took place September 21–22, 1987, at Gorsley Baptist Church.

216. Editor's note, in Slater, *Perspective on Baptist Identity*, 5.

217. Haymes has developed his argument for a renewed Baptist identity with Ruth Gouldbourne and Anthony R. Cross in their book *On Being the Church*.

218. Haymes, "Still Blessing the Ties That Bind," 91.

commitment to historic traditions.[219] In the immediate background is also the impact of restorationism upon Baptist churches in the early 1980s.[220] For Haymes, the problem is not conservative evangelicalism, but what he calls a rise in "non-rational conservatism" which has little time for questions of belief and practice and is focused only on what feels right.[221] This reflected his earlier concern in *A Call to Mind* that there was a dangerous growth of unthinking Christianity. Stephen Ibbotson interpreted Haymes's target here as churches of the renewal and restorationist movement.[222] Haymes argued for an evangelical theology in terms of the grace of God, but not an evangelical label.[223] Haymes's third change is what he called "the rise of personality cults"[224] and the loyalty to an individual rather than a commitment to Christ. He is opposed to those looking for strong or charismatic leaders. For each of these reasons, he sees Baptist identity as under threat, and so the rest of the chapters are a reminder of the tradition from which Baptists come and in which there is something to treasure. Haymes develops his account of Baptist identity around the themes of ecclesiology, questions of authority, the tradition of dissent and the importance of right belief.

In the Baptist understanding of the church Haymes makes nine interrelated points. (1) The church is important in the purposes of God. It is not an optional extra. (2) It is God who calls the church into being, who makes covenant against any human-centered religion. (3) God is gracious and we are recipients of his grace. (4) Our motivation for evangelism is that God is gracious, not for the sake of church growth. (5) Baptism affirms the saving grace of God and as such we should see baptism as sacramental. (6) Baptism and church membership are joined together, because baptism is always ecclesial, and discipleship is also ecclesial. (7) Furthermore, this means associating with other congregations is should not be "marginal" to our life. "We need a renewal of trust, a larger sense of Christ and his church." (8) The church does not equal the kingdom. The church is part of the purposes of God, of which the goal is that all things find their life in the kingdom. (9) At the center of the church is Christ, but the edges are blurred.

When Haymes turns to authority, he says Baptists have sought to hold together creatively three things: (1) Authority belongs to Christ; (2) The Bible is authoritative; and (3) The local church has liberty to discern the mind

---

219. Haymes, *Question of Identity*, 3.

220. For one account of this see Millward, "Chalk and Cheese?"

221. Haymes, *Question of Identity*, 4.

222. Ibbotson, "Variety of Worship," 64.

223. Haymes, *Question of Identity*, 9.

224. Haymes, *Question of Identity*, 4.

of Christ, and is not bound by anyone else.[225] The upshot of this, Haymes says, is if Christ is authoritative, then we have to recognize our Christologies for what they are, human words, which cannot be "equated with" Jesus.[226] This seems to be a comment on the Michael Taylor affair, and those that wanted the union to have much clearer statement of Christology. Haymes sides against those who were advocating this view.[227] When Haymes turns to the authority of the Bible, he does so as one who takes seriously historical criticism, and as such that shapes how we understand its authority. He argues that the Bible is "authoritative because it is the basic resource for those who believe Jesus Christ is the living Word of the liberating God."[228] Yet, he says, the writers of the Bible were human and to treat it otherwise is to practice "bibliolatry," in which we worship the Bible, rather than God.[229] For Haymes, the authority of the church, seen in the church meeting, needs to be shaped by trust and humility among the members, and at the same time, they should not hand over the making of decisions to ministers, deacons or elders. The final point, being that the local church should be open to and actively seek the wisdom from the wider church.

Haymes's discussion of dissent argues that there is no private religion, that the church exists by God's grace for the sake of the world, and therefore the church will be engaged in "social, political and economic dissent."[230]

The final chapter is an argument for Baptists to confess their faith as a "creative and useful task."[231] Belief, he says is both a believing in and a believing that. Baptists practice the former, but fear the latter. The result of this is that Baptists fail to do theology and it is theology that brings renewal. Haymes criticizes a "spirit of pragmatism"[232] and simple slogans that fails to recognize the reality and complexity of belief. He says, "I wish we could take the task, the practice of theology, more seriously amongst us,"[233] following our Baptist forebears.

The Mainstream essays find much in common with Haymes's presentation. Where they diverge are in terms of their view of restorationism,

225. Haymes, *Question of Identity*, 14–15.

226. Haymes, *Question of Identity*, 15.

227. Haymes and Taylor were colleagues for several years at Northern Baptist College.

228. Haymes, *Question of Identity*, 16.

229. Haymes, *Question of Identity*, 16–17.

230. Haymes, *Question of Identity*, 25.

231. Haymes, *Question of Identity*, 26.

232. Haymes, *Question of Identity*, 28.

233. Haymes, *Question of Identity*, 29.

church growth, and the place of Scripture. Tidball's response is the most important as it is the most directly critical. Tidball says the lack of emphasis on mission in *A Question of Identity* is a "serious omission."[234] A key distinctive of Baptist identity, says Tidball, is "our sense of mission."[235] He disagrees with Haymes that a desire for church growth is human-centered and instead sees evangelism as a response to God's grace *and* a desire for the church to grow.[236] Tidball's "fundamental questions" for Haymes center on the grace of God, the authority of Christ and also that of the Bible. In terms of grace, Tidball is concerned that Haymes has not said enough about sanctification, that is, the grace of God is not indifferent to right doctrine and right living. Tidball says what Haymes says with regards Christ is in danger of "a wooliness of doctrine."[237] He wants to argue that there are some parameters to christology and if there are not, then we are left with the authority of Christ not meaning very much. On the Bible, Tidball presents a more "evangelical hermeneutic" that finds language of a "basic resource" and a "major resource" as too weak, at least with how Baptists have usually spoken.[238] Tidball concludes with worries that to follow Haymes's call to theological thinking may be to make Christianity too intellectual and academic. Finally, Tidball suggests the changes in church life, might be because this is what people want and that Haymes's remedies may not be the answer. On this point, I suggest, Tidball speaks as an evangelical first, rather than as a Baptist.

The Mainstream essays in particular by Derek Tidball, Alastair Campbell, Nigel Wright, and Stephen Ibbotson argue more positively about the emergence of restorationism, as something from which Baptists must learn.[239] There is a suggestion that the Restorationist churches have become more baptistic than Baptist churches in terms of the strength of their networks and their desire to be New Testament churches. There is, as expected, a strong positioning of Baptists as evangelical, and in the case of Campbell, even a claim that being evangelical is more determinative than being Baptist in terms of Christian identity.[240]

---

234. Tidball, "Response to *A Question of Identity*," 11.

235. Tidball, "Response to *A Question of Identity*," 11.

236. Tidball, "Response to *A Question of Identity*," 11.

237. Tidball, "Response to *A Question of Identity*," 13.

238. Tidball, "Response to *A Question of Identity*," 14.

239. Wright, "Baptist Way of Being Church," 43–44.

240. Campbell, "Grounds of Association," 37.

Conclusion

This chapter has demonstrated that through the 1980s two streams of renewal were being advocated. While they had different emphases: one was
more focused on the institution of the denomination, and so political in
nature, the other was more on the need for theology; both streams were advocating positively for a renewal of life and thought among Baptists. There
was only limited interaction between the two streams. The clearest engagement was that between Haymes's book and the Mainstream response. This
was to be expected because the second stream did not occupy an ongoing space in Baptist life outside of its occasional publications. Mainstream
in this regard was the more well-known and was able through its regular
newsletter and annual conference to push for the changes they wanted to
see.[241] The Champion stream was more modest, much smaller in size and
was apolitical in terms of the structures: it made no attempt to fill posts
with regards national appointments, but it did come to dominate the role
of principals in the colleges. As principals they exercised influence over the
many ministerial students who trained at their respective colleges[242] and
the role also gave them a profile at a national level. Those in stream 2, with
a perceived sense of disappointment, reflected later that their work "hardly
caused a ripple" and "prompted little discussion" and wondering if they
should have be more "polemical."[243]

It is not straightforward to compare the two streams, because Mainstream, through their newsletter, were not doing the kind of theological
work present in the stream 2. In this stream 2 were unique in the theology
they were producing in the 1980s. The two streams might be compared in
terms of their theological background. Fiddes, Haymes, Hayden, and Clements were all from the Bristol-Oxford tradition.[244] Kidd while he trained

241. In addition they also made use other outlets in the Baptist constituency like the
Baptist Times and *Fraternal.*

242. See Goodliff, *Ministry, Sacrament and Representation,* 80–81, for some
evidence of this in terms of understandings of ministry. At Spurgeon's the impact of
the second stream was more limited, although this changed as John Colwell, another
significant Baptist theologian, joined the staff in 1994. During the 2000s, as Tutor in
Christian Doctrine and Ethics, his theological work shared similar concerns. Colwell
would publish in *Promise and Presence: A Sacramental Theology,* identifying him in the
growing circle of "catholic" Baptists, alongside Fiddes and others.

243. Fiddes et al., "Doing Theology Together," 8–9.

244. The two colleges formed a partnership in 1936 where students would do the
BA in theology at Bristol, before going onto Oxford. See Moon, *Education for Ministry,*
78. This continued into the 1990s with Janet Tollington and Sean F. Winter, who both
went from Bristol on to Oxford to do a DPhil. Under the principalships of Champion,
West, and Haymes (at Bristol) and Child, White, and Fiddes (at Regent's) there was a

for ministry at Spurgeon's did his DPhil at Regent's. The Bristol-Oxford tradition was more open ecumenically and liturgically and represented a more high church Baptist stream. Those involved in Mainstream had a higher number of members from the more conservative evangelical colleges of Spurgeon's, London Bible College and All Nations: Coffey, Brown, Wright were all trained at Spurgeon's, while McBain and Tidball were trained at London Bible College and Goodland at All Nations. Beasley-Murray trained at Northern, but he was already a convinced evangelical by the time he arrived and his time there did little to shape him theologically. There was a definite division in terms of theological and spiritual education between the two streams. However this cannot be pressed to far, because White, Campbell, Ramsbottom were all trained at Regent's and Grange at Northern, which shows that Mainstream at least had support from across the colleges, apart from Bristol. While stream 2 was the more academic, a number of those associated with Mainstream would gain PhDs in the 1990s,[245] although apart from Wright they made few continuing academic contributions.

Through the 1980s those associated with both stream 1 and stream 2 began to become more nationally recognized figures. It was though in the 1990s that they moved into positions of influence: Coffey in becoming general secretary and Wright through *Challenge to Change* and later chairing the Task Group on Associating; Fiddes in becoming chair of the Doctrine and Worship Committee and Haymes in becoming president of the union in 1993 and chairing the Review Group on Superintendency. In addition both Wright and Haymes began to write regular comment pieces in the *Baptist Times*.

Subsequent chapters will explore how the two streams and those associated with them were at the heart of the conversation and renewal of Baptist life that became the focus of the decade.

---

shared theological outlook.

245. Terry Griffith, Alistair Campbell, Nigel Wright all completed doctorates and of course Beasley-Murray, Brown, White, and Tidball all had doctorates as well.

Chapter 3

Sources of Renewal

The Place of Tradition

THIS CHAPTER WILL EXAMINE the sources being used in the theology of Nigel Wright and Paul Fiddes, representing the two streams of renewal described in the previous chapter.[1] In so doing I am asking to what or who do they appeal, that is, in what concepts or traditions are their theological claims for the renewal of Baptist life grounded. While there is a view among some Baptists that they only need the Bible,[2] both Wright and Fiddes find a place for tradition in their arguments. In recent years there has been a renewed interest among Baptists in the place and role of tradition and an acceptance that we cannot *just* read the Bible. In this there is a simple acknowledgment, as Stephen Holmes states, that we cannot escape our "historical locatedness"[3]—tradition of some kind is unavoidable for those who claim the name Christian. What judgment and authority is given to tradition is of course a matter of debate. If tradition is unavoidable, it is at the same time not static, rather it is a "diachronic and synchronic process of continuity and change."[4] Baptists can point to elements of continuity with their forebears and also point to places where they have changed.

---

1. Both Fiddes and Wright are included as the only British theologians considered as "New Voices in Baptist Theology" in Garrett, *Baptist Theology*, 676–83, 686–90.

2. See for example Ted Hale's critical review of Kidd, *Something to Declare*, in *BT*, August 29, 1996, 7, 12.

3. Holmes, *Listening to the Past*, 6.

4. Medley, "Stewards, Interrogators, and Inventors," 81.

In a discussion of how to use tradition, Mark Medley suggests that the skills we need are those of stewardship, interrogation, and invention. The first is about the importance of continuity, the second and third point to the ongoing task of renewal. Stewardship receives "the tradition with charity and cherish[es] its wisdom,"[5] while interrogation examines the tradition and considers how it might require "re-evaluation,"[6] and lastly, invention seeks ways in which a tradition might be reappropriated or reconfigured for the present.[7] In all of this theology and history come together and there is a tension between what B. R. White called "the problem of deciding the balance between the guidance given by tradition horizontally and the guidance given in the present by the Holy Spirit vertically."[8]

For Wright, "any renewal movement . . . searches for roots in the past"[9] and for this reason in *Challenge to Change* at different moments he draws attention to points in Baptist history where an "insight" is "considered to be crucial."[10] The purpose of engaging with a tradition is the "recovery"[11] of beliefs and values that will help renew the church in the present. For Wright, his interest is not personal—how am I connected to these people—but for the purpose of discovering what will lead the present church into greater "obedience to Jesus."[12] Later he says, "the value of reading history is that it sheds light upon the present and gives signposts for the future."[13] For Wright, tradition is something that can be held and passed on. As such he can speak of the Baptist "genetic code" in which Baptist identity is carried.[14]

Fiddes's discussion of tradition uses the language of "tracks" by which he explains "there are pathways trodden in the past which still have definite meaning and relevance for the present."[15] He combines this with "traces," which "hint at uncertainty, at ambiguity."[16] For Fiddes, "scripture and tradition always belong together"[17] because of the ongoing activity of reading

5. Medley, "Stewards, Interrogators, and Inventors," 83.
6. Medley, "Stewards, Interrogators, and Inventors," 84.
7. Medley, "Stewards, Interrogators, and Inventors," 87.
8. White, "Task of a Baptist Historian," 403.
9. Wright, *Challenge to Change*, 19.
10. Wright, *Challenge to Change*, 16.
11. Wright, *Challenge to Change*, 16.
12. Wright, *Challenge to Change*, 17.
13. Wright, *Challenge to Change*, 212.
14. Wright, *Free Church*, 40.
15. Fiddes, *Tracks and Traces*, 1.
16. Fiddes, *Tracks and Traces*, 1.
17. Fiddes, preface to *Tradition*, xi. Cf. Fiddes, "Learning from Others," 56–64.

and interpreting the Scripture by the church. Following the North American Baptist theologian James McClendon, Fiddes argues that we should understand tradition as a "complex set of enduring, but not changeless, practices"[18] in which the church indwells and participates. The implications, says Fiddes, in contrast to Wright, are that Baptist identity or heritage cannot be reduced to an agreed set of values or beliefs. There is no founding Baptist document,[19] rather the Baptist tradition is about an ongoing shared life in "the tradition of the gospel."[20] Tradition for Baptists is something held by the community and as such the ongoing engagement with tradition, says Fiddes, occurs most commonly in the task of preaching and in the act of gathering in church meeting.[21]

Wright's three key sources of renewal are Anabaptism and early Baptist history, the charismatic movement and evangelicalism. *Challenge to Change* is an argument for a renewed Baptist identity. Wright believes there is a Baptist identity, but it needs renewing and it needs recovering. What needs recovering are a set of values and principles and he looks back to "the emergence of the continental Anabaptists . . . and English Baptists"[22] for their source, what he calls elsewhere the Baptist genetic code. He identifies four key insights which, if "recovered" and "re-appropriated," would lead to a "renewal of local churches and of wider denominational relationships."[23] The four insights are: the supreme authority of the Bible; the true church is composed of believers and therefore baptism should be a sign of freely chosen faith; the priesthood of all believers and the autonomy of the local church; and freedom of conscience and the separation of church and state.

Alongside this source is the claim that Baptists are evangelical, demonstrated by the place they give Scripture. Wright thus argues that the Baptist denomination needs "to recover explicitly its evangelical identity."[24] Here then is a second source for renewal: evangelicalism as a "theological tradition" and not he says as a "party."[25] This tradition prioritizes Scripture, grace, and faith. Wright carefully refuses to define being evangelical with any more

18. Fiddes, preface to *Tradition*, xii.

19. "Baptists have never been much interested by historic moments and places in their story," Fiddes, *Tracks and Traces*, 21.

20. Fiddes, preface to *Tradition*, xii.

21. Fiddes, preface to *Tradition*, xv. In this description Fiddes is echoing something of Alasdair MacIntyre's description of "living tradition," *After Virtue*, 222. See also McClendon, *Ethics*.

22. Wright, *Challenge to Change*, 22.

23. Wright, *Challenge to Change*, 22.

24. Wright, *Challenge to Change*, 160.

25. Wright, *Challenge to Change*, 161.

precision. There is room for diversity with regards "the priority of scripture." He suggests that the Baptist Union be viewed "as a coalition of conservative, liberal and radical evangelicals."[26]

For Wright, a third source of renewal is charismatic renewal. Wright can say churches "should experience the renewing work of the Spirit."[27] The charismatic movement is thus important because it contains within it "the spiritual renewal of the believer and the cultural renewal of the church."[28] Baptists need a "*glasnost*" with regards the Spirit. Wright can say "that Baptist Christians ought to listen carefully to the voice of the Spirit in charismatic renewal."[29] Wright argues that Baptist worship should be more charismatic and that its evangelism should follow the power evangelism of John Wimber, that is, preaching should be joined with signs and wonders.

Turning to Fiddes, the key source of renewal he believes is the "idea of covenant." This he says was a "theological theme that was of central importance for several centuries" and is being recovered today.[30] Fiddes looks back to the English Separatists and early Baptists as the location in which this covenant theology is developed.[31] Another source for Fiddes is what might be termed a Baptist Catholicism, associated most prominently with Ernest Payne. Fiddes says of Payne that "he exemplified in himself the Baptist vision which places the community of Baptist Christians clearly within the fellowship of the church universal."[32] Fiddes understands his own work as a continuation of that particular Baptist vision.[33]

If recovery of covenant is central to Fiddes vision of renewed Baptist life, he seeks to bring it into relation with a second source that of a theology of *koinonia* rooted in the triune God.[34] The doctrine of the Trinity takes a significant place within Fiddes's theology and he offers his own unique understanding of it in conversation with a wide range of other theologians. Fiddes also reaches back and reaches out to ecumenical theology that has recovered the doctrine of the Trinity and argued for its implications for the ministry and life of the church.

26. Wright, *Challenge to Change*, 161.
27. Wright, *Challenge to Change*, 49.
28. Wright, *Challenge to Change*, 50.
29. Wright, *Challenge to Change*, 54.
30. Fiddes, *Tracks and Traces*, 17.
31. Fiddes, *Tracks and Traces*, 78–82.
32. Fiddes, *Tracks and Traces*, xvi.
33. Fiddes, *Tracks and Traces*, xv.
34. Fiddes, *Tracks and Traces*, 78–82.

A final source of renewal is that of mission. This is most closely associated with Coffey, but it also finds a place within Wright and Fiddes, as will become evident in the next chapter.

For both Fiddes and Wright there is a reaching back to retrieve something from the past[35] and a reaching out to something considered helpful in the present. In terms of sources some of them are shared across the two streams—the theology of mission and to a lesser degree anabaptism. Other sources are unshared and particular to the different streams. So the concept of covenant and the emphasis on catholicity is present in the theological renewal stream, while evangelicalism is emphasized in the denominational renewal stream. This demonstrates that the conversations in the 1990s found places of convergence but also of divergence and dispute. A third point can also be recognized in that some of the sources are those generating ideas and some are those generating traditions. The theology of covenant and the theology of mission are sources of ideas that Fiddes and Wright are using as building blocks for their vision of renewal. While evangelicalism and catholicism are traditions in which Wright and Fiddes situate themselves to locate and orientate their respective visions. Having given a brief description of the key sources that the two streams look to, in the rest of this chapter I want to engage more closely with each of them.

Anabaptism

The seeds of Wright's Anabaptist interest lie in a visit in 1980 (his first sabbatical) to a Mennonite community in Pennsylvania. He says that as a result of that visit

> a firm interest . . . had begun to take root . . . These groups of radical, revolutionary disciples caught my imagination . . . Here was a historical vantage point . . . which provided a lens through which to view the contemporary Church in both its traditional and its innovative modes of life.[36]

Elsewhere he has also said,

> When I reflect about what has drawn me to Anabaptism I can identify certain strengths which resonate for me as a Baptist and

35. For a helpful discussion of what it means to retrieve something theologically see Sarisky, "Tradition II."

36. Wright, "Pilgrimage in Renewal," 26.

which exert a magnetic pull on the ways in which I wish to do theology and, indeed, pursue discipleship.[37]

In *Challenge to Change*, Wright suggests that the Anabaptist vision, with its emphasis on discipleship, evangelism, zeal, and peace, has something from which Baptists can learn.[38] In an increasingly post-Christian context the Anabaptists, believes Wright, provide some tracks to follow. At the same time, Wright does not shy away from recognizing negative traits in Anabaptism. For example, where it was sometimes too literalist in its readings of the Bible or where its concern to be the true church led it to be unable to be open to sinners. In terms of the latter, Wright claims that an Anabaptist emphasis on separation needed to be balanced by an equal emphasis on mission.[39] Wright is interested in those Anabaptists who were what he calls evangelical: those associated with Conrad Grebel, Menno Simons, Jacob Hutter, and Pilgram Marpeck. This chapter on Anabaptism is not essential to Wright's chief argument for change, but its inclusion demonstrates its importance—the magnetic pull—to Wright's own theology, signified by his regular use of the word "radical." Wright's ongoing interest in Anabaptism can be seen in his doctoral studies which compared the ecclesiologies and missiologies of John Howard Yoder and Jürgen Moltmann and published as *Disavowing Constantine*. His broad thesis was that the Baptist attitude to the state should incline itself more toward Anabaptism (Yoder) than Reformed Christianity (Moltmann). Wright argues for a political and missiological theology that restates Anabaptist ideas for the present context. Wright's Anabaptist learnings can also be found in *The Radical Evangelical*, although more muted,[40] and in *Free Church, Free State*, which he says is "in many ways . . . a more accessible version" of *Disavowing Constantine*.[41]

Wright returned to the importance of Anabaptism in 2006 in a contribution to a set of essays on Baptist spirituality. Here he claims Anabaptism as a "resource on which we [Baptists] may draw for understanding the forms of piety we have espoused and for shaping our spiritual practices

37. Wright, "Spirituality as Discipleship," 82.

38. Wright suggests that early Anabaptists can be compared to the present day Restorationist or house-church movement, from which Wright also believed Baptists could learn.

39. Wright, *Disavowing Constantine*, 3.

40. He says, "As this book proceeds, my own indebtedness to some of the radical aspects of evangelical history will emerge, in particular that type of radical Protestantism which has taken form first in Anabaptism and then in the Free Churches of English history," Wright, *Radical Evangelical*, 11.

41. Wright, *Free Church, Free State*, xviii.

for the future."[42] He draws out three aspects of Anabaptist spirituality he believes Baptists should give attention to: the centrality of Christ, the primacy of the congregation and the theme of following after Christ. This is a reminder that Wright's concern has generally been at the congregational level and only after that to wider structures that might serve the health and growth of the local. Anabaptist theology is helpful to this aim and he largely approaches the tradition in the mode of a stewardship, unearthing its relevance for the present.

Anabaptism as a source of renewal can also be set against the background of the Anabaptist Network which was launched in Autumn 1992 with a new journal, *Anabaptism Today*, and several study networks.[43] Its roots came from an earlier smaller study group called the Radical Reformation Study Group that had been set up in the 1980s by Alan Kreider[44] and Wright.[45] Kreider and Wright with Stuart Murray[46] and others were influential in setting up the Anabaptist Network.[47] The network was cross-denominational, but, in addition to Wright and Murray, several key Baptists were involved during the 1990s. The book *Coming Home: Stories of Anabaptists in Britain and Ireland* tells the stories of some of those who have been involved in and impacted both by Anabaptism and by the network.[48] Among those whose stories are included are Brian Haymes, Keith Jones, and Anne Wilkinson-Hayes.[49] Over a thousand people at one point were members of the network, of which the largest number were Baptists.[50]

What the stories in *Coming Home* and Wright's work demonstrate is that the impact of Anabaptism has been one which has largely affected

42. Wright, "Spirituality as Discipleship," 80. The chapter was first given in 2006 at the Baptists Doing Theology in Context Consultation held at Luther King House, Manchester, and was then published in 2008.

43. *BT*, September 24, 1992, 10; *Spurgeon's College Record* 103 (Spring/Summer 1993) 9.

44. Alan Kreider was a member of staff at both Northern Baptist College and then Regent's Park College, Oxford in the 1990s. He and his wife Eleanor were Mennonites, who originally came to the UK as missionaries under the Mennonite Boards of Missions based in the 1980s at the London Mennonite Centre.

45. Nigel Wright was Tutor in Christian Doctrine, Spurgeon's College, 1987–1994, and then principal at Spurgeon's College, 2000–2012.

46. Stuart Murray was Tutor in Church Planting and Evangelism, Spurgeon's College, 1992–2001.

47. Others involved were Eleanor Kreider, Judith Gardiner, Noel Moules, Trisha Dale, David Nussbaum, and Nelson Kraybill.

48. Murray and Kreider, *Coming Home*.

49. Anne Wilkinson-Hayes was Social Action Advisor, Baptist Union, 1992–1997.

50. Randall, "Anabaptism and Mission," 148.

individuals—shaping their spirituality and theology—and the congregations to which they belong, and with regard to the latter, often only in limited ways. All those Baptists involved in the Anabaptist Network have remained Baptists. There has been no planting of Anabaptist churches. The network has also always been ecumenical as *Coming Home* demonstrates. I would contend Baptists in general have not shifted in a more Anabaptist direction. They have not become a union of *radical* Baptists. Instead it has remained within the union largely a fringe interest, albeit deeply significant for those who have identified with the Anabaptist Network. Ian Randall says Anabaptism has "made an important contribution" as a source of renewal for "effective mission."[51]

Wright's interest in Anabaptism was not shared by many in Mainstream. There was no argument made, even by Wright, for Mainstream to become more Anabaptist.[52] Anabaptism as a movement or its ideas were never directly discussed within the *Newsletter*, although Alan Kreider was a speaker at the 1984 conference. Wright's radical evangelicalism then was fairly unique among the mix of evangelicals within Mainstream, at least to the extent that it was derived from an engagement with Anabaptism.

From the second stream, Brian Haymes was a member of the Anabaptist Network. He was both a colleague and a friend of Kreider but had already come to appreciate Anabaptism during his preparation for ministry. In his contribution to *Coming Home*, Haymes writes that it was the Anabaptist "emphasis on the practice of discipleship that struck me as significant."[53] Haymes also speaks of his interest in Anabaptists expressed through the work of John Howard Yoder and Stanley Hauerwas[54] and in his essay on baptism as a political act, both theologians feature in support of his argument. Haymes's Anabaptist interest is also evident in that he co-wrote with Kyle Gingerich Hiebert, *God After Christendom?* in the Anabaptist series of books edited by Stuart Murray.[55] Outside of this Anabaptism has not shaped significantly Haymes's contributions to Baptist life. It is in the background rather than in the foreground of his work. Like with Mainstream, Anabaptist thinking is marginal to the second stream's work.

The third person who must be mentioned in this brief consideration of Anabaptism as a source of renewal is Keith Jones. Jones was also a member

51. Randall, "Anabaptism and Mission," 164.

52. He notes in *Challenge to Change* that "my enthusiasm for Anabaptists is not shared by everyone," 212.

53. Haymes, "Longing for Authentic Christian Belonging and Discipleship," 63.

54. Haymes, "Longing for Authentic Christian Belonging and Discipleship," 64.

55. Although in the introduction, Haymes and Hiebert are critical of some of the aspects of Murray's slant on the move from Christendom to Post-Christendom.

of the Anabaptist Network and for some time convenor of the Anabaptist Theological Study Circle. In his contribution to *Coming Home* he says, "I contend passionately that the believers' church needs to act radically to become the sort of missionary congregations which can have an impact in our post-modern, post-Christendom world."[56] In 1998 as he moved from being deputy general secretary of the union to being rector of the International Baptist Theological Seminary, Jones published *A Believing Church*. In this booklet he precisely asks the question how might the Anabaptists help renew the church today.[57] He writes, "I am persuaded that unless we look carefully at our history and learn from it, we might well miss something of a larger vision and the opportunity to connect with our roots."[58] Jones understands that a recovery of Anabaptist thinking can help us see what it means to be "the missionary people of God."[59]

From his account of the Anabaptists, Jones highlights features of their thought as places to ask questions of Baptist life today—they were radicals, they were marginalized, they practiced a christological hermeneutic, alongside being a consultative community, with a distinctive lifestyle; they were also inclusive, especially with regards the role of women, they were ecumenical, concerned for human rights, and for peacemaking and they were missionary.

Two years earlier, ahead of the denominational consultation, Jones gave an address to the annual assembly of the Bristol and District Association of Baptist Churches on his thoughts for the future of the union. An edited version appeared in the *Baptist Times*. In this address he specifically draws on Anabaptist thought.[60] He begins his reflections with the kingdom rather than the institution of the church. He argues that it is easy to get "drawn into a veritable spider's web of an ecclesiological institution . . . which requires preservation for its own sake." The Kingdom provides a different starting point, a missional one, focused on "prophetic, Gospel-focused living." He offers four themes—first, a gospel performed and embodied not just proclaimed; second, a willingness to learn from the world church, that is, being open to a "cross-fertilisation of mission"; third, a willingness to be a more inclusive church, especially with regards women, but also in terms of race; and fourth, a willingness to embrace a much wider ecumenism. Some of these themes are apparent in the later *A Believing Church*. While it is true

56. Jones, "Believers' Church Needs to Act Radically."

57. Jones, *Believing Church*, 2.

58. Jones, *Believing Church*, 7.

59. Jones, *Believing Church*, 7.

60. *BT*, July 4, 1996, 12.

to say that this kind of vision found some connection with the outcomes of the denominational consultation, an Anabaptist way of being Baptist did not emerge, at least not at a conscious level. Jones on becoming rector of the International Theological Baptist Seminary in 1998 went on to encourage Anabaptist theology and practice among the students.

If Anabaptist thinking had an impact in the Baptist institutional life in the 1990s it was perhaps in the document *Five Core Values*. This sought to offer a description of what it was to be a gospel people, that is, a people "determined by the life of Jesus" and "living in *radical* commitment to him."[61] The five core values were identified as prophetic, inclusive, sacrificial, missionary, and worshiping. These were the values, arising out of the person of Jesus Christ that should be visible among Baptists in community. Each of the values had implications, the document argued, for local churches, for the denomination and in society and the world. Whether consciously or not this was a document that sounded some Anabaptist themes, none more so than in the suggestion that being a missionary community might mean becoming a "Peace Church." One of the members of the task group that wrote *Five Core Values* was Anne Wilkinson-Hayes, another member of the Anabaptist Network. Wilkinson-Hayes writes in her contribution to *Coming Home* that "the commitment to recovering Anabaptist principles of community, peace and radical lifestyle within my own Baptist tradition has grown over recent years."[62] In the *5 Core Values Bible Study Pack*, David Coffey claims that the core values were a means of "call[ing] us back to that biblical non-conformity and prophetic dissent which lies at the heart of our calling as God's people."[63]

Evangelicalism

The 1990s was the decade when the Baptist Union began to more consciously reflect an evangelical identity. In 1991 84 percent of Baptists identified as evangelical.[64] Immediately it must be asked what is meant by evangelical? David Bebbington argues that "from the eighteenth century onwards most [Baptists] were Evangelicals."[65] Ernest Payne, David Russell, and Bernard

61. *Five Core Values*, 4.

62. Wilkinson-Hayes, "Lending Greater Integrity to Being Church," 133.

63. *Five Values Bible Study Pack*, 1. In a book on spirituality in the churches of CTE, the Baptist contribution (probably written by Myra Blyth) describes *Five Core Values* as taking up a "radical evangelical Baptist commitment," Lampard, *Such a Feast*, 12.

64. Randall, "Baptist Growth in Britain," 63–64.

65. Bebbington, *Baptists Through the Centuries*, 2.

Green were all happy to use the word evangelical to describe Baptists.[66] Brian Stanley argues that this may reflect that among the Free Churches "a broad range of theological opinion continued after the Second World War to lay claim to the label 'evangelical' . . . extending as far as the early 1970s."[67] What changed is that the word evangelical by the 1980s and 90s had come to mean something more conservative than it had previously. So Bebbington suggests that between the 1970s and end of the 1980s the phrase "'conservative evangelical' . . . was . . . dropped by most adherents of the movement in favour of the simpler 'evangelical.'"[68] Faith Bowers, a Baptist historian has said:

> Many Baptist friendships are made with fellow Evangelicals, who do not always move most readily in ecumenical circles. The term "Evangelical" is now often used just of those who have a conservative approach to the Bible and not much else. Some Baptists resent this hijacking of the term by part of the denomination. Coming from a less conservative wing of the denomination, I am frequently reminded, by my own reactions when in ecumenical contexts, that I am an Evangelical Christian—yet some Baptists would begrudge me that label.[69]

This is a similar point to that Haymes makes in *A Question of Identity*, where he speaks of evangelical becoming a party label, wanting to distinguish between the term evangelical and evangelicalism. The word evangelical has thus been used differently by Baptists. So while Baptists are evangelicals, for many this is in terms of a broad theological and historical tradition.[70] The majority of Baptists had not identified with what Pete Ward calls "transconfessional evangelicalism" which focused on "strategy and organizational power."[71] Some Baptists have been hesitant or even resistant to belonging to or identifying with any of the "tribes of evangelicalism." It is this that began to change in the 1990s as Mainstream had grown a more tribal evangelicalism within the union, which began to dominate. Stanley considers that the growth of evangelicalism among the Free Churches was connected to how

66. In Payne's 1977 presidential address he says, speaking of Baptists: "as activists and evangelicals by nature and tradition," *BT*, April 1977. In an article for the *Baptist Times*, Russell begins, "Baptists stand firmly in the evangelical tradition," *BT*, September 5, 1974, 1. Green said, "For at heart we Baptists are all an evangelical people in the best and right sense of that word," *BT*, October 8, 1981, 16.

67. Stanley, *Global Diffusion of Evangelicalism*, 44.

68. Bebbington, "Evangelical Trends," 99.

69. Bowers, "Unity in Legitimate Diversity," 58.

70. See Bebbington, *Evangelicalism in Modern Britain*, 2–3.

71. Ward, "Tribes of Evangelicalism," 27.

much Free Church identity was a "more potent force than pan-evangelical sentiment."[72] By the late twentieth century, a pan-evangelicalism had replaced a Free Church identity.[73]

During the 1980s and into 1990s Baptists move from being what I will call evangelical with a small "e," representing a broad evangelicalism, committed especially to the Bible and the need for conversion, to being Evangelical with a capital "E," representing a moderate conservative evangelicalism[74] with lots in common with Clive Calver's EA[75] and Spring Harvest.[76] Baptists became part of the emerging Evangelical subculture.[77]

What happened in the 1980s, I suggest, was that a growing confident evangelicalism confronted a less confident sense of being Baptist.[78] Neither Payne nor Russell built bridges to those in the conservative evangelical wing of the church,[79] which was not a big problem until Michael Taylor's address opened up a doctrinal crisis.[80] This provoked the more moderate conservative evangelicals into action.[81] In an amendment to the 1971 November council resolution which asserted the council belief in the deity of Christ, Payne sought to differentiate Baptists from Evangelicals, making a clear

72. Stanley, *Global Diffusion of Evangelicalism*, 46.

73. There appeared no significant champion of a Free Church identity in this period. This is reflected by the waning influence of the Free Church Federal Council, which in 2001 became the Free Churches Group within CTE.

74. It is important to qualify the version of conservative evangelicalism as "moderate" because it would not have been recognized by the Baptist Revival Fellowship of the 1960s and '70s, with its anti-ecumenical and anti-union stance, which were deemed theologically liberal.

75. In percentage terms by the late 1990s Baptists churches made up about 25 percent of all churches in membership with the Evangelical Alliance, see Warner, *Reinventing Evangelicalism*, 48.

76. From its beginnings 30 percent of those attending Spring Harvest have been Baptists, Warner, *Reinventing Evangelicalism*, 67.

77. Pete Ward has described some of the evangelical subculture especially with regard to worship music in *Growing Up Evangelical* and *Selling Worship*.

78. Connected to this is the influence of charismatic renewal and the restorationist churches.

79. Stanley, *Global Diffusion of Evangelicalism*, 46. Sadly Percy Evans, the principal of Spurgeon's College died two months before Payne took office as general secretary. Evans, a friend and supporter of Payne's, would have been Payne's link to the Spurgeonic tradition, that is, the conservative evangelicals, West, *To Be a Pilgrim*, 73, 74, 76.

80. Stephen Holmes says, "Billy Graham had re-invigorated conservative evangelicalism in the 1950s, and an older, broader tradition of Baptist life still persisted, especially, perhaps on the committees of Baptist Church House. At some point a public disagreement was inevitable," Holmes, "Dangers of Just Reading the Bible," 126.

81. Most notably George Beasley-Murray and Cyril Black and also in the background Douglas McBain.

statement that in his view that being Baptist did not mean simply being evangelical.[82] The amendment which called for toleration and mutual respect did not pass but was included as an addendum.[83] To the 1972 assembly, a further resolution was brought by Cyril Black and passed which affirmed that the Declaration of Principle should be understood as declaring Jesus as truly God and truly man and that all ministers must give their assent to it.[84] An attempt by Champion, and seconded by Green, to remove the particular paragraphs about the Declaration of Principle and the Ministerial Recognition Rules was defeated.[85] Writing to Russell, Cyril Black said, "Most of our ministers are much more conservative . . . The strength of this conservative element in the denomination can no longer be ignored."[86] Beasley-Murray records that

> there are those who see 1972 as the moment when the tide actually began to turn even though it was some years before the tide began to come in. The ethos of the denomination began to change.[87]

In an article for the Alpha magazine in 1991 Warner wrote that "the evangelical Baptists are growing."[88] He puts the growth of evangelical Baptists down to the impact of Mainstream. He concludes his article by saying,

> At every level—numerical growth, senior appointments, increasing number of trained leaders and ambitious evangelistic strategy—the evidence is clear. We are witnessing an evangelical resurgence among Baptists which is unprecedented this century.[89]

---

82. Randall, *English Baptists*, 374. The addendum by Payne began: "This Council declares that whilst asserting and cherishing its special affinities with those of the Evangelical tradition, our denomination has always claimed a place in the one holy universal church and desires the closest possible fellowship with all who love and trust our Lord Jesus Christ."

83. The full resolution with the addendum can be found in Hill, *Baptist Revival Fellowship*, appendix 9, 205–6.

84. This resolution can also be found in Hill, *Baptist Revival Fellowship*, appendix 13, 216–17.

85. Randall, *English Baptists*, 380–81.

86. Letter cited in Randall, *English Baptists*, 382. Cf. Beasley-Murray, *Fearless for Truth*, 159–60.

87. Beasley-Murray, *Fearless for Truth*, 160.

88. Warner, "British Baptists," 18.

89. Warner, "British Baptists," 20.

Coffey was a self-confessed evangelical, a member of the EA and its council.[90] He was one of the speakers at the 1996 National Assembly for Evangelicals. Many of the presidents of Baptist Union during these years were also identifiable evangelicals—Tidball, Gaukroger, James, McBain, Bochenski, and Wright. In 1986 the Evangelism Committee became a member of the EA[91] and in 1996 the Mission Department as a whole joined the EA.[92] Several prominent Baptists wrote books about evangelicalism—Tidball, *Who are the Evangelicals?*; Wright, *The Radical Evangelical*; Warner (with Clive Calver), *Together We Stand*; and Bebbington in 1989 had written *Evangelicalism in Modern Britain*.

In November 1999, the EA requested a meeting with the union to explore membership of the union with the EA.[93] This emerged from the fact that the Baptist Union of Scotland and the BMS had both recently become members.[94] At the November 2000 council meeting Christopher Ellis reported back on the meetings between the EA and members of the Faith and Unity Executive. Ellis said that the union had had a relationship with the EA for many years, but had "drawn back from a commitment to sign the EA declaration of faith as being inappropriate to its status as a representative Union of individual churches."[95] Ellis went on to say that another argument might be that "formal membership might underline the evangelicalism of the BUGB and could encourage fruitful links with other evangelical groupings and churches."[96] Fiddes in the discussion pointed out that the EA's dec-

90. Coffey joined the council in 1988, see Minutes of Evangelism Committee, October 12, 1988. Also on the council, at different times were Gaukroger, Tidball, Wright, Warner, and Robert Amess. Ian Coffey (David's younger brother) worked for EA between 1988–1992.

91. Minutes of the Evangelism Committee, September 10, 1986, 2.

92. Randall, *English Baptists*, 497. Darrell Jackson, "BUGB Churches and EA Membership," February 1997. In an email Jackson, who was a mission advisor in the Mission Department, explained to me that "during 1997 (I don't recall the details) it was agreed that on the basis that many Baptist churches identified more closely with the EA than with either CTE or CTBI (of which we were full members) it would be desirable to have a more formal relationship with the EA . . . It was decided with the Management Team of BUGB that the Evangelism Desk of the Mission Department should become a 'member' of the EA, enabling me to engage with a number of EA-led evangelistic initiatives. This occurred under Keith Jones's oversight of the Department and the EA membership was renewed for each year that Derek Allan remained Head of Department." Private email dated December 6, 2016.

93. Minutes, Baptist Union Council, November 1999.

94. For the story of BUS membership with the EA, see Moyes, *Our Place among the Churches*, 126–27.

95. Minutes, Baptist Union Council, November 2000, 18.

96. Minutes, Baptist Union Council, November 2000, 19.

laration of faith contained Scripture as its final authority, where the union's Declaration of Principle stated that Jesus Christ, as revealed in Scripture, was our final authority. He also said that there was an issue of how an ecclesial body related to a non-ecclesial body; the same point that had been made about the relationship between the union and BMS. The Baptist Union has still not joined the Evangelical Alliance.[97]

Wright argued that an "agenda for the union" should include seeing itself unambiguously and self-consciously as an evangelical and evangelistic organization. The debates on Baptist identity of recent years lead us inescapably to a debate on evangelical identity since being evangelical is of the essence of being Baptist. It is not a word to be shy of, therefore, but to be rejoiced in. The Reformation distinctives of Scripture alone, faith alone, and grace alone need to be distinctive of Baptist Christians and embraced with assurance and joy. Within the evangelical spectrum there is plenty of room for the free debate and disagreement that have also come to be important to us. But the health of the union is tied up with its evangelical faith.[98]

Wright understands evangelical in *Challenge to Change* in relation to the authority of Scripture: Baptists recognize the authority of Scripture and in so doing they are evangelical. Although this is only one point of the Bebbington Quadrilateral, it is arguable that it is the primary marker from which the others flow. Stott also said that "the supremacy of Scripture has always been and always will be the first hallmark of an evangelical."[99] The same argument is presented again in Wright's *New Baptists, New Agenda*. He says it is incorrect to suggest that among Baptists there are evangelicals and liberals. To be Baptist he says is to be "some kind of evangelical."[100] Within evangelicalism there is variation and Baptists are "a coalition of emphases within evangelical boundaries."[101] Wright traces the history of Baptists to the Reformation and to the Puritan movements, which held to a high view of the authority of Scripture over tradition.[102] In an even more recent paper Wright has argued that evangelical identity is "logically prior to our Baptist identity."[103] Here he means that our belief in God, Christ, atonement,

97. Although at least one more meeting took place between representatives of the union and of the EA in October 2002. By then it was agreed that "Baptist Union membership of the EA was not a priority."

98. Wright, "Agenda for Baptist Christians," 2.

99. John Stott cited in Edwards, "Evangelical Alliance," 49.

100. Wright, *New Baptists*, 13.

101. Wright, *New Baptists*, 14.

102. Wright, *New Baptists*, 15.

103. Wright, "Sustaining Evangelical Identity," 221.

and election come before our particular convictions about church, baptism, and ministry.

Wright's view is for a broad evangelicalism that in the past was able to embrace both Arminianism and Calvinism, and in the present to hold together what are termed conservative, radical, and liberal evangelical traditions. There are Baptists that hold to each of these views. While Wright is arguing that Baptists are always evangelical, he acknowledges that during the final years of the twentieth century the Baptist Union "has become more evangelical,"[104] which he had of course worked for. Stanley has argued that the Baptist Union embraced a more conservative evangelicalism when it appointed David Coffey in 1991.[105] This reflected the increasing impact that the union's explicitly evangelical wing Mainstream was having. In Wright's view, writing in 2002, he claims that

> Baptists tend to express a centrist form of evangelical life and witness, which in general terms, is progressive, ecumenically open (but not particularly enthusiastic about formal ecumenism), holistic in its approach to mission and often profoundly engaged in social action and regeneration projects alongside evangelism.[106]

This certainly reflects Wright's own evangelicalism and that of Mainstream and this largely reflects the evangelicalism of the EA.

Wright and others in Mainstream wanted Baptists, and the union to draw on the growing resurgence of evangelicalism that was taking place across the churches and seen clearly in the growth of the EA under the leadership of Clive Calver,[107] who had also cofounded the increasingly popular annual Spring Harvest weeks. This was a mainstream evangelicalism that helped introduce charismatic worship, a greater concern for social action and which had a provided a general positive belief about the future of British Christianity. Into the 1990s, Alpha, with its evangelical theology, became a key tool for Baptists in doing evangelism.[108] As the 1980s gave

104. Wright, *New Baptists*, 21.

105. "Among the historic English Free Churches conservative evangelicalism retained its strongest base in the Baptist Union . . . However, conservative theology was not widely reflected in the higher echelons of the denomination until the appointment in 1991 of a conservative evangelical, David Coffey, as general secretary of the Union," Stanley, *Global Diffusion of Evangelicalism*, 45.

106. Wright, *New Baptists*, 21.

107. On Calver see Edwards, "Evangelical Alliance," 51; Randall and Hilborn, *One Body in Christ*, 283–308. A more critical assessment can be found in Warner, *Reinventing English Evangelicalism*, 41–66.

108. See Darrell Jackson, *The Impact of Alpha on Baptist Churches* (Didcot: Baptist

way to the 1990s it was a good time to be an evangelical, highlighted by the expectancy of revival—see here Warner's inclusion of it as a key marker of evangelicalism[109]—from the mid-1990s to the end of the decade. This kind of pan-evangelicalism was embraced by Baptists, arguably alongside a less-ening interest in the particularities of Baptist history and practice, despite attempts made by the union to emphasize these things.[110]

Warner argued for a more evangelical attitude among Baptists when he distinguished between evangelical Baptists and Baptist evangelicals. The former are committed to denomination first, the latter to evangelicalism first.[111] Warner described himself a charismatic reformed evangelical, who came to faith in an Anglican church, who has become a Free Churchman by conviction and trained and served as a Baptist minister (then in 1996) in a New Frontiers' church that has retained its Baptist roots.[112] On the back of his books he is never described as a Baptist, instead it speaks of him "lead[ing] a growing, multi-congregational church in South London."[113] Warner's vision was for a uniting of evangelicals—"the nation can only be reached if all evangelicals work together" and "my hope is for the nation and the world that all evangelicals, charismatic and non-charismatic and *without regard to denomination*, will together find a new zeal to take the good news of Jesus to every home."[114] It is this that concerned Phil Hill when he says, "The history of evangelical life has encouraged solidarity through non-denominational rather than denominational involvement."[115] Identity was being found in the evangelical ecumenism of Keswick, Spring Harvest, and March for Jesus.

It is helpful at this point to consider the work of Fiddes and Haymes who generally avoid the evangelical label.[116] Haymes in 1986 speaks of hav-

---

Union, 2002), cited in Randall, "Baptist Growth in England," 62–63.

109. Warner, "Evangelical Convictions," in Warner and Calver, *Together We Stand*, 99–100.

110. See the various Baptist Union sponsored publications: *Baptist History and Heritage*, by Hayden; *Radical Believers*, by Beasley-Murray; and an updated set of the pamphlets on *Baptist Basics*.

111. Warner, "Baptist Evangelicals and Evangelical Baptists," 1. Cf. Warner, "Evangelical Identity," 107–15.

112. Warner, "Evangelical Identity," 121.

113. Back cover of Warner, *21st Century Church*.

114. Warner, "British Baptists," 20.

115. Hill, *Church of the Third Millennium*, 9.

116. The only place I can find Fiddes using it is part of a feature on the Baptist colleges in the *BT* in January 1990. He begins his piece on Regent's Park College by saying, "Being evangelical involves using the best tools of biblical scholarship to find and communicate the Good News of Christ for our world today." I suggest he is using it here,

ing a "serious regard for that conservative evangelicalism that took questions of doctrine, truth, belief and order seriously,"[117] which is not the same as saying he views himself as an evangelical. Furthermore, he is critical of a "non-rational conservatism" that he saw as influential. This is a criticism, it seems, at least, of some kinds of evangelicalism. Later he argues that the "true Church is evangelical not as a theological party label but in the proper sense of living in, by and with the call of the gracious God."[118] In Wright's language we might see Haymes as on the liberal end of the evangelical spectrum. Tidball, in his response to Haymes, has fundamental questions about how Haymes articulates the grace of God, the authority of Christ and the authority of the Bible.[119] Tidball writes as a conservative evangelical and it is this that shapes his criticisms.[120] With regard to the grace of God, he claims that Haymes is "in danger of making God's love out to be loose and sentimental"; with regard to the authority of Christ, he is concerned that without qualification, there is potential to lead to a "wooliness of doctrine" and with regard to the Bible, Tidball is not satisfied by Haymes's description of the Bible as a "basic resource" or a "major resource."

Fiddes sees Baptists as part of the church catholic as well as being particularly children of Reformation.[121] He speaks positively of Andrew Fuller's "evangelical Calvinism," but the sense from Fiddes is that there are other ways, or to use his language, other "tracks" of being Baptist. In the case of Haymes and Fiddes they are more concerned for *Baptist* identity and do not include the label evangelical in their description. This does not mean they necessarily reject evangelicalism, instead perhaps they see it as having become unhelpful, or too much, as Haymes suggests, a party label.

This decision not to use evangelical, for perhaps understandable reasons, has meant that Fiddes and Haymes missed an opportunity to reach out to the majority of Baptists for whom evangelical was a meaningful and important term. It meant that an opening for a broader conversation with

following Barrie White, as a means of maintaining bridges to the whole of the union. Likewise on only one occasion can I find Haymes using it in a chapter on Baptist and Pentecostal churches. He says, "Baptist and Pentecostal Churches are both expressions of evangelical Christianity," "The Baptist and Pentecostal Churches," 107.

117. Haymes, *Question of Identity*, 4.

118. Haymes, *Question of Identity*, 9.

119. Tidball, "Response to *A Question of Identity*," 12–15.

120. Tidball studied theology at London Bible College and was later both a lecturer and principal. He has described himself as "having been born and brought up in an evangelical subculture and having now been at the heart of national evangelicalism for over thirty years," Tidball, "What's Right with Evangelicalism?," 253. See also his brief biography at the beginning of *Who Are the Evangelicals?*, 1.

121. Fiddes, *Tracks and Traces*, 1.

Mainstream was missed. The impact of this is, I suggest, that Fiddes's and Haymes's work was not considered important by some in stream 1 in the discussion about the future of Baptist life and witness.[122]

Charismatic Movement

Writing in 2014, Wright argued that "we are now living in a 'post-charismatic' world."[123] He explains that by this he means "much of what [the charismatic movement] imparted to the church is now widely received and taken for granted."[124] This describes something of the impact of charismatic renewal upon Baptists. For during the 1970s and into the early 1980s the denomination was "only reluctantly involved."[125]

From his introduction to the charismatic movement as a university student it has been an important part of Wright's theological make-up,[126] although some of the language associated with charismatic theology is less prominent in Wright's later work—*New Baptists, New Agenda* and *Free Church, Free Church*.[127] Early on in Wright's life his experience of the charismatic remained a "personal experience" and, he says, the implications "were not immediately obvious for the corporate life of the church."[128] He found some answers in the Restoration Movement which he considered helpful but, where this might have resulted in him leaving the Baptist tradition, it aided him instead to becoming more committed to it. The result was that he took on board some of the character of the Restorationist churches translating them into his Baptist context. Wright's charismatic experience and theology took a new step when he and his church at the time came into contact with John Wimber's power evangelism.[129] Through these new experiences Wright felt the calling to become a theological teacher and it was from this point on that he began an ongoing positive but now also critical relationship with charismatic renewal, seen in his friendship with

122. Haymes was also beyond the pale for some because he was principal of Northern Baptist College until 1994 and had been a friend and colleague of Michael Taylor.

123. Wright, "Charismata and the Second Naïveté," 129.

124. Wright, "Charismata and the Second Naïveté," 129.

125. McBain, *Fire Over the Waters*, ix.

126. In 2014 he says, "I write as an active participant, past and present, in charismatic life, but not as an uncritical one," Wright, "Charismata and the Second Naïveté," 138.

127. Wright has offered accounts of the Holy Spirit in *The Lord and Giver of Life* and *God on the Inside*.

128. Wright, "Pilgrimage in Renewal," 25.

129. For Wright's view on Wimber see Wright, "Baptist Evaluation."

Tom Smail and Andrew Walker and the book they collaborated on called *Charismatic Renewal: The Search for a Theology.*

As a source of renewal in Wright's vision the charismatic movement is most clearly evident in *Challenge to Change.* Here the argument is that churches need to "experience the renewing work of the Spirit"[130] and not just personally, but as congregations and as denominations. He speaks of a "call for *glasnost*,"[131] for openness to the Spirit; it is this, he believes, which will bring the change that is necessary. Alongside renewal, he argues for restoration and with that he contends that "Baptist Christians ought to listen carefully to the voice of the Spirit in charismatic renewal."[132] For this reason he goes on to say that charismatic renewal is "an aspect of the total work of God from which we genuinely desire to benefit."[133] He laments where Baptists have been too cautious or simply indifferent to charismatic Christianity. Joined to the principles of renewal, reformation, restoration, Wright adds revival: every Christian and church should have a "profound sense of our need for God and the comings of his Spirit."[134] He quotes the great evangelical preacher and charismatic Martin Lloyd-Jones in support of this need for revival and the Spirit's power.

Wright concludes *Challenge to Change* in the language and mood of charismatic renewal:

> The Holy Spirit is brooding over Baptist churches and their denomination, seeking somewhere to rest and fulfill his mission. Yet we imprison him within our attitudes, traditions and structures and fail to allow him to express through us the life and power which reaches out. We grieve him by our unwillingness to change and be changed, and the consequence is not that the Spirit falls asleep, but that his work among us is quenched. We must see that it could all be so different and that by taking up the challenge to change, Baptist churches and associations of churches could become a major means of the Spirit's transforming activity.[135]

This is Wright at his most bold and is similar to the same kind of call that Douglas McBain had made in *No Gentle Breeze.* By 2002 and *New Baptists*, it is less obvious that charismatic renewal is an ongoing source of renewal

130. Wright, *Challenge to Change*, 49.
131. Wright, *Challenge to Change*, 50.
132. Wright, *Challenge to Change*, 54.
133. Wright, *Challenge to Change*, 54.
134. Wright, *Challenge to Change*, 55.
135. Wright, *Challenge to Change*, 246.

to Wright's work. In a chapter on evangelism there is no reference as in *Challenge to Change* to Wimber and power evangelism. Wright still mentions the work of the Spirit but now in a more Trinitarian key.[136] There is no call to restoration or revival, instead Wright says his "expectations are modest," and while he might share hopes of revival he is doubtful it is going to happen.[137] There is a sense in Wright that he came to see that the charismatic movement, while not disowning it or moving beyond it, could only renew the church so far. He would write in 1993, reflecting on the charismatic movement, that "progress into the future comes from owning the good things that belong to the past and yet seeing them within ever new and ever fuller contexts."[138] Of course it was not just Wright who was a charismatic among Mainstream. This was a shared label for many, although not all. Prominent advocates of charismatic renewal within Mainstream were McBain in the 1980s and Warner in the 1990s. Warner in 1995 in *Prepare for Revival* would say, "Nothing is needed more by the world and the Church at the end of the twentieth century than this: a mighty outpouring of the Spirit of God in revival power."[139] Coffey also gave a tentative welcome to the "Toronto Blessing" and argued that "we must retain the conviction that the church which takes no interest in the Holy Spirit is the sleeping church."[140] The future of the church for the first stream was a charismatic one.

Covenant

Fiddes has been the leading advocate for the rediscovery of covenant within Baptist theology.[141] Covenant is the thread that runs throughout his *Tracks and Traces*. Its most detailed presentation, to date, appears in the essay Fiddes wrote in honour of the Baptist historian B. R. White: "'Walking Together': The Place of Covenant theology in Baptist Life Yesterday and Today."[142] It was White who helped draw new attention to covenant in his

136. See his 1993 paper where he writes, "Having emphasized the Spirit and sought to give a him place, there is now an entirely consistent and appropriate need to become fully trinitarian," Wright, "Pilgrimage in Renewal," 31.

137. Wright, *New Baptists*, 1–2. See also Wright, "Does Revival Quicken or Deaden the Church?"

138. Wright, "Pilgrimage in Renewal," 30.

139. Warner, *Prepare for Revival*, 175.

140. Coffey, "When the Spirit Comes."

141. Darrell Jackson says the renewed interest in covenant is a "revisioning of Baptist theology," Jackson, *Discourse of "Belonging*," 65.

142. Fiddes, *Tracks and Traces*, 21–47. Reprinted earlier in Brackney et al., *Pilgrim Pathways*, 47–74. Fiddes historical studies of covenant have continued more recently

own work and that of some of his students.[143] Fiddes seeks to demonstrate the "strategic significance" of the recovery of a theology of covenant. He believes that in its recovery and its acceptance as a central concept is the source of renewal for Baptist life.

Fiddes begins by suggesting that the covenant made by the English Separatists at Gainsborough in 1606 or 1607 is a "defining" moment in the Baptist story.[144] The pastor of this congregation was John Smyth who, with Thomas Helwys, would found the first Baptist church in 1609. The language of the Gainsborough covenant is both vertical and horizontal; it is "both *with* God and *with* each other."[145] It is a covenant that expresses both a deep commitment to one another and at the same time an openness to how and where that commitment may lead—it speaks of "walking together in ways known and yet to be made known." Fiddes acknowledges that the story that unfolded is one that resulted in dissension and separation. He argues that the practice of covenanting together was to bear fruit in later seventeenth-century Baptist life and its recovery in the present is vital to an understanding and practice of Baptist ecclesiology today.

Fiddes's discussion of covenant theology identifies "four threads of significance" that together offer a thick account of covenant for English Puritans and Separatists.[146] The first thread is to recognize that "covenant" was a reference to the covenant that God has made with humanity for their salvation in Jesus Christ: an eternal covenant of grace. The key figure behind this concept of covenant is Calvin, who sees Christ as the mediator of God's covenant both in the Old Testament and in the New Testament.

The second thread is to see this divine covenant as a "transaction" between God the Father and God the Son; the Son submits to the will of the Father to save the elect. The covenant of grace is understood to be made between the persons of the Trinity. The covenant is primarily a covenant within God in which humanity benefits "second Hand" as the Particular Baptist theologian Benjamin Keach describes it.[147]

The third way covenant is used, says Fiddes, is as a reference to how God makes an agreement with his church or with particular churches.

---

with "Covenant and the Inheritance of Separatism."

143. Fiddes speaks of White's "pioneering work in this area" and the "notable further works . . . by two of his doctoral pupils at Oxford, R. T. Kendall and Stephen Brachlow," *Tracks and Traces*, 23.

144. Fiddes, *Tracks and Traces*, 21–22.

145. Fiddes, *Tracks and Traces*, 22.

146. Fiddes, *Tracks and Traces*, 23.

147. Benjamin Keach, *The Display of Glorious Grace* (1698), 294, cited in Fiddes, *Tracks and Traces*, 27.

While having similarities with the first understanding of covenant, there is a difference in that covenant is here recognized as conditional, rather than unconditional. This conditional use marks "God's partnership with a particular, visible church,"[148] the unconditional eternal covenant of grace with the invisible church. If this appears to be too tidy a distinction, Fiddes refers to Keach and (John) Gill who argue that there can only be "one gracious covenant of God."[149] At this point in the essay Fiddes says that there is some register of mystery and ambiguity among theologians of the period over these matters.[150]

The fourth way covenant is used is as "an agreement undertaken and signed by church members."[151] Smyth writes of a church as being "joyned together by covenant with God & themselves."[152] Covenants are made both vertically with God and horizontally with one another.

Historically, early Baptists did not make covenants, despite John Smyth, but they did become much more widespread in the later seventeenth century following covenants made and published by Benjamin and Elias Keach. Even where covenant language was not prevalent in the middle of the seventeenth century, at least in the fourth sense outlined above, Fiddes does note that there remained a "*concept* of a local covenant," in language such as "by mutual agreement" and "walking together."[153] This covenant ecclesiology marked Baptist understandings of church for two centuries, before declining in the nineteenth century, according to John Briggs, because it was felt too sectarian, in an age where churches were working together in a variety of ways.[154]

Fiddes argues that these four covenant threads are "woven together,"[155] that is, while they can be distinguished from one another, there is definite overlap and connection. Fiddes agrees with White who sees in the theology of John Smyth a clear example of the eternal covenant God makes and a "local" covenant made by a church as "fused" together.[156] Crucially, Fid-

---

148. Fiddes, *Tracks and Traces*, 28.

149. Fiddes, *Tracks and Traces*, 29.

150. Fiddes, *Tracks and Traces*, 29.

151. Fiddes, *Tracks and Traces*, 29.

152. John Smyth, *Principles and Inferences concerning the Visible Church* (1607), printed in W. T. Whitley (ed.), *The Works of John Smyth* 1 (Cambridge, 1915), 254, cited in Fiddes, *Tracks and Traces*, 29.

153. Fiddes, *Tracks and Traces*, 31.

154. Fiddes, *Tracks and Traces*, 43, referring to Briggs, *English Baptists in the Nineteenth Century*, 15–20.

155. Fiddes, *Tracks and Traces*, 31.

156. Fiddes, *Tracks and Traces*, 32.

des presents this as an argument for the church universal: "covenant and catholicity belong together."[157] A covenant made by a particular local church is always a "manifestation" of God's eternal covenant.

Robert Browne, the Separatist, brings the third and fourth references of covenant together—the covenant God makes with his church is "simultaneous" also to the covenant made by the church.[158] Covenant-making is understood as both a divine and a human action. The contribution of Smyth is to suggest that the first understanding of covenant is also part of God and the church covenanting together. The covenant being made by God and by the church is the covenant of grace; the covenant making of a local church is caught up in the covenant God makes with humanity in Christ. Fiddes finds similar references in Keach. Fiddes sums up his presentation by claiming that "Smyth and Keach, at two ends of a century, offer a dynamic account of participation in God's covenant of grace through mutual covenant-making."[159]

Fiddes continues his development of a theology of covenant by turning next to the contribution of Karl Barth. Barth challenges a notion of the eternal covenant as an "absolute decree" and instead pushes it to be understood as "a grace that enables the human response of 'yes' to God's 'yes' to us."[160] In addition, Barth goes further by arguing that covenant is a matter of God's being as well as his act, that is, "the covenant of grace is thus *integral* to the communion between Father, Son and Holy Spirit."[161] God determines to freely be God for us. Fiddes argues from this that we can speak of a covenant within the Trinity: "as God the Father makes covenant of love eternally with the Son in the fellowship of the Holy Spirit, so simultaneously God makes covenant in history with human beings."[162] Fiddes believes that this adds important "theological depth" to how Baptists use covenant, that is, covenant is not just how we relate to God, but how we participate *in* God.[163]

In the final third of "Walking Together," Fiddes discusses the implications of this covenant theology in relation to a Baptist understanding of salvation, the notion of church as a voluntary society and how covenant differs from the practice of assenting to confessions of faith.

---

157. Fiddes, *Tracks and Traces*, 32.

158. Fiddes, *Tracks and Traces*, 33.

159. Fiddes, *Tracks and Traces*, 35.

160. Fiddes, *Tracks and Traces*, 35.

161. Fiddes, *Tracks and Traces*, 35.

162. Fiddes, *Tracks and Traces*, 36.

163. Fiddes develops the notion of participating in God in a number of places but most significantly in *Participating in God*.

In terms of a doctrine of salvation, Fiddes presents a specifically Baptist understanding of salvation that emerges from the weaving together or "fusing" together of both conditional and unconditional notions of covenant. There is both a Calvinist notion of salvation as an act of the grace of God (unconditional) and an Arminian notion that salvation requires a personal response (conditional) contained in the making of a church covenant. While there is for Baptists, who believe in and practice believers' baptism, an emphasis on personal salvation, this is not "held in isolation from life in relationship with others."[164] Those called to be baptized are called into membership in Christ's body.

The concept of Baptist churches as an example of a voluntary society is apparent throughout their history. Fiddes finds it evident in the writings of Browne, Smyth, a revision of Keach's *Baptist Catechism* by Benjamin Beddome, Gill, and Joseph Angus. They all refer in some form or another to the idea of the principle of voluntarism.[165] Angus, the Baptist historian, quotes with approval John Locke's description of a church as a "free and voluntary Society." However, Fiddes contends that this is only one side of a church that covenants together. Fiddes argues that alongside, and even preceding, any practice of voluntarism is the initiative of God.[166] For Baptists, Christ *gathers* those who covenant together.[167] Fiddes cites the Second London Confession which speaks of believers "consent[ing] to walk together according to the appointment of Christ";[168] Christ calls and the church covenants. The more recent 1948 English statement on the Baptist doctrine of the church refers to churches being "gathered by the will of Christ."[169] This is strong evidence to resist an understanding of Baptist churches as merely voluntary societies. Fiddes states strongly it is "positively misleading to call a local church a 'voluntary society'"[170] and in a more recent essay argues that "covenant always resists autonomy."[171] For John Locke the church as a voluntary

---

164. Fiddes, *Tracks and Traces*, 233.

165. Fiddes, *Tracks and Traces*, 41–42.

166. Miroslav Volf's discussion of covenant fails to recognize the divine initiative within Smyth's theology, Volf, *After Our Likeness*, 175–76. This is something mentioned by Colwell, "Church as Sacrament," 57.

167. "When Christian disciples make covenant with each other . . . they are not just drawing together, but being drawn together," Fiddes, "Not Anarchy but Covenant," 146, 148.

168. Fiddes, *Tracks and Traces*, 42.

169. *The Baptist Union Doctrine of the Church* (1948), cited in Fiddes, *Tracks and Traces*, 42.

170. Fiddes, *Tracks and Traces*, 42.

171. Fiddes, "Communion and Covenant," 130.

society was an expression of the liberty of the members to join of their own free will, what today is another example of the "market-place of choice."[172] Fiddes says this is to describe the church without reference to the place of Christ. Baptists understand the local church as standing "under the rule of Christ," which both frees, but also binds, the church in relationship to Christ. It *frees* in the sense that it resists a hierarchy within the church and externally in terms of some kind of ecclesial authority, but it *binds* in the sense that the church sits under the authority of Christ, which shapes the church members' freedom in the way of shared discipleship.

Not only, says Fiddes, is it misleading to call a local Baptist church an example of a voluntary society, it is also unhelpful to say Baptist churches are independent entities that only associate with other churches on the basis of pragmatism or alliance. As we noted above, for Fiddes covenant and catholicity go together. Baptist associations are an expression of catholicity grounded in covenant, for the reason that "if a local church is under the direct rule of Christ as king then it is necessarily drawn into fellowship with all those who are under Christ's rule and so part of his body."[173] It is Fiddes's contention that a union of churches, like the Baptist Union of Great Britain should see itself as in covenant relationship, that is, as "a means of exploring the purpose of God in the world."[174]

Fiddes ends his discussion of covenant theology by arguing against the necessity of church confessions as the "*required* basis"[175] for covenant making. The Baptist understanding of covenant, centered in the language of "walking together" is relational language and implies openness and trust and a notion of journey. Fiddes approaches this covenant theology using both the skill of stewardship and invention, in that he believes there is a tradition that needs to be picked up again, but he also wants to build upon the covenant theology of the past and see it extended in new ways.

"Catholic" Baptists

Fiddes dedicates *Tracks and Traces* to the memory of Ernest A. Payne, who, he says, "exemplified in himself the Baptist vision which places the

---

172. Fiddes, *Tracks and Traces*, 42. Fiddes elsewhere writes how Arnold sees Nonconformity as "a seedbed of anarchy . . . where the voluntary principle, the stressing of individual choice and self-will were placed at the center of religion as much as in politics and industry," Fiddes, "Not Anarchy but Covenant," 146.

173. Fiddes, *Tracks and Traces*, 44.

174. Fiddes, *Tracks and Traces*, 45.

175. Fiddes, *Tracks and Traces*, 47.

community of Baptist Christians clearly within the fellowship of the church universal."[176] I think this is significant in the Baptist theological vision that Fiddes expounds in his book.[177] Payne, not only as general secretary of the Baptist Union but also as a scholar, was an immense presence in the middle decades of the twentieth century. He was both a committed Baptist and a committed ecumenist[178] and these two principles shaped his work and those who he encouraged. Payne should perhaps be seen as one of the earliest adherents to those who have been called "Baptist catholics."[179] In his book, *Towards a Baptist Catholicity*, Steven Harmon has argued that catholic Baptists have seven identifying marks: tradition as a source of authority; a place for creeds in liturgy; liturgy as a context for formation; community as a locus of authority; a sacramental theology; a constructive retrieval of tradition; and a thick ecumenism. Payne's work has in it all seven marks to lesser or greater degrees.[180] His perhaps most important treatment of Baptist ecclesiology was *The Fellowship of Believers: Baptist Thought and Practice Yesterday and Today*, first published in 1944 and then revised and enlarged in 1952. The origins of this book were as a rebuttal, although unnamed, of Arthur Dakin's *The Baptist View of Church and Ministry*, also published in 1944. Payne believed it to be "one-sided and even inaccurate"[181] as a description of Baptist thought. In his chapter on "The Visible Church" Payne concludes:

> From the seventeenth century Baptists have regarded the visible Church as finding expression in local communities by the election of officers, the observance of baptism and the Lord's Supper, and Christian discipline, and who find an extension

176. Fiddes, *Tracks and Traces*, xvi. Payne had presided over Fiddes's ordination.

177. Fiddes would have got to know Payne well during the final years of his life when Payne moved back to Oxford in 1976.

178. "[Payne] accepted that he had to live in the creative tension of his denominational loyalty, which was unswerving, and his ecumenical commitment, which was total," West, *To Be a Pilgrim*, 203.

179. See Harmon, *Towards Baptist Catholicity*, 1–21, and Freeman, "Confession of Catholic Baptists."

180. See in particular Payne, *Fellowship of Believers*; *Free Churchmen: Unrepentant and Repentant*; *Thirty Years of the British Council of Churches* and with Stephen Winward, *Orders and Prayers for Church Worship*. Of the latter Myra Blyth has said that it is "a classic resource of high Baptist liturgy . . . Ecumenical in spirit, it encourages ministers to treasure reformation principles and Baptist convictions . . . it draws inspiration from ancient sources and extensively borrows from the prayers of the church through the ages," Blyth, "Visible Unity," 131. See Andy Goodliff, "Ernest Payne—Forerunner of Catholic Baptists," *Baptist Quarterly* (forthcoming) for a fuller account of how Payne's work demonstrates these seven marks.

181. West, *To Be a Pilgrim*, 60.

and expression of their life in free association, first, with other churches of their own faith and order, but also with all other groups of Christians loyal to the central truths of the apostolic Gospel. This, in outline, is the Baptist doctrine of the Church as visible. It is something different from the exaggerated independence, self-sufficiency and atomism which have sometimes been favoured of recent days. It is high churchmanship in its emphasis on the faith . . . it is high churchmanship in its assertion of the Lordship of Christ . . . It is high churchmanship in its loyalty to the "ordinances of the gospel" . . . It is high churchmanship in its inner urge towards communion, fellowship and unity with all those other Christians who together make up the Church Catholic.[182]

Here we pick up the clear argument of Payne's view of Baptist ecclesiology—local and interdependent, sacramental and catholic. Bebbington suggests that the reemergence of what he calls "high churchmanship" among Baptists can be seen in the context of an engagement with: biblical scholarship, the Genevan movement among Congregationalists,[183] the liturgical movement, and greater ecumenical contacts.[184] Randall says there was "cross-fertilisation" between the Congregationalists and Baptists.[185] Baptists like Payne were being influenced by these movements. He was, according to Densil Morgan, "a-typical of Baptists though representative of a younger generation of ministers in holding to a higher ecclesiology than was usual, a more pronounced sacramentalism and a historical sense that went beyond the stark Biblicalism of much of his tradition."[186] Payne's connection with the "Genevan" movement can be seen in his membership of a group of Free Churchman who wrote *The Catholicity of Protestantism*, which Morgan describes as "a magisterial account of the Word-centred revelation theology and ecclesiological seriousness of the new Nonconformity."[187] When Payne's *Fellowship of Believers* was reviewed in the *Presbyter*, the journal associated

182. Payne, *Fellowship of Believers*, 36–37.

183. The "Genevan" movement or "Orthodox Dissent" was a group of Congregationalist ministers, largely based at Mansfield College, Oxford who were "orthodox, scholarly and liturgically minded" (Bebbington, *Evangelicalism in Modern Britain*, 251) and reacted against a liberal Christianity. The three leading thinkers were Nathaniel Micklem, John S. Whale, and Bernard Manning. See Randall, *Evangelical Experiences*, 174–98. Cf. Grant, *Free Churchmanship in England*.

184. Bebbington, *Baptists Through the Centuries*, 192–93.

185. Randall, *Evangelical Experiences*, 184.

186. Morgan, *Barth Reception in Britain*, 229. Arguably this can also be said, to some degree, of Payne's teacher Henry Wheeler Robinson.

187. Morgan, *Barth Reception in Britain*, 219.

with the Genevan movement, described it as "the Baptist version of the Church Order."[188] *The Fellowship of Believers* at several points makes reference to Micklem, Whale, and Daniel Jenkins.

Payne was influential on a younger group of scholars,[189] particularly Alec Gilmore, Stephen Winward, Morris West, and Neville Clark.[190] This group had been meeting regularly and already published together in 1960 (with others) a book on baptism,[191] which Payne had written an introduction for. The authors expressed their appreciation to Payne for his "counsel and guidance." Three years later the group published *The Pattern of the Church* which was a treatment of Baptist beliefs with regards to church and the ministry, but firmly from an "ecumenical perspective" and an "ecumenical context."[192] Again, Payne is thanked for "his wise counsel and willing helpfulness."[193] The final chapter of the book is a call to ecumenical church unity following the previous chapters calling for denominational reform in a more catholic direction. The book thus follows in the tradition already laid down by Payne, with a high view of church, ministry, and sacraments, which I suggest can be called catholic. It logically led to a positive concern for ecumenism for a "vision of contesting catholicity."[194] This line of thought which is developed by Payne, but could also be traced back to Shakespeare, has been concerned for the importance of the union. It has favored a level of centralization, or in more theological terms has argued for a strong expression of interdependence to balance the liberty of the local church.[195] An ongoing argument through the twentieth century occurred between those who emphasized the individual autonomous church and those who claimed that Baptists have always held to a vision of the church catholic and as a result argued for ways

188. Morgan, *Barth Reception in Britain*, 229. The Church Order was founded in 1946 as a means of encouraging liturgical renewal within Congregationalism. Micklem would also be among those who attended a House of Commons dinner held in Payne's honour at his retirement, West, *To Be a Pilgrim*, 157.

189. Brackney, *Genetic History of Baptist Thought*, 188.

190. Winward, West, and Clark all trained or studied at Regent's Park College, during Payne's tenure as a tutor.

191. Gilmore, *Christian Baptism*.

192. Foreword to *The Pattern of the Church*, 10. At this point all four were in local church ministry, although West would later become principal of Bristol Baptist College and Clark Principal of South Wales Baptist College, while Winward would become a lecturer at Selly Oak Colleges, Birmingham. Gilmore would become involved in publishing and Christian literature.

193. "Appreciation," in Gilmore, *Pattern of the Church*, 6.

194. Freeman, *Contesting Catholicity*, 19.

195. See also Walton, *Gathered Community*, and Underwood, *History of the English Baptists*, 265.

to strengthen the union in that direction. The influence of Payne can be traced through to Fiddes and stream 2 who are located in this more catholic "track" as the preface to *Tracks and Traces* demonstrates.

Doctrine of the Trinity

By the second edition of Colin Gunton's *The Promise of Trinitarian Theology* published in 1997, Gunton could remark "suddenly we are all trinitarians, or so it would seem."[196] This is just one example of how across theological traditions the doctrine of the Trinity had become a central doctrine for constructive theology and with it an ecclesiology shaped by the concept of *koinonia* (translated as communion or fellowship). Fiddes draws on this trinitarian-shaped ecclesiology, representing how Baptists were engaging with the wider ecumenical and theological conversations taking place. Alongside Fiddes, the doctrine of the Trinity was also present in the work of Wright and Haymes.[197]

Fiddes was the Baptist member of the British Council of Churches Study Commission on Trinitarian Doctrine Today that wrote the 1988 report *The Forgotten Trinity*.[198] This commission met ten times between 1983 and 1988. *The Forgotten Trinity* report begins "there is a feeling abroad that the doctrine of the Trinity is an irrelevance," which perhaps reflects the change that had taken place by 1997. In an accompanying selection of papers from the commission, Fiddes contributed a paper on the atonement and the Trinity, which drew from his theological work in *The Creative Suffering of God* and *Past Event and Present Salvation*. Fiddes's particular account of the doctrine of the Trinity was already apparent at this point, but would be more fully articulated in his 2000 work *Participating in God*. For our purposes here we draw attention to how the doctrine of the Trinity is a source of renewal in terms of Fiddes's doctrine of the church. Harmon argues that "Fiddes's participatory account of Trinitarian *koinonia* is . . . central to his systematic theological program."[199] Where Fiddes stands out is that he allows ecumenical theology to influence and shape his own theology. He does not just react to it from a Baptist perspective but practices what

196. Gunton, *Promise of Trinitarian Theology*, xv.

197. For Haymes's account of the Trinity see *Transforming Superintendency*, 9–13. More recently he has said that he finds himself in agreement with Fiddes, see Haymes, "Trinity and Participation," 12.

198. Others on the committee were Sarah Coakley, Colin Gunton, Tom Smail, James Torrance, and John Zizioulas.

199. Harmon, "Trinitarian *Koinonia* and Ecclesial *Oikoumene*," 19.

is called "receptive ecumenism"[200] and in this way he has done constructive theology like few other Baptists.

Key to Fiddes's account of the doctrine of the Trinity is the word "participation" already in play in *The Creative Suffering of God*[201] and developed fully in *Participating in God*. Fiddes argues that the doctrine of the Trinity be understood as an account of the three divine Persons as relations, that is, God understood as a "movement" or "event" of relationships, in which God enables humanity to participate. He calls this a "relational" rather than "social" doctrine of the Trinity.[202] This event of relationships, what Zizioulas calls "being as communion,"[203] Fiddes suggests can be thought of in covenantal terms, there is both an eternal covenant within God (developing an insight from Barth) and God's covenant with humankind, so that, "we are participating not only in God's covenant with us, but in the inner covenant-making God."[204] Fiddes goes on to work out this "ecclesiology of participation"[205] in relation to ministry, baptism, the Lord's Supper, and mission. More recently Fiddes has developed the links between a theology of *koinonia* and covenant—drawing together the communion ecclesiology of the ecumenical movement with the particular covenantal ecclesiology of the Baptists.[206]

In 1993 Wright wrote that "a most encouraging sign in modern theology is the place given not only to the doctrine of the Trinity but to the trinitarian shape of Christian existence and of all truly Christian thought."[207] Wright had been reading Barth since the late 1980s and in the early 1990s had begun his doctorate on Moltmann and under the supervision of Gunton. All three were significant trinitarian thinkers shaping Wright's thought. In *The Radical Evangelical* he argues that evangelicals can gather round a

---

200. See Fiddes, "Learning from Others."

201. Fiddes, *Creative Suffering*, 141.

202. See Fiddes, *Promised End*, 268, distancing himself from the likes of Moltmann. Cf. Fiddes, "Relational Trinity," 160.

203. Zizioulas, *Being as Communion*. Fiddes cites Zizioulas's work regularly when he is discussing the Trinity: *Tracks and Traces*, 73; *Participating in God*, 15; *Past Event*, 163; *Promised End*, 263;

204. Fiddes, *Tracks and Traces*, 79. This citation comes from a 1996 paper, "Church and Trinity: A Baptist Theology of Participation," originally published in a festschrift for the German Baptist Wiard Pokes.

205. Fiddes, *Tracks and Traces*, 66.

206. See Fiddes et al., *Baptists and the Communion of Saints*, 127–55. Cf. Fiddes, "Church Local and Universal"; Fiddes, "Koinonia," 37–49.

207. Wright, "Pilgrimage in Renewal," 31.

shared recognition of "the primacy of the Trinity."[208] The chapter on the Trinity comes before the chapter on Scripture (which is also preceded by a chapter on election). He commends the report *The Forgotten Trinity*. In this he affirms a broadly social doctrine of the Trinity, following Zizioulas.[209] The doctrine of the Trinity is also present in both *Disavowing Constantine* and *Free Church, Free State*. In the former he describes Moltmann's account of the Trinity,[210] but more important is Gunton and Miroslav Volf.[211] Wright argues that the Trinity is the fountainhead of all theology, and so a theology of mission and of the church. Following Gunton he says, "The being of God as communion is the ontological basis for the church which is that being's echo within history."[212] Wright then goes beyond this to claim that the "church is an icon of the Trinity"[213] which is very similar to Volf's language of "image."[214] It is "image" language Wright uses in *Free Church, Free State*.[215] What is evident in Wright is a clear connection between the Trinity and church. He will speak of the church participating in God and praises the "excellent exposition" of this in Fiddes.[216] If the church is an image of the Trinity then, he argues, we should beware of hierarchical accounts of the Trinity because this will lead to a hierarchical church, which is not a Baptist view.[217]

There is much in common between Fiddes and Wright on the Trinity, although Fiddes's emphasis on the church participating in the triune God is not the same as Wright's description of the church as imaging the triune God.[218] What is common to both Wright and Fiddes is to see the doctrine of the Trinity as useful.[219] From the doctrine of the Trinity we can move to the doctrine of the church, which for Fiddes means the church is immersed

208. Wright, *Radical Evangelical*, 13.

209. Wright, *Radical Evangelical*, 25.

210. Wright, *Disavowing Constantine*, 129–36.

211. Wright, *Disavowing Constantine*, 193–94nn3 and 4. Wright had by 1994 read an article by Volf published in 1989 in which much of his trinitarian ecclesiology was already conceived, prior to it appearing in his monograph *After Our Likeness*. See Volf, "Kirche als Gemeinschaft." Wright says he drew "inspiration" from Volf in Wright, "'Koinonia' and Baptist Ecclesiology," 370.

212. Wright, *Disavowing Constantine*, 180.

213. Wright, *Disavowing Constantine*, 180. Cf. Wright, *Free Church, Free State*, 233.

214. Volf, *After Our Likeness*, 196–97.

215. Wright, *Free Church*, 4–6.

216. Wright, *Free Church*, 21n24.

217. Wright, *Free Church*, 6–7.

218. See Rees, "Trinity and the Church," which compares Volf and Fiddes.

219. I owe the language of "useful" to Holmes, "Three Versus One?," 81.

in the life of God's divine relating and for Wright means the church is an image of the Trinity. It is this attempt, among others, that fellow Baptist Stephen Holmes has questioned. Holmes argues that the attempts to make the doctrine of the Trinity useful are "overstated and at best questionable."[220] The broader point, Holmes claims, from his careful reading of the tradition, is that the social, and the relational version of Fiddes's, accounts of the doctrine of the Trinity are not continuous with the tradition, but a development or adaption of the tradition.[221]

As systematic theology in the 1990s continued to see a flourishing of interest in the doctrine of the Trinity, so Fiddes and Wright were part of this engagement[222] and both streams can be said to be highlighting the importance of understanding God as triune.

Mission

One final source of renewal, which we might connect first with Coffey, but is also present in Wright and Fiddes, is the concept and theology of mission. In the summer 1992 edition of *Baptist Leader* Coffey praised the work of David Bosch and his book *Transforming Mission*.[223] This indicated that Coffey had a good grasp from Bosch (if he was not already aware,) of how the word mission had been changing. As indicated in the introductory chapter mission was at the heart of Coffey's vision for the Baptist Union.

In the late 1960s a series of reports and addresses had put mission into the consciousness of Baptist life and thought. In a paper for the 1970 denominational conference, Peter Clark spoke of mission being the "'in' word."[224] This reflected the impact of what was happening in the WCC with regards to a theology of mission. At the International Missionary Council Conference at Willingen in 1952, what Geoffrey Wainwright calls, "a profound rethinking of the nature of 'the missionary obligation of the Church' was under way."[225] Bosch began his now classic *Transforming Mission* by remarking that "since the 1950s there has been a remarkable escalation in the

220. Holmes, "Three Versus One?," 84.

221. Holmes, *Holy Trinity*, 2. Colwell has also been critical of Fiddes doctrine of the Trinity but for different reasons, see Colwell, "In the Beginning," 50.

222. Unsurprisingly in terms of those that they were engaging with in their theological work—Barth, Moltmann, Zizioulas, Gunton, etc.

223. Coffey, "Towards 2000," 1. It is also mentioned that Bosch had been invited to speak at the 1993 Baptist Assembly. He tragically died in April 1992.

224. Clark, "Evangelism Now" in *The Denominational Conference of the Baptist Union of Great Britain and Ireland. Handbook for Delegates*, 19.

225. Wainwright, *Lesslie Newbigin*, 164.

use of the word 'mission' among Christians."[226] At Willingen, says Bosch, a shift from church as sender to being the one sent begins to occur.[227] By 1958 the new consensus, summarized by Newbigin, was: 1. The church is the mission; 2. The home base is everywhere and 3. Mission in partnership.[228] In the 1960s another shift in understanding of the goal of mission was taking place, in that the goal was "shalom" or "humanization," with the result that "mission became an umbrella term for health and welfare services, youth projects, activities of political interest groups, project for economic and social development."[229] In other words, mission as social action, rather than primarily evangelism. Bosch also highlights another "element" of what he calls "the emerging ecumenical missionary paradigm," which becomes central to a theology of mission, that of, the *missio Dei*. The mission of the church is God's mission. Again it was at Willingen that the idea first surfaced and has been, says Bosch, "embraced by virtually all Christian persuasions."[230]

Brian Stanley argues that these changes were "less immediately apparent in the BMS than in other strands of the Protestant missionary movement" and he says that this is because of the "conservative theological alignment of most British Baptists" that evangelism and conversion remained the goal of mission.[231] What was true for the BMS was true for the union. While the language of mission was being embraced in different writings of the 1960s it remained focused on evangelism. The 1969 report of the Evangelism Working Group, *Call to Obedience*[232] acknowledges that the mission of the church is to share in the mission of God and that this mission is to be a sign of "reconciled community," but "most specifically" the mission is evangelism.[233] Norman Jones, who became head of the department of Mission in 1972, wrote that "the church is mission," but that means "it is always engaged in presenting the Gospel of our Lord Jesus Christ."[234] However, George Beasley-Murray's 1968 presidential address, "Renewed for Mission,"[235] is a direct engagement with the new understandings of mission. He begins by stating the new views that mission is God's and the importance of action alongside

226. Bosch, *Transforming Mission*, 1.

227. Bosch, *Transforming Mission*, 370.

228. Bosch, *Transforming Mission*, 370. See Wainwright, *Lesslie Newbigin*, 169–73.

229. Bosch, *Transforming Mission*, 383.

230. Bosch, *Transforming Mission*, 390.

231. Stanley, *History of the Baptist Missionary Society*, 504.

232. *Call to Obedience*.

233. *Call to Obedience*, 6–7.

234. Jones, *Preparation for Mission*, 3.

235. Beasley-Murray, *Renewed for Mission*.

word. Beasley-Murray sees service in action as "expressive" of proclamation and in that way evangelism takes priority: "to continue this proclamation, and action commensurate with it, is the essence of Christian mission."[236] He goes on to challenge those (in ecumenical circles) who were arguing that mission was wherever people engaged with social action. "Contrary to the strange contemporary fashion of Churchmen belittling the Church, we affirm that our task is to plant and build the Church through the Gospel, that in turn it may become a mighty force in the hand of the Lord for the accomplishment of his mission in the world."[237] Beasley-Murray does engage with the voices that were arguing that the church needed to change. He mentions Newbigin's argument that the structures of the church emerged when it was contracting rather than expanding, and Beasley-Murray agrees the church needs to establish a "go-church" structure rather than a "come-church" one.[238] He suggests that what is required is for the Church to understand itself not "simply [as] a gathered congregation, but a gathered *ministry*."[239] He moves this image to a military one, "the Church in our land needs to be on a war footing" in which everyone is "enrolled in Christ's Army."[240] This Church renewed for mission needs "dedication" and the "blessing of the Holy Spirit."[241]

What helped many Baptists embrace a wider vision of mission was no doubt the work of the leading evangelical John Stott.[242] In 1975, following the Lausanne Conference and its Covenant in 1974, he published *Christian Mission in the Modern World*.[243] Here Stott lays out an argument that the Great Commission "must be understood to include social as well as evangelistic responsibility."[244] He says the "truly Christian" way of stating the relationship between social action and evangelism is to see them as "partners,"[245] this is what the life of Jesus demonstrates. The church's mission has a "double vocation."[246] Of course, the chapter that follows the one on

236. Beasley-Murray, *Renewed for Mission*, 8.

237. Beasley-Murray, *Renewed for Mission*, 11.

238. Beasley-Murray, *Renewed for Mission*, 14.

239. Beasley-Murray, *Renewed for Mission*, 15.

240. Beasley-Murray, *Renewed for Mission*, 16.

241. Beasley-Murray, *Renewed for Mission*, 18.

242. Indicated by Coffey himself, see Randall, *English Baptists*, 472. See also Tidball, *Who are the Evangelicals?*, 193–94.

243. Timothy Dudley-Smith suggests that this was "a courageous book" because "it would diminish in some Free Church and Independent circles his reputation for unswerving evangelical orthodoxy," Dudley-Smith, *John Stott*, 242.

244. Stott, *Christian Mission*, 37.

245. Stott, *Christian Mission*, 43.

246. Stott, *Christian Mission*, 48.

mission is on evangelism, and Stott begins by saying, "yet I think we should agree with the statement of the Lausanne Covenant that 'in the church's mission of sacrificial service evangelism is primary.'"[247]

During the 1980s mission was not something reflected on by Baptists in any significant manner. Paul Beasley-Murray on several occasions argued for the importance of evangelism. In his address to the 1985 Mainstream conference he argued that evangelism should come "top of the agenda" and be "a national priority."[248] Here the use of mission is used interchangeably with that of evangelism. Beasley-Murray advocates the "adoption of church growth insights" and the "restructuring of denominational structures."[249] On the latter, Beasley-Murray notes that the union was putting evangelism on a level again with social action,[250] but argues that there is still only a single person in the Mission Department dedicated to evangelism, out of five with other interests. In his opinion, he believed that the union should invest more in evangelistic appointments. A later article, balances this concern for evangelism with social action: "Evangelism does not exhaust the church's mission."[251] Beasley-Murray is not convinced that this "broader understanding of mission" has been fully "taken up by all Baptists."[252] He mentions Colin Marchant and his work on urban mission, who argued that the Great Commission be joined to the Nazareth Manifesto.[253] Beasley-Murray argues that evangelism is a resurrection gospel, which emphasizes the Lordship of Christ, which, he says, could be "the bridge" between the evangelical emphasis on conversion and "the more radical understanding of mission" from the WCC which saw salvation as about justice and dignity.[254]

The BU Council agreed a National Mission Strategy in March 1993, which was one of the objectives of *Towards 2000*. In a section on theology, it says while there might be differences, there is "a core theology which would unite us all."[255] This is defined as "everything that Jesus sends his people into the world to do and accomplish in his name."[256] It argues that mission

247. Stott, *Christian Mission*, 55.

248. Beasley-Murray, "Evangelism—a National Priority," 17.

249. Beasley-Murray, "Evangelism—a National Priority," 20.

250. This is a reference to the appointment of Tom Rogers as Secretary for Evangelism in 1986.

251. Beasley-Murray, "Toward a Biblical/Theological Framework," 18.

252. Beasley-Murray, "Toward a Biblical/Theological Framework," 18.

253. Marchant, *Signs in the City*. Marchant was president of the Baptist Union in 1988.

254. Beasley-Murray, "Toward a Biblical/Theological Framework," 22.

255. *A Ten Year Plan Towards 2000*, 14.

256. *A Ten Year Plan Towards 2000*, 14, citing Wright and Slater, *A Theology of*

is holistic, meaning it is both evangelism and social action and it cites John 20:21 and then the Nazareth Manifesto, the Great Commission, the Great Commandment and the parable of the sheep and goats. "A biblical strategy for mission embraces the whole of life and seeks to allow the redeeming love of God to affect all things. The church is called to exercise an evangelistic and prophetic ministry in society: to be a living witness to the kingdom of God." The methods for achieving this view of mission are centered on the local church, planting new congregations, special areas (i.e., rural, inner city, multi-ethnic, special ministries) and associations. The Strategy is summarized as wanting "to let the missionary imperative shape the life of our churches at every level."[257]

The conversation about the meaning and scope of mission were ones both streams were aware of and engaged with. In 1990 Wright would write for the union's AiM programme *A Theology of Mission*, with both Newbigin and Stott appearing in the footnotes. In *A Call to Mind* and *Bound to Love* Hayden and Haymes, respectively, had written on the church's mission in the context of pluralism.

Conclusion

The two streams represented by Fiddes and Wright drew from a range of sources in order to describe the renewal of Baptist life they believed was needed. While drawing from the Baptist tradition, they also reached out to wider voices attuned to twentieth-century theological developments and renewal movements. Significant to both streams were the broader traditions in which they placed their visions—evangelicalism and catholicism—which were important for shaping their trajectories. Both Fiddes and Wright demonstrate the skills that Medley says are important in engaging with tradition and this is especially the case with Fiddes.[258] In this way Fiddes and Wright see the importance of tradition and connecting with the past as a source for the present. For each of them there is an element of recovery or retrieval of something that Baptists in the present had overlooked or become ignorant of from among their forebears. Fiddes and Wright believe it important to articulate again particular concepts and ideas for the task they saw of renewing contemporary Baptist church life, both locally and for the union.

Mission, 8.

257. *A Ten Year Plan Towards 2000*, 22.

258. Medley, "Stewards, Interrogators, and Inventors," 81–83.

Chapter 4

The Center of Renewal

IN THE 1990S THE modes of renewal were centered around two concepts: mission and covenant. Stream 1, particularly in the person of Coffey, saw that the denomination should be renewed by an emphasis on mission. This reflected a view of the union as a resource agency for mission in the churches. This was advocated by Wright in *Challenge to Change* and especially in the report *Relating and Resourcing*. Stream 2, particularly in the person of Fiddes, saw that the denomination should be renewed by an emphasis on covenant. This reflected a view of the union as an ecclesial body joined in Christ. This was supported by Haymes in the report *Transforming Superintendency*. The first stream was thus more pragmatic in its approach, while the second stream sought to give a firm theological basis for its proposals.

This diverging emphasis on mission and on covenant would work itself out in the reform of the union's structures in terms of associating and oversight, which will be the focus of a later chapter. Here the renewal of the union was most keenly contested, although attempts were made to reconcile the two visions. In the background were also the implications for the union with regards to ecumenism. The twentieth century has been called the "ecumenical century"[1] and although some Baptists would have been quite content to sit on the sidelines, the union did engage and the 1990s saw a new ecumenism emerge. Here the two streams were both generally positive ecumenists, but for differing reasons and stream 2 wanted to go further ecumenically than stream 1 were comfortable to travel.

---

1. As Brian Stanley notes in *Christianity in the Twentieth Century*, 127.

Mission

Mission and the Missionary God

When Coffey became general secretary the word mission was consistently one he used.[2] It was, in his words, the "consistent core."[3] This is most clearly seen in his introduction of the language "Missionary God." In 1996 in writing about the upcoming denominational conference Coffey used the phrase the "Missionary God." This description of God had already been used in a hymn written by Christopher Ellis for the 200th anniversary of the Baptist Missionary Society in 1992 which had been sung at that year's Baptist Assembly.[4] Coffey himself had already used it in an address to the Mainstream Conference in 1989. The phrase can be found once in Bosch's *Transforming Mission* (which was published in 1991), where he writes: "In the new image mission is not primarily an activity of the church, but an attribute of God. God is a missionary God."[5] Its origins are probably in a paper by Stott. Stott first used the phrase "Missionary God" in a chapter, "The Living God Is a Missionary God," published in 1979, and reprinted in 1981 in a missionary reader.[6] Stott's argument is that the Bible, from Abraham onward, demonstrates that God has a mission and as such he is the missionary God. In 1992, Stott would repeat the argument in *The Contemporary Christian*, where he says, "Christian mission is rooted in the nature of God himself. The Bible reveals him as a missionary God (Father, Son, and Holy Spirit), who creates a missionary people, and is working towards a missionary consummation."[7] It is likely that Stott or Bosch, or both, are the source for Coffey's new expression. Coffey never unpacks what it means to call God missionary. For the most part the phrasing by Coffey reflected the desire to shift the Baptist Union in a more missionary direction, so alongside missionary God, the language of missionary people, missionary union, missionary communities, and missionary purposes through the 1990s becomes part of the Baptist

---

2. This emphasis on mission was also being heard within the Church of England reflected in the Lambeth 1988 call for the Church of England to become "a movement for mission," Thomas Butler, preface to Warren, *Building Missionary Congregations*.

3. Coffey, "The Way Ahead: The General Secretary's Report to SMT 3 January 1997," 2, Denominational Consultation Papers.

4. *Baptist Union of Great Britain Annual Report 1992*, 10.

5. Bosch, *Transforming Mission*, 390. Coffey gives it a "five-star recommendation" in "Towards 2000," 1.

6. Stott, "Living God is a Missionary God," 10–18.

7. Stott, *Contemporary Christian*, 325.

shared vocabulary.[8] The underlying argument being developed is the idea that if we can confess God as missionary, then the union and churches must also be missionary. By 2005 the then new service book of the union, *Gathering for Worship*, uses the language of "Missionary God" as part of prayers offered for the commissioning of a missionary overseas;[9] for the celebration of Pentecost;[10] and in the introduction to the section on ministry where it is said that "all Christians share in the ministry of the missionary God."[11]

When in 1995 Coffey and Jones called for a denominational consultation, this emerged out of what they perceived was "the challenge of being a missionary people to a needy world."[12] Mission, Coffey, and Jones argued, was "the prime factor" and the consultation was an opportunity to be a kind of "missiological prism" in which the structures of the union might be viewed and challenged.[13] It is here that Coffey used for the first time the expression "missionary God." The link is made that missionary activity must be judged in the light of the doctrine of God: "As a Union, surely we need a fresh vision of God."[14] An invitation is made to reflect on mission theologically.

The concept of the missiological prism understood the Baptist Union as a light which was being passed through the prism that was God's missiological imperative. The purpose intended was that this might offer insights into how the union might be transformed. This missiological imperative was described as "God's revelation to lost humanity." Although Coffey and Jones had described mission in holistic terms, a document which set out to explain the concept of the missiological prism, described mission as evangelism.[15] Explaining this imperative emphasized that everything begins with God and what God is already doing. The imperative is about revelation which was understood as meaning the Bible. The Bible was both a tool for evangelism and a guide to how to do evangelism. The imperative is thirdly about "lost humanity" which was understood as taking seriously that outside of the gospel, humanity is lost. Important in the thinking around the

8. It was used by numerous people, especially in Baptist Union publications. For example, Anne Wilkinson-Hayes, "Time for Change," *Infomission* 11 (1996).

9. Ellis and Blyth, *Gathering for Worship*, 182.

10. Ellis and Blyth, *Gathering for Worship*, 392.

11. Ellis and Blyth, *Gathering for Worship*, 114.

12. Coffey, "Denominational Consultation."

13. Coffey, "Denominational Consultation." The other factors were financial, frustration, and ferment.

14. Coffey, "Denominational Consultation," 2.

15. "The Missiological Prism" BU Denominational Consultation papers. This document I think was an internal one and was not ever published.

missiological prism is the work of the Anglican Robert Warren on *Building Missionary Congregations.*[16] Warren's argument was that the church was the "primary agent of mission."[17] He argued both that there was a cultural shift taking place which required the church to move out of what he called "pastoral mode" to a "missionary mode."[18] This pastoral mode was "deeply clerical" and "function[ed] primarily as an organisation."[19] The mission mode is defined as: restoring purpose to the nature of the church; restoring spirituality to the heart of Christian community; recovering the prophetic dynamic of the gospel; recovering the baptismal identity of every believer; renewing the community character of church life; and a shift from a church life to a whole life focus.[20] Warren's analysis and proposal had resonances with Baptist understandings of the church and mission.[21]

The implications of this shift to put mission at the center were reflected in two areas that of the union's mission department and the relationship with BMS. At the March 1997 council it was agreed that the Mission Department would be renamed as the Department for Research and Training in Mission. This was partly initiated by the inability to replace the head of the department after Derek Tidball had moved to become principal of London Bible College in 1995, but also from some of the outcomes of the 1996 denominational consultation.[22] This had seen 258 people[23] vote for changing the Mission Department into a training, coordinating resource. In the proposal that followed there was a belief that what churches and associations needed was a "small specialised team to engage in research, development and training" in order that "the latest thinking in holistic mission and in adult learning" might be shared. This reflected Houston's address at the denominational consultation that spoke about the union becoming a

16. Warren's definition of a missionary congregation is "a church which takes its identity, priorities, and agenda, from participation in God's mission to the world," Warren, *Building Missionary*, 4.

17. Warren, *Building Missionary*, 2.

18. Warren, *Building Missionary*, 3.

19. Warren, *Building Missionary*, 15.

20. Warren, *Building Missionary*, 17–27.

21. See "What Is a Missionary Congregation?" Tony Peck presented a paper (unpublished) on "The Missionary Congregation" at the 1999 consultation on "Doing Theology in a Baptist Way" and Wright would reference Warren and missionary congregations in Wright, *New Baptists*, 86.

22. The detailed advice from the consultation saw some suggesting that the Mission Department be closed and replaced by regional, others that it had a more research and training role.

23. See chapter 1's discussion of the denominational consultation for who the 258 people were.

"learning organization" in "strategic alliance" with others.[24] The department
had historically existed as a team of people holding specialist subject areas
(evangelism, social affairs, education, youth). The vision for the new team
was centered around mission advisors working together and in partnership
with colleges and associations to "develop a more holistic mission and encourage the congregations in the journey towards mature discipleship." At
the heart of this was what was called "a move away from Committee driven
programmatic work, to an experience-reflection-action model."[25] The view
expressed in this decision was that mission was local but needed resourcing.

The consultation had strongly argued for a closer relationship between
the union and the BMS. This ranged from uniting the two (260–20),[26] to a
covenant relationship (279–81) and to the BMS becomes the mission arm
of a Federation of British Baptists (265–24). This reflected a long history of
seeking to see the union and the society come closer together. The planned
joint headquarters were finally realized in 1989, after permission had been
given in 1961 by the assembly and a stated desire to this end by the council as early as 1936.[27] Some had wanted not just a joint headquarters but a
closer working together and for Ernest Payne a desire to see the joining of
the two organizations into one.[28]

While there was an evident desire from the consultation to see a new
kind of relationship emerge, by March 1999 little progress had been made
and the DCRG asked whether the union and the society could create a forum to continue a conversation.[29] There had been an attempt in the Fellowship of British Baptists (FBB)[30] to explore a new kind of relationship and
Brian Stanley wrote a paper in 1996 for discussion.[31] Stanley offered four

24. *Towards a Department for Research and Training in Mission.* DCRG/97/6.

25. *Towards a Department for Research and Training in Mission.* DCRG/97/6.

26. Numbers for and against in the votes taken at the consultation.

27. See Sparkes, *Offices of the Baptist Union of Great Britain.*

28. "When . . . I became Secretary of the Union I indicated my conviction that the
Baptist Union and the Baptist Missionary Society should be brought together," Payne,
Between Yesterday and Tomorrow, 6.

29. *Continuing the Journey*, 5.

30. In 1994, the Fellowship of British Baptists (FBB) had been established between
the different unions and the society with a covenant that expressed a commitment to
"strengthening of fellowship and developing of partnership." See *SecCheck* 8 (Spring
1994). Prior to the FBB there had been a Joint Consultative Committee, see Stanley,
History of the Baptist Missionary Society, 521.

31. Stanley, "Looking Towards the Future." Stanley was a Baptist and church his-
torian, who had taught at Spurgeon's until 1991 before moving first to Trinity College,
Bristol, and then in 1996 to Cambridge Director of the Currents in World Christianity
Project.

possible options: (a) BMS and BUGB merger; (b) BMS becomes overseas mission department of FBB; (c) BMS remains a voluntary society within the FBB; and (d) the creation of a Baptist Mission Fellowship replacing BMS, FBB, and in some measure the three national unions.

Stanley discounted option A, because BMS related to more than just the BUGB. Option B has strengths, especially that it would enable clearer ways for global Baptist partners to relate to British Baptists missionally. Stanley says there are problems in that BMS might lose some independence, and that the FBB is too remote from local churches, for local churches to be content with BMS having authority to speak for Baptists. He says the same problems would be present and possibly at an "even greater measure" if the BUGB denominational consultation suggestion of BMS being an arm of a Federation of British Baptists were implemented. Option C was to keep things as they were, but Stanley suggested a good proportion of British Baptists would "remain dissatisfied," although not those who only saw the unions as voluntary non-ecclesial entities. Stanley did argue that even here that BMS should become the Baptist Mission Society rather than Missionary Society, reflecting the change of understanding with regards mission.[32] Option D is Stanley's own suggestion. It is based on four principles: historically structures have been organized around mission; eliminate dualism of mission global and ministry local; a desire in Baptist churches for simpler structures which have a mission priority; and churches should redefine themselves in missionary terms. As the Baptist Mission Fellowship, there would be an expression of *koinonia* for the sake of mission. The BMF would give a sense of movement over the static language of union. Mission would be understood as not just evangelism or church growth, but in terms of the kingdom of God. Stanley recognizes that some unions might feel a loss of national identity and in addition that the new Mission Fellowship might be too large for churches to feel connected, especially in light of the denominational consultation for smaller bodies. Stanley felt the language of "fellowship" was one degree less than being ecclesial and so should calm fears of creating a British Baptist *Church*.

When the FBB discussed Stanley's paper there was some openness to explore options B and D, apart from Alistair Brown, the then new BMS general director, who believed the unions were like BMS in being voluntary societies and saw no need for change.[33] The minutes suggest that Coffey was open to something more radical. By the next meeting of the FBB

32. Here some change did happen in March 2000 when the Baptist Missionary Society renamed themselves BMS World Mission, reflecting some of Stanley's suggestion.

33. Minutes of the Sixth Council Meeting, FBB, December 16–17, 1996.

Stanley's proposals found no enthusiasm and so the relationship of the national unions to BMS remained in option C.[34] Stanley came back to the topic in his 2011 Dr. George Beasley-Murray Memorial Lecture where he argued that "the challenge is to be willing to re-conceive the mutual relations, and perhaps even structures of our national Baptist Missionary fellowships."[35] He goes on to comment, perhaps including his own experience, of "a protracted and not particularly edifying history of relationships between the Union and the Missionary Society."

Despite all the talk of mission, a theology of mission was much slower to emerge. On becoming moderator of the Doctrine and Worship Committee in 2002, Sean Winter suggested that it would be appropriate for the committee to look at mission "as the main area not yet considered" in the life of the union: "Since the language of mission was dominant throughout the union, it seemed potentially useful to consider the underlying theology."[36]

Ahead of the 1996 denominational consultation the union's Doctrine and Worship Committee prepared a set of bible studies called *Beginning with God*. In the preface, Ellis, who was the then chair of the committee, argues that the consultation should not begin with problems or even vision, but with God.[37] *Beginning with God* makes it quite clear that this God is the "missionary God." The study concludes with the hymn "Missionary God" written by Ellis and first used back at the 1992 Baptist Assembly. Ellis, in the preface, says that mission is God's and this appears to be the basis for naming God as missionary. Each verse of Ellis's hymn begins "Missionary God" but the rest of the verses speak more of asking God to breathe, help, open, give, and remake and fill the church in God's mission. God has a mission, but the church carries it out. The question this raises becomes: is it appropriate then to call God missionary?

Also written ahead of the consultation was *Something to Declare: A study of the Declaration of Principle* jointly written by the principals of the four English Baptist colleges.[38] Here was a significant contribution from stream 2. In his foreword, Coffey writes of the need for pastor-theologians who will "address how faithfully the Church of today is reflecting the nature

34. Minutes of the Seventh Council Meeting, FBB, May 1997.

35. Stanley, "Renewing a Vision for Mission among British Baptists," 200.

36. Minutes of the Doctrine and Worship Committee, Friday January 9, 2004, 5.

37. *Beginning with God*, 3.

38. The four principals at the time were Paul Fiddes, Brian Haymes, Richard Kidd, and Michael Quicke. The idea for a study of the Declaration of Principle came from the principals to which Coffey and Jones added their encouragement, see Fiddes et al., "Doing Theology Together," 14–15.

and purposes of the missionary God."[39] In the introduction, Kidd says that what the principals are doing in *Something to Declare* is a contribution "to think more deeply about the 'missionary God' and to focus our explorations through a so-called 'missiological prism.'"[40] In the third section of the study under the heading the "Question of Mission," which discusses the third article of the Declaration of Principle,[41] the principals understand discipleship as "a participation in the energy and life of the missionary God."[42] This participation is made possible through baptism. They recognize the influence of Bosch in the development of the theology of *missio Dei*. The principals make a helpful observation that the language of "mission of God" is ambiguous as it can mean that mission is what God calls us to go and effect and it can also mean that mission is that in which God is the chief player, not just that God sends, but that God is active in mission.[43] It is the former that seems to lie behind most usages of "missionary God" by Coffey and Ellis. The principals argue that we should hold on to both, mission is both that which God does *and* that which God calls us to participate in.

Through the "mission of God" prism the principals suggests three characteristics of what mission looks like: interactive, diverse, and corporate. The story of God's mission in Jesus is interactive, that is, it is a "venture of risky and vulnerable love" in which Jesus calls followers. The story of God's mission in Jesus is diverse, that is, Jesus' ministry sees each person as they are in their particular need and context. The story of God's mission in Jesus is corporate, that is, mission flows both ways in that there is no longer a clear sense of sender and receiver. As we see in Jesus, mission is shaped by weakness and vulnerability and as such this is "the measure for once and for all."[44] This leads to the conclusion that the mission of God must be "determinative" for the mission of the church; how we carry out mission should reflect the way God in Christ does mission.[45] The principals here embrace the "missionary God"[46] but seek to begin to provide a thicker

---

39. Kidd, *Something to Declare*, 7.

40. Kidd, *Something to Declare*, 9.

41. The third article of the Declaration of Principle is that "it is the duty of every disciple to bear personal witness to the Gospel of Jesus Christ, and to take part in the evangelization of the world."

42. Kidd, *Something to Declare*, 48.

43. Kidd, *Something to Declare*, 49.

44. Kidd, *Something to Declare*, 50–51.

45. Kidd, *Something to Declare*, 51.

46. There appears to be some slight hesitation by the principals in using the language of missionary God. In the introduction it is in quotation marks and then it is only used once more on the last page, although this time without quotation marks. The

theological description that does not see mission as overly concerned with success or numbers, but with faithfulness to God.[47] In other words the importance of mission is theological not only a pragmatic response to declining church attendance.

A third piece of work that also contributed some reflections on God and mission is the report *Transforming Superintendency* (*TS*). In the terms of reference given to the review group, they were asked to set their report "within the perspective of the Mission of God."[48] The group took this seriously and began the report with a theological reflection on the doctrine of God.[49] This report, in common with the others mentioned, is content to describe God as the "triune missionary God." Like *Beginning with God*, *TS* argues that "Christians must always begin with God."[50] To speak of God, they claim, is to speak of Father, Son, and Holy Spirit. The triune God is by nature relational and is "always 'going out' in love to others."[51] This "going out" takes shape as "a will to save" and as a result seeking to restore relationship with humanity. The triune God through Jesus calls the church and this is an invitation to "share the life and mission of God."[52] The church is marked by fellowship with God and comprises those who are the body of Christ in the world.[53] The church is described as those who share in God's missionary purposes. One way God does this is through the gift of ministry; ministry is defined as the "enabling of the Church in every place to be the Church."[54] The mission of God is made evident through the preaching of the gospel and the witness of the church.[55]

Toward a Theology of Mission

It was not until the middle of the next decade that some more work was done, as mentioned above, to reflect further on the language of missionary God. Here John 20:21 is taken as the key biblical text by Fiddes, Stephen

chapter on mission continually uses the phrase "the mission of God."

47. Kidd, *Something to Declare*, 52.

48. *Transforming Superintendency*, 51, cf. 7.

49. The structure of the report, beginning with the doctrine of God, was probably due to the group's chair, Brian Haymes, who went on later to write a book which made the same move: Haymes et al., *On Being the Church*.

50. *Transforming Superintendency*, 9.

51. *Transforming Superintendency*, 9.

52. *Transforming Superintendency*, 10.

53. *Transforming Superintendency*, 10.

54. *Transforming Superintendency*, 12.

55. *Transforming Superintendency*, 13.

R. Holmes and John Colwell.[56] We look first to Fiddes's chapter on mission published in *Tracks and Traces* in 2003.[57] Fiddes begins with John 20:21 which he interprets as meaning the church shares in the mission of God. The church is "apostolic" because the church is "sent" and sent in the same manner and form of Christ: "*as* the Father sent me."[58] Fiddes goes further than simply saying that mission is the church imitating Christ to claim that mission is "a *participation* in the Father's own sending of the Son."[59] Mission is not a task but a call to share in God's work. The sending of the Son by the Father, according to Fiddes, was "God's mission from eternity."[60] Mission is the way the church is, because it is the way God is in himself. If the church is apostolic, it is also catholic says Fiddes, for it is the church's being-sentness that is an expression of its catholicity.[61] Fiddes has already described mission in participatory language, before he also introduces another key word in his theology, "covenant." A theology of covenant lies at the heart of Fiddes's doctrine of God, developed from Karl Barth: the covenant God makes with us through Jesus is an expression of the eternal covenant between Father and Son and Holy Spirit. The covenant that God makes with us through Jesus is a missionary act—the Father sends the Son.[62] For Fiddes the missionary God is also the covenant-making God. This means mission must always be "relational" and focused on "making communion and community."[63] Furthermore, mission that is shaped by covenant must always be intentionally open, that is, a church participating in the mission of God can never seek to create a homogeneous unit, because God seeks covenant with all people, not a select group.[64]

Holmes's starting point is to test the claim that "a missionary church worships a missionary God." While the wider church has widely accepted the language of the *missio Dei*, that God has a mission, it has been more

56. Colwell was Tutor in Christian Doctrine and Ethics at Spurgeon's College from 1996–2009. He had completed a PhD on Karl Barth at King's College London in the mid-1980s and in 2005 published a significant work on sacramental theology: *Promise and Presence.*

57. The origins of this chapter are a paper presented first in 1997 as part of conversations between the Baptist World Alliance and the Orthodox Ecumenical Patriarchate of Constantinople.

58. Fiddes, *Tracks and Traces*, 250.

59. Fiddes, *Tracks and Traces*, 251.

60. Fiddes, *Tracks and Traces*, 251.

61. Fiddes, *Tracks and Traces*, 252.

62. Fiddes, *Tracks and Traces*, 252–53.

63. Fiddes, *Tracks and Traces*, 253.

64. Fiddes, *Tracks and Traces*, 253.

reluctant, or it is at least rarer, for the wider church to speak of God as missionary. Holmes seeks to provide a rationale for Baptists confessing God as missionary.[65] His paper also begins with John 20:21. A reading of John's gospel demonstrates, says Holmes, that the sending of the disciples is linked, is continuous, with the sending of the Son by the Father.[66] The disciples and Jesus share in the same work. It is this point that gives scope to name God as missionary. The means of the church's participation in the mission of Jesus is through the Holy Spirit, which John's gospel records Jesus breathing on the disciples. As Jesus is sent by the Father, there is a parallel mission or sending of the Holy Spirit that connects the church to Jesus. Having made these brief exegetical comments on John 20:21–23, Holmes turns to the theology of Augustine as "the *locus classicus* discussion of divine missions."[67] Holmes's engagement with Augustine raises the question that while we might say that mission belongs to the economic Trinity (the means in which God acts), there remains a question of whether we can speak of mission belonging to the eternal life of God. The former means we can speak of God's mission; the latter would mean we can affirm missionary as an attribute of God. Augustine argues strongly for the *missio Dei*, that the Son and the Spirit are sent by God, but these are "anomalous events" and not integral to who God is in himself.[68] Augustine is concerned to protect the divinity of the Son from the suggestion that being sent implies ontological subordination. He believes that we cannot divide the actions of God, it is God who acts, and so the Son is involved in his own sending.

In order to speak then of God as missionary, Holmes turns first to Basil of Caesarea. Basil argues that we can differentiate the acts of the Trinity on the basis of the relationships of origin. Basil says that each divine act has its origin in the Father, therefore we can say that redemption is initiated by the Father, carried out through the incarnation of the Son and brought to completion by the Spirit's work in the church.[69] If Basil is right, and Holmes believes that he is, this also helps us to see that it must be possible to speak of the Son and the Spirit "defer[ing] to the authority of the Father" and that this is a "necessary consequence of the particular relationships of origins within the Trinity."[70] Turning back to John 20:21, Holmes can see that there

65. Holmes, "Trinitarian Missiology," 72. Holmes's paper was published in an academic journal which means it has not been widely read by many Baptists. It was originally presented to the Doctrine and Worship Committee in 2004.

66. Holmes, "Trinitarian Missiology," 74.

67. Holmes, "Trinitarian Missiology," 76.

68. Holmes, "Trinitarian Missiology," 79.

69. Holmes, "Trinitarian Missiology," 80.

70. Holmes, "Trinitarian Missiology," 82.

is room to claim that the sending of the Son by the Father is ontological, within God's own life, and not just economic. This is strengthened by the earlier conversations between Father and Son in John chapters 13–17 which many read as an intra-trinitarian conversation.[71]

On this basis Holmes argues his case for describing God as missionary. He goes on though to distinguish his claim from the likes of Jürgen Moltmann. Holmes says if the events of the gospel story do reveal God's eternal life, it does not entail that these events are definitive of God's life. Where Moltmann argues that the crucifixion is definitive for God's eternal life, Holmes contends instead that the crucifixion is "a repetition of the pattern of God's eternal life."[72] At this point Holmes discusses the Fiddes paper explored above as an example of someone following the Moltmann line, but one alert to the theological pitfalls that Moltmann arguably falls into. That is, Fiddes is the best example of a Moltmannian theology, but Holmes argues that we do not need to follow this trajectory to enable us to say the triune God is missionary.[73] Holmes suggests that following Barth is more helpful. Barth takes the doctrine of election and places it within his doctrine of God, which means the history of Jesus is not a separate act, but "part of who God is, not just what God has done."[74]

In the final sections of Holmes's article he draws his argument together. To speak of the missionary God is to say that the relations of Son and Spirit to the Father are not just a "movement of origination, but a movement of purposeful sending."[75] Holmes says the character of these relations according to John 20:19–23 is of "gracious generosity."[76] Jesus speaks words of peace over the disciples and speaks of forgiveness of sins. To attribute mission to God's character is also to suggest that God's own life is orientated outward, although Holmes is more cautious than Fiddes (in his view) to not give any ground that God needs something outside of himself. Yet in the way that love says something about how God relates to creation, so being missionary gives rise to a movement of God that goes beyond concern to action in order to realize his loving purposes.[77] Holmes's final observations are around how a doctrine of God that includes being missionary affects ecclesiology. If God is missionary in himself then the church cannot truly be itself without

71. Holmes, "Trinitarian Missiology," 82.

72. Holmes, "Trinitarian Missiology," 83.

73. Holmes, "Trinitarian Missiology," 84.

74. Holmes, "Trinitarian Missiology," 85.

75. Holmes, "Trinitarian Missiology," 86.

76. Holmes, "Trinitarian Missiology," 88.

77. Holmes, "Trinitarian Missiology," 88.

it too being missionary. The doctrine of God, as we explored above in the works from the mid-1990s, does shape what it is to be the church. Mission becomes a mark of the church, alongside one, holy, catholic, and apostolic.[78] Holmes's final point says that for a missionary God mission never comes to an end, mission is not temporal, but eternal. Holmes finds no reason for this not to be the case, and some hints in the book of Revelation to support it.[79]

Holmes's article, while subtitled as only "Towards a Theology of God as Missionary," remains among Baptists the most extensive argument thus far for the confession that Coffey, Ellis, and others have made, and continue to make, about the identity of God.[80]

John Colwell's shorter paper "Mission as Ontology" originated at the same time as Holmes's and was also first presented to the Doctrine and Worship Committee. Colwell's paper covers similar ground to Fiddes and Holmes, but he makes his own argument. Colwell's concern is that language of the church "doing mission" is theologically ungrammatical.[81] To talk about mission, we must, like others, begin with God. Following Bosch, he says that the language of mission was first used "exclusively" with reference to the doctrine of the Trinity. He refers to Bosch's claim that mission is an attribute of God and affirms this in terms of the economic Trinity, but *pace* Holmes, not with reference to God *in se*. Colwell is concerned that to make mission an attribute of God's nature is to ultimately make the object of that mission eternal too.[82] Therefore, Colwell steps short from speaking of God as missionary.

Colwell's constructive point is to argue that the Son and the Spirit's sending is ontological rather than functional.[83] Who the Son and Spirit are is defined by their being sent by the Father, not primarily by what they do. The same is true of the church, says Colwell, and he supports this point with reference to John 20:21.[84] The church is sent as a witness to the Son and this corresponds to the sending of the Spirit. The mission of the church reflects more the mission of the Spirit than that of the Son. The sending of the Son is unique. The church does not continue the Son's sending but is related to the

78. Holmes, "Trinitarian Missiology," 89.

79. Holmes, "Trinitarian Missiology," 89–90.

80. Coffey continues to speak of a missionary God in his Dr. George Beasley-Murray Memorial Lecture delivered in 2006 and published in 2014 in Wright, *Truth Never Dies*. Ellis also continues to speak of God as missionary in "Spirituality in Mission."

81. Colwell, "Mission as Ontology," 8.

82. Colwell, "Mission as Ontology," 8.

83. Colwell, "Mission as Ontology," 8.

84. Colwell, "Mission as Ontology," 9.

Son through its witness to the Son.[85] The mission of the church, like that of the Son and the Spirit is ontological rather than functional. Colwell's point is that the mission of the church is not dependent on what it does but on its being sent into the world. Anything the church does is an outworking or an outcome of its mission. Its mission resides in who it is, those gathered and sent into the world by the Son in the power of the Spirit.[86]

Colwell goes on to comment that the language of mission has largely replaced the language of evangelism, and this points to a fresh understanding that evangelism, as in proclamation, must be accompanied by social and political action.[87] While on the one hand this might be applauded, Colwell expresses concern that this is probably more about evangelism becoming something the church is uneasy about. More importantly all the church's talk of mission as that which is done as activity creates a separation between the church and mission.[88] It creates an "and" where there should be no "and."[89] It identifies some of the church's life as mission and parts as non-mission, often what might be termed "worship." Colwell wants to stress that the church is a "missionary people," at no point does mission start or stop.[90] Mission is what the church is as it indwells the gospel story through Baptism and the Lord's Supper.[91] As such it is itself a sign and a sacrament—a witness to the Son.[92]

Wright has also written on the relationship between God and mission. In *Disavowing Constantine* he affirms the *missio Dei* and argues that "the sending of the Son and Spirit reveal God's self-giving love and expresses the centrifugal movement of God's being."[93] Mission defines God's being and as a consequence the church's. Like Colwell, he speaks of the church as a sign, sacrament, and instrument.[94] In Wright's later work *Free Church, Free State* he argues that mission is a priority of the church, it is the "defining essence of the church."[95] He then provides an extended quote from Daniel Migliore,

85. Colwell, "Mission as Ontology," 9.

86. Colwell, "Mission as Ontology," 9.

87. Colwell, "Mission as Ontology," 10.

88. Colwell, "Mission as Ontology," 10.

89. I borrow this point from a similar one Stanley Hauerwas makes in *A Better Hope*, 155–61.

90. Colwell, "Mission as Ontology," 11.

91. Colwell, "Mission as Ontology," 11. Colwell develops his argument of "indwelling" in *Living the Christian Story*.

92. For more on the church as sacrament, see Colwell, "Church as Sacrament."

93. Wright, *Disavowing Constantine*, 9.

94. Wright, *Disavowing Constantine*, 10.

95. Wright, *Free Church*, 16.

in which Migliore says that "the triune God is a missionary God."[96] He returns to mission and the church toward the end of the book and describes the mode of mission as declaring truth through persuasion. The church's mission follows the pattern of its Messiah and Wright suggests it is less the "agent" of mission than the "locus," that is where God is at work.[97] This echoes Colwell that the church does not primarily do mission but is mission, where the gospel is present. Stuart Murray is critical of Wright's theology of mission for its brevity.[98] Despite the language of the "priority of mission" and the church as a "missionary, messianic community," Wright does not include mission in his description of what he considers the "ecclesial minimum." Evangelism and mission are strangely muted themes in both Wright's key accounts of Baptist identity *Challenge to Change* and *Free Church, Free State*. They are present, but not up-front and central. Wright's shorter book *New Baptists, New Agenda*, which was written in between the other two mentioned, is where he offers some further comments on mission. Here he distinguishes evangelism as a subset of mission. Mission is the holistic action of God to seek and restore all that was lost.[99] Mission is the imperative of the church, that is, churches are, or should be, missionary congregations.[100] Mission is "participation in God's saving purposes for the world."[101] Mission is congregational says Wright, for conversion is a trinitarian and ecclesial experience, it is to be gathered into God and as such gathered into the church.[102] He does not say it, but the suggestion is that we must speak of missionary congregations but not missionary associations or unions. The role of the association or union is to relate and resource the local church in mission.[103]

Summary

To summarize we have seen that the confession of a missionary God is supported by Fiddes and Holmes, although in different ways. Colwell supports the concept of missionary God in terms of how God acts but resists the move to say this of God's eternal life. For Colwell though mission is ontological

96. Wright, *Free Church*, 16, quoting Migliore, *Faith Seeking Understanding*, 200–201.

97. Wright, *Free Church*, 234.

98. Murray, "Church Planting, Peace and the Ecclesial Minimum," 132.

99. Wright, *New Baptists*, 31.

100. Wright, *New Baptists*, 65.

101. Wright, *New Baptists*, 65.

102. Wright, *New Baptists*, 81–82.

103. Wright, *Free Church*, 189.

rather than functional, such that to speak of a missionary church is not to speak of what a church does, but who the church is in God.

At the level of formal theology—the theology of the denomination's theologians—there was an understanding of mission as ontological for God and the church, but at the level of the operant theology within the union and its churches there was a more functional view of mission. Mission was the church's purpose: what it should be doing.[104] Mission was thus prone to what Ian Stackhouse has called "faddism."[105] Underlying this was a functional understanding of mission, where the union was seen as a resource agency generating ideas for mission, creating a need for the latest and most novel, that which will "work."[106] The concern to "turn the tide" in terms of numbers lent itself to a "concerted effort to arrest the process of atrophy by further activity."[107] What emerges is a theology of mission that begins with God combined with a "deep-seated anxiety about the uncertain future of the church."[108] I would contend that it was a concern for numbers that took precedence so that despite Coffey arguing that what was needed was "a moratorium on all our activity" in order for it to be judged "in the light of our Doctrine of God,"[109] this task was largely left undone as the Doctrine and Worship Committee observed in 2003.

Covenant

The Doctrine and Worship Committee

Where Coffey and stream 1 were arguing for mission as a central organizing concept, Fiddes and stream 2 were looking to covenant to take this place. It was first introduced by the report *The Nature of the Assembly and the Council of the Baptist Union of Great Britain* presented in 1994 that sought to provide a theology of the union with covenant as the key theological idea. In 2001 the union published *Covenant 21*, which was a set of materials,

104. The language of formal and operant theology comes from Cameron et al., *Talking About God in Practice*, 53–56.

105. Stackhouse, *Gospel-Driven Church*, 8–31. Stackhouse says this faddism is a consequence of a charismatic evangelical mix of revivalism and activism and programmatic mission.

106. In the 1990s Baptist churches were encouraged to be involved in AiM; Challenge 2000; On Fire; Church Planting; Willow Creek and seeker services; Alpha; Sowing, Reaping Keeping.

107. Stackhouse, *Gospel-Driven Church*, 10.

108. Goodliff, *Shaped for Service*, 230.

109. Coffey, "Denominational Consultation."

including a worship service that was used at the 2001 Baptist Assembly and offered also for use by local congregations. This might suggest that Baptists had embraced a theology of covenant to understand their shared life together. However this section will tell a much more complicated story in which "covenant" did not ultimately find wide acceptance, instead it remained a contested term, despite several attempts to argue for it historically, biblically, and theologically.

The story begins with the Doctrine and Worship Committee, which was established in 1992 as part of the new Faith and Unity Executive.[110] The document, *A Ten Year Plan*, describes the purpose of the committee "as a small advisory group providing the biblical, historical and theological framework for our discussions on Baptist identity."[111] Its first chair was Paul Fiddes and other members included Faith Bowers (secretary), Gethin Abraham-Williams,[112] Christopher Ellis,[113] Brian Haymes, Peter Hicks,[114] Douglas McBain, David Roberts, Nigel Wright, and ex officio both David Coffey and Keith Jones. The make-up of the committee included people from both the denominational and theological streams: Paul Fiddes, Brian Haymes, and also Christopher Ellis[115] representing the theological renewal stream and Nigel Wright and Douglas McBain the denominational renewal stream. Out of the 1992 council *Structures Report* came a question of the ecclesiological nature of the Baptist Union, and the Doctrine and Worship Committee were asked to prepare a report on this matter.[116] This would be

110. In April 1990, Barrie White had suggested to the ACCR that a "doctrine commission" be set up for the union. Minutes of ACCR, 24 April 1990. It was Keith Jones though who was instrumental in its setting up. He was the prime author of the 1992 *Structures Report*.

111. *A Ten Year Plan Towards 2000*, 6.

112. After pastoring three Baptist churches, Abraham-Williams had been Ecumenical Officer to the Milton Keynes Council and from 1990 the general secretary of the Covenanted Churches in Wales.

113. Chris Ellis had trained for ministry at Regent's Park College in the 1970s and had pastored three churches and by 1992 was minister at Cemetery Road Baptist Church, Sheffield. He had completed an MA in theology at the University of Sussex and also published *Together on the Way: A Theology of Ecumenism*. He would later complete a PhD on Baptist worship at the University of Leeds and in 2000 become principal of Bristol Baptist College.

114. Peter Hicks was a Baptist minister and from 1991 Director of Ministry at London Bible College. He had previously been Lecturer in Philosophy at the college between 1981–1985. He had a PhD (University of London 1986) on the philosophical concepts in the thought of Charles Hodge.

115. Ellis was a member of the group that contributed to Fiddes, *Reflections on the Water*, which had begun meeting in 1990.

116. This was one of three reports Jones encouraged the committee to prepare, the

the first report from the committee and it was presented to council in March 1994 and then discussed in November 1994.

The Nature of the Assembly and the Council

The Nature of the Assembly and the Council of the Baptist Union of Great Britain attempted to provide a theology of the union and in so doing describe theologically the relationship between the assembly and the council, the purpose of those meetings and in addition how we might speak of spiritual leadership in the union. The report was largely written by Fiddes and then debated and revised by the committee over several meetings. The theology of the union it presents is centered on the concept of covenant. As an earlier chapter has already demonstrated Fiddes and the group who had produced *Bound to Love* had already retrieved covenant as an important Baptist theological idea. In *Bound to Love* Hayden had remarked that the Baptist Union "has been in search of a theology which will authenticate the organised national life of Baptist churches."[117] The essays in *Bound to Love* sit in the background to *The Nature of Assembly*, providing some of the argument from which Fiddes borrows.

The *Nature of Assembly* argues for the union to be viewed as an ecclesial body in which the assembly and the council are "two expressions of covenantal relationship between the churches."[118] The underlying argument is to extend the covenant relationship in a local congregation to that which is between churches in the union. The commitment to "walk together and watch over one another" is a response to the initiative of Christ to gather churches together: the union is an expression of *being* church.[119] The report seeks to distinguish between a church (local congregation), the Church (universal) and what it is termed *being church* that is the union. The point being claimed is that the Baptist Union is an ecclesial body which should be understood theologically. Churches, associations, and colleges within the union are bound together by God and expressed in the affirmation of the BU's Declaration of Principle, which is understood as a covenant document.[120]

---

other two were on ministry and baptism. When he was secretary of Yorkshire Baptist Association he had overseen similar kinds of theology work and he carried this into his new role as deputy general secretary. Its purpose being to help the union think more theologically and also be in a better place in terms of ecumenical engagement. Email to me from Keith Jones, August 6, 2018.

117. Hayden, "Baptists, Covenants and Confessions," 31.

118. *Nature of the Assembly*, 15.

119. *Nature of the Assembly*, 10.

120. *Nature of the Assembly*, 16. In *Bound to Love*, Hayden suggests that "perhaps

The assertion that the union is ecclesial leads to the argument that as a local congregation meets in church meeting, so must the union as it gathers in assembly and council. Therefore, "a national assembly must by nature be 'deliberative.'" The report rejects the view that the assembly is analogous to the church meeting and the council to the deacons' meeting. Instead it argues that the constitution sets them "side-by-side"—they are two mutual expressions with the same purpose. The purpose of assembly and council being to seek the mind of Christ, as is the purpose of the local congregation. The former do not have authority over the latter, but a covenantal understanding of the union will see the local congregation take seriously the wisdom of assembly and council. In terms of the relationship between assembly and council, there is a difference in authority. The council made up mainly of representatives from the associations has its "own covenantal character, its own way of representing the church and its own authority" and yet the "Assembly is a more comprehensive expression of the Union."[121] At the heart of these covenantal relationships is what the report calls a "balance of mutual trust."[122] What characterizes the union as it meets in assembly and council and as local congregations is the importance of seeking to "listen carefully," and the "willingness to search for the mind of Christ together."[123]

The report moves its arguments on to the implications of this covenantal understanding for the union, and for the meetings of assembly and council. For assembly, the report contends that it should be emphasized that the purpose of the assembly meeting is that those in covenant relationship "seek the purpose of Christ for the life of the churches and the health of the society." The report criticizes the way that deliberation has been marginalized in favor of seeking to be inspiring and celebratory. It further laments that in becoming the Baptist Assembly, rather than the assembly of the Baptist Union, there had been a loss of the covenantal character—the "obligations and privileges" upon delegates.[124] The report highlights the problem that the BU and BMS are not the same, the union being ecclesial and BMS

we should see the Declaration of Principle as being comparable to the 'covenant document' in the local church in a previous century," 35.

121. *Nature of the Assembly*, 20.

122. *Nature of the Assembly*, 20.

123. *Nature of the Assembly*, 22.

124. In 1984 the name of the assembly was changed to the Baptist Assembly and became a joint assembly of the Baptist Union and the Baptist Missionary Society, *Baptist Union Annual Report 1984*, 9. Some of this was no doubt due to that both secretaries of the BU and BMS—Bernard Green and Reg Harvey—were "long-standing personal friends," Randall, *English Baptists*, 426. Morris West had made similar soundings to the report, see Beasley-Murray, "Notes of a Conversation with Morris West re the Baptist Union Assembly, 8/2/92." Paul Beasley-Murray papers.

being a voluntary body. The report argues that the annual assembly of the
BU is restored, but to take place in a wider event called the Annual Baptist
Congress. This had the potential of retaining some of the character of the
present assembly, and at the same time, making clear that assembly of the
BU was a particular kind of moment—one for those bound in covenant.
A third point is to argue that more time be given to deliberation of critical issues: this would allow "the covenant relationship of the Union to be
actualised."[125] A final point is that the assembly should give considerable
time to debate the work of council, as presented in its annual report.

The Response to The Nature of Assembly

The Nature of Assembly was the first attempt to give a clear argument for
a theology of the union around the concept of covenant. The report was
not received well, neither by the council nor from wider responses after
it was published. The minutes of the January 1995 Doctrine and Worship
Committee indicated that it was felt "a negative response had come from
the constituency overall."[126] It further noted that the committee believed
that "the report showed excellent theology but poor communication." The
question the committee identified was how best to communicate, especially
where, it was deemed, "there was cultural vandalism evident in the resistance to theological terms."[127] This was a strong indictment on the ability
of Baptists to do theology together. The committee continued to discuss the
report and in September 1995 presented a response to the responses, which
went to all those who had written to comment on the report. This included
a letter from Fiddes, accompanied by a list of "misunderstandings" of and
"disagreements" with the report, a short paper by Kidd[128] on the importance
of covenant[129] and another short paper by Wright on the spiritual leadership
of the general secretaries. The report returned to council for discussion in
November 1995, where it was accepted, but, according to the Doctrine and
Worship Committee minutes, was met with "total silence."[130] The result was
that most of the content of the report was sidelined and nothing was done

125. *Nature of the Assembly*, 27.

126. Minutes of the Doctrine and Worship Committee, January 9, 1995, 3.

127. Minutes of the Doctrine and Worship Committee, January 9, 1995, 3.

128. Kidd was appointed to the committee in 1995. He course is another key member of the theological renewal stream.

129. This was later published as Kidd, "Why 'Covenant' Remains a Crucial Word for
Baptists," in *Theology Themes* (*Theology Themes* was a journal published by Northern
Baptist College between 1992–1997).

130. Minutes of the Doctrine and Worship Committee, January 3, 1996, 1.

with it.[131] This was due in part to its poor reception and also because the agenda had by then moved on, that is, the moment had passed.

The misunderstandings listed saw some responding to the report as an attempt to centralize power and turn the union into a church and as such subordinate the local church to the union. There was a problem or misunderstanding with the description of the union as "being church" and the word "ecclesia"[132] and so the committee decided to try the language of the union having a "churchly" kind of character.[133] The disagreements listed included a view that church cooperation beyond the local congregation was essentially pragmatic but not theological; a rejection of covenant as a relationship between persons; a claim that covenant relationships require a doctrinal basis; that the assembly and council are not like a church meeting, because decisions are only binding when made by a local congregation; and that the assembly should remain inspirational, rather than deliberative. Fiddes saw the disagreements as the place in which further discussion could take place.

Kidd's paper sought to be a longer reply to the disagreements over whether covenant is used in the Bible with reference to relationships between persons and to whether covenant requires an accompanying confession of faith. With regard to use of covenant in the Bible, Kidd acknowledges that there is a predominance of use to speak of a "vertical" relationship, but he says the purpose of covenants made by God is "the formation of a *people*," that is, there is a corporate nature to the covenant, which is not only vertical but also horizontal.[134] He also argues that the new covenant through Christ is most clearly seen at the communion meal, which again has vertical and horizontal dimensions that are "*both* sharply in focus."[135] At the Lord's

131. In 2000 Sean Winter (who had been appointed chair of the Doctrine and Worship Committee) prepared a briefing paper for the committee where he says, "It seems to me that the following issues, arising out of [*The Nature of Assembly*] . . . are still with us, and warrant further consideration." Dated June 22, 2000. Winter from 2000–2008 was Tutor in New Testament at Northern Baptist College, Manchester.

132. The committee had seen that "technical terms, like ecclesial . . . were clearly not acceptable in the constituency," Minutes of Doctrine and Worship Committee, May 15, 1995, 3.

133. Minutes of Doctrine and Worship Committee, July 1995, 3 [*sic*, May 15, 1995]. The phrase "churchly character" was first used by the report *Visible Unity in Life and Mission*, in the same context: "nor should such wider 'conciliar' forms and organs be denied this 'churchly' character," 8. It is not clear whether the committee is borrowing from this earlier report, but it is very likely.

134. Kidd, "Why 'Covenant' Remains a Crucial Word," 13 (page numbers are from the published version in *Theology Themes*).

135. Kidd, "Why 'Covenant' Remains a Crucial Word," 13.

Supper, we remember the covenant God has made with us (vertical) and at the same time, as those who share bread and wine, we understand the congregation as the body of Christ (horizontal). These biblical insights were grasped, says Kidd, by the early Baptists and as a result "are fundamental to our roots as Baptists" and "remain uniquely significant for Baptists."[136] This covenant understanding of the local church is also present in the Baptist practice of association, that is, historically, a "similar covenant language occurs at the level of Association."[137] Its use in the report with the reference to the union, Kidd accepts is new, but he says that this is "one of the bold, and creative suggestions in the [report]."[138] In terms of a confession of faith, he says that "it would be a retrograde step"[139] to try and write one in which to covenant around, instead he favors giving more attention to the Declaration of Principle, as the report suggests. This short paper by Kidd is very much developed in the next attempt to present the centrality of covenant.

Something to Declare: A Study of the Declaration of Principle

In the lead up to the denominational conference in 1996, the four principals of the English Baptist colleges—Fiddes, Kidd, Haymes, and Quicke[140]—published *Something to Declare*. A foreword was written by Coffey commending the booklet as a "major contribution" and a "significant offering."[141] An exposition of the Declaration of Principle had been suggested in *The Nature of Assembly* and the process of writing that report gave the impetus to give a "detailed examination"[142] of the union's basis of unity. Viewing it as a covenant document also provided a fresh opportunity to argue once again for covenant.

    Something to Declare begins by accepting that the term "covenant" had been a "clear focus of disagreement." It goes on to acknowledge that the "objections were voiced with energy and commitment" and therefore *Something*

---

136. Kidd, "Why 'Covenant' Remains a Crucial Word," 14.

137. Kidd, "Why 'Covenant' Remains a Crucial Word," 14.

138. Kidd, "Why 'Covenant' Remains a Crucial Word," 14.

139. Kidd, "Why 'Covenant' Remains a Crucial Word," 15.

140. The four principals had been meeting regularly together since 1994. Quicke was appointed principal of Spurgeon's College in 1993 and Kidd to Northern in 1994, as Haymes moved to Bristol that year, Fiddes had been principal at Regent's since 1989. The regular meetings emerged from a shared friendship and what they described as "a strong commitment to the Baptist Union." Quicke had trained at Regent's at the same time as Fiddes.

141. Coffey, foreword to Kidd, *Something to Declare*, 6.

142. Editor's introduction to Kidd, *Something to Declare*, 8.

to Declare is a new attempt to argue for the place of covenant to those that had been unconvinced.[143] The first section "Baptists and Covenant" is a reprint of Kidd's earlier paper, although now reaching a wider audience.[144]

The second section of the booklet is a history of the development of the Declaration of Principle, through its various versions. The principals argue that while not a full Confession of Faith, the Declaration is theological and biblical. Theological because of its trinitarian and christological emphases and biblical in its echoing of the Great Commission found in Matthew 28:18–20 with clauses on authority, baptism, and mission. This says that the "basis of the union" is not pragmatic, but theological. It is the Baptist Union, not the Baptist Society, and, the authors says, "implicit in this was the significance of being together in Christ in the purposes of the triune God which amounted to more than just creating an organisation."[145] The principals are strongly making the case for the union as an ecclesial and not just a pragmatic body. They go on to claim:

> The Declaration clearly proclaims the basis of our congregational and denominational life as being in the triune God, our Creator, our Saviour, and Source of transforming grace . . . The Declaration . . . strengthens [the theology of the union] by asserting one clear centre, Jesus Christ.

This is an implicit reply to those like Hayden and George Beasley-Murray[146] who had argued Baptists needed a new confession of faith. It is the principals' view, as it was the Doctrine and Worship Committee's view in *The Nature of Assembly*, that the Declaration of Principle is theologically adequate, when properly read and understood and that therefore in it is "something important for our present and future life."[147]

Something to Declare was promoted at the 1996 Baptist Assembly and every delegate to the denominational consultation was given a copy.

143. Kidd, *Something to Declare*, 12.

144. This might suggest that Kidd's paper had been discussed by the principals prior to its presentation to the Doctrine and Worship Committee in July 1995 and they may have had an input into its argument.

145. Kidd, *Something to Declare*, 24.

146. Roger Hayden had said that "the formulation of a contemporary Confession of Faith would be a difficult, but not unworthy, task for Baptist Christians," Hayden, "Baptists, Covenants and Confessions," 35. In the minutes of the Doctrine and Worship Committee, May 15, 1995, 2, there is a reference to Hayden especially arguing strongly that "covenant required a confession of faith or it was useless." George Beasley-Murray had argued for "Baptists in Britain to produce a Confession of Faith for today," "Confessing Baptist Identity," 84.

147. Kidd, *Something to Declare*, 25.

It probably has been the most widely read of all the publications from the theological renewal stream. It was reviewed in the *Baptist Times* by Nigel Wright and Ted Hale. Wright is largely appreciative of the booklet and is in agreement with them on the point that covenant can refer to our relationship with God and with each other in the church. This is perhaps to be expected as someone who was a member of the Doctrine and Worship Committee that had produced *The Nature of Assembly*. He does end his review with the conclusion that he thinks that the Declaration of Principle does need rewriting because he finds some of exegesis done by the principals to go beyond the original meaning of the words, which, he says, "has the effect of highlighting the deficiencies of the original text."[148]

Ted Hale's review is much more critical.[149] He begins by describing *Something to Declare* as giving support to what he calls the "Didcot Position,"[150] which he implies is being pushed onto churches. He does not think the principals provide any New Testament basis for their presentation of covenant, rejecting their references to the Lord's Supper and Acts 10 as having "nothing whatever to do with covenant."[151] He argues that covenant as they understand it "does not exist."[152] He observes that covenant has never been used in the various versions of official Baptist declarations of principle. It is Hale's view that the theology of covenant proposed replaces the centrality of the witness of the New Testament: "It is supremely through our study of the New Testament that we seek to know the mind of Christ."[153] Hale's review reveals that his position is against any notion of the union usurping what he calls (borrowing from Henry Cook's *What Baptists Stand For*) the "congregational principle"[154] and interprets *Something to Declare* (and the whole discussion happening within the union) as an attempt to give the union and its officers power over the local church. Hale continued

---

148. *BT*, August 29, 1996, 6.

149. Ted Hale had trained for ministry at Northern and had been minister at Higham Way, Burbage, and from 1982 minister at the Abbey Centre, Northampton. He had received a PhD from the University of Nottingham in 1994.

150. Didcot being a reference to the location of Baptist House, where the union's officers and staff were based from 1989 onward.

151. *BT*, August 29, 1996, 7.

152. *BT*, August 29, 1996, 7.

153. *BT*, August 29, 1996, 7.

154. *BT*, August 29, 1996, 7, 12, citing Cook, *What Baptists Stand For*, 77. Cook was general superintendent for Metropolitan Area, 1939–1954 and president of the union in 1955. For many years *What Baptists Stand For* was "regarded as the definitive statement of Baptist beliefs," Cross, *"To Communicate Simply,"* 398n127.

in numerous letters to the *Baptist Times* and to Coffey to reassert his views in opposition to the denominational consultation and its process.[155]

On the Way of Trust

A year later, the principals produced a second booklet, *On the Way of Trust*, a sequel to *Something to Declare*, which itself could arguably be seen as a sequel to *The Nature of Assembly*. Both *Something to Declare* and *On the Way of Trust* are much more clearly written and argued than *The Nature of Assembly*. The latter was reaching for clarity, which, I suggest, it never quite found, and so perhaps goes some way to explain its reception. The context of *On the Way of Trust* was the situation after the denominational consultation and the council meeting in November 1996 which had "generated a plethora of interconnected consultations, task groups and reviews"[156] that were overwhelming. There was a danger of division and a "competitive and potentially destructive spirit."[157] Instead what was heard at that November council meeting was the need for a "theology of trust,"[158] to which the principals sought to respond. Baptists, they argue, are those who choose "mutual trust" over institution or hierarchy. A theology of trust is a theology of covenant. Covenant is a holding together of grace and trust.

The argument is thus made again scripturally and then historically for the importance of covenant to how Baptists understood their being church. On this occasion the example is from the Gainsborough covenant of 1606. From this church the first Baptist church in England led by Thomas Helwys would emerge. Here the word covenant was used: ". . . joined themselves by a covenant of the Lord into a church determined in the fellowship of the Gospel." This is clear evidence that the covenant made had both vertical and horizontal dimensions. The principals claim that this practice of covenant making would be typical in Baptist life until the nineteenth century when they "fall into disuse."[159] For the principals, the Baptist way of being church was all understood from the starting place of the covenant made between God and each other.

---

155. *BT*, December 31, 1998; February 11, 1999; April 8, 1999, and letter to David Coffey and Keith Jones, June 3, 1996, which included an address given to Broad Alliance for Radical Baptists Meeting at the Baptist Assembly, 1996. He had already exchanged letters with Paul Fiddes in the *Baptist Times*, see *BT*, December 14, 1995; January 4, 1996; and January 25, 1996.

156. Kidd, *On the Way of Trust*, 8.

157. Kidd, *On the Way of Trust*, 8.

158. Kidd, *On the Way of Trust*, 8.

159. Kidd, *On the Way of Trust*, 18.

The principals seek a fresh attempt to define the union theologically. The union is not a Church, but they say, it does contain the "marks of the church."[160] This begs for further definition, but is left as a statement. The reason for not calling the union a church reflects that for some Baptists, like Hale, who held strongly to the congregational principle, only the local church is the visible church. Other Baptists, and implicitly I interpret this to be the position of the principals, refrain from the calling the union a church for ecumenical reasons: "It also keeps open the possibility of discovering through pilgrimage with other Christian people what a true Church in visible unity might be like."[161] While avoiding the word "Church," the word "covenant" they believe is the "essential one" in speaking about intermediate structures, i.e., associations and union.[162] The principals admit that the word "covenant" itself has rarely been used, but the language of "walking together and watching over one another" is they believe deeply covenantal.[163] It was a mark of the fact that Baptist churches believed that the purposes of Christ could be received not only in a local church meeting, but also in the meeting of churches together. Local congregations trusted that Christ was present in assembly and not just in the local church meeting, which of course required them to take seriously the wisdom that might be offered from the churches together, always with the acceptance that this could never be imposed.

At the denominational consultation there was some suggestion that the union should become an alliance. The principals emphasize the retention of the word "union." Alliance has a pragmatic understanding, whereas union has a more ontological meaning and picks up the Reformed language of "union in Christ." Union in Christ also speaks of the union between Father and Son in the Godhead. For the principals covenant and union belong together. In their rejection of the word alliance, they are careful not to say that there is not a place for bodies like the Evangelical Alliance, not named, but definitely being referenced here. Their point is that alliance and union are not equivalent, and the latter is to be preferred if holding to a covenantal understanding of what it is to be Baptist churches, associations, and colleges together: "Alliances are good, but no substitute for covenant."[164]

---

160. Kidd, *On the Way of Trust*, 21. The marks of the church being "one, holy, catholic, and apostolic" as defined in the Nicene Creed.

161. Kidd, *On the Way of Trust*, 21.

162. Kidd, *On the Way of Trust*, 21.

163. Kidd, *On the Way of Trust*, 21.

164. Kidd, *On the Way of Trust*, 26.

They continue by contrasting "covenant union" and "strategic alliances."[165] They take three forms of strategic alliance in the business world: networking, sharing resources, and joint ventures. In each case, while there might be something important in networking, sharing resources, and joint ventures, there is also, they argue, something different and more valuable in a covenant union. A covenant union will value the weakest member, it will value the quality of life together more than the resources provided, and it will value diversity and risk, for "covenant is about walking together in pilgrimage."[166]

In these three documents we see a developing theology of covenant that is an appropriately faithful way of understanding shared Baptist life in the local church, in association, and in the union. A case is made biblically, theologically, and historically. Its reception though was contested and despite *Covenant 21*, which we will come to below, a theology of a union as covenant failed to embed itself in the language and practice of the union. The final report of the Denominational Consultation Reference Group treats covenant as one topic among others[167] and it is not mentioned in the concluding reflections. What emerged in 1998 was the report of the Task Group on Core Values, which was adopted by council and published as *Five Core Values for a Gospel People*. In their concluding reflections the DCRG wrote:

> As a group we echo the welcome in many churches for the *Five Core Values for a Gospel People*. We believe that in the midst of what could look like mainly structural changes, it has been important to [sic] have a statement of the values which we hope will be foundational to our life together as a Union of churches, Associations and Colleges . . . It is our hope that they will act as a reference point to guide future developments, constantly challenging us to seek first God's kingdom and so to become a more authentic gospel people.[168]

Covenant 21

Covenant 21 had its roots in a proposal made by Roger Hayden to the council meeting in November 1995 for a Millennium Covenant, which would have four emphases: thanksgiving, prayer, mission, and financial giving. Hayden set it in the context of a similar challenge at the end of the nineteenth century

165. Kidd, *On the Way of Trust*, 23.
166. Kidd, *On the Way of Trust*, 26.
167. *Continuing the Journey*, 4, 6.
168. Kidd, *On the Way of Trust*, 7.

to create the Twentieth Century Fund, which had made so much possible at the beginning of the last century.[169] A Millennium Covenant Task Group was set up to develop the idea.[170] Hayden described the Covenant as "a programme which centres upon the approaching third millennium, and will provide a launch pad for the demands of a new century."[171] He hoped that an "educational programme of informing, encouraging and challenging the Christian Baptist family to increase and sustain its giving to rainbow mission and ministry will bring us sustainable new opportunities in the early years of the new Millennium." This was set in the context of mission:

> The Millennium Mission Covenant gives opportunity for a response to the challenges of contemporary mission with a covenant to Pray—for the world; Care—for the world; Serve—in the world; Encourage—the church in mission; and Give—to release trained mission ministers into the churches for mission development.[172]

It was met with enthusiasm at that meeting, but was put on hold at the March council meeting in 1996 due at that point to there not being enough support.[173] This was a new concept of covenant, less about relationships than about finance.

Following the denominational consultation in September 1996, the idea of a covenant was made part of the terms of reference of the Task Group on Associating (agreed in November 1997), although the financial aspect had now been set aside.[174] The task group, in their report *Relating and Resourcing* (*RR*), state that it's their view that "an annual renewal of commitment is impracticable," but go on to argue that "there is value in a renewal of commitment focused on the millennium." *RR* proposed "the preparation of a covenant for the first decade of the new millennium around which the churches, associations and colleges of our Union might constructively gather." The report explains that "the millennium offers a focal point

169. *BT*, November 16, 1995, 2. For an account of the Twentieth Century Fund see Shepherd, *Making of a Modern Denomination*, 25–28.

170. Aide Memoire, Millennium Covenant Task Group, Wednesday, November 8, 1995.

171. Hayden, "Millennium Covenant: Questions and Answers," January 1996 (unpublished in DCRG papers).

172. Keith Jones, "Millennium Mission Covenant," February 1996 (unpublished, in DCRG papers).

173. Minutes, BU Council, March 1996. See also *BT*, March 28, 1996, 3.

174. The task group were asked to "determine a method of annual review of commitment between churches, Associations and colleges and the officers and staff of the Union," appendix 1 of *Relating and Resourcing*, 17.

at which the various elements of the Denominational Conference might be drawn together." From this a Covenant Task Group was set up, convened by Hayden,[175] and reporting in November 1999. It was too late for a millennium covenant and so the date had shifted to 2001. The report with some changes was published at the end of 2000 as *Covenant 21: Covenant for a Gospel People.*[176]

The introduction speaks of "fellowship-sharing" and that a covenant service is "an opportunity to express this fellowship and actually to *make it deeper.*"[177] The language of fellowship was first used in connection with covenant in *The Nature of Assembly.* The next second section describes covenant in Scripture, Baptist thought, and Baptist practice. Once again the case is made for covenant being at the heart of Baptist life. For the first time it is stated that the making of covenant between church members was "a development of the biblical concept of covenant."[178] Yet, it is claimed it was not unbiblical, in that it was "in accord with the Old Testament demand that people should imitate the nature of God in showing *hesed,* covenant faithfulness, to each other."[179] It is also acknowledged that while there is no explicit case of associations making covenants, there is evidence of covenant language, for example, in the language of "walking together." The section concludes that although this is "a new step for churches in the Baptist Union, to enter together into a covenant-renewal service, it is a step which has a firm foundation in Baptist thought about covenant through the years."[180]

Coffey in writing about *Covenant 21* at its publication, sets it in the context of the "journey of reform and renewal" taking place and sees covenant as ensuring that this journey is one that "gives priority to the spiritual relationship over the institutional organisation."[181] *Covenant 21* for Coffey draws the threads from the last ten years of reports and consultations into a new beginning. He writes, "I trust that through *Covenant 21,* we will personally sense in our time the new thing that God is doing in our Union of churches, associations and colleges."[182] At the assembly, in his address Cof-

175. Other members of the group included Kingsley Appiagyei, Christopher Ellis, Paul Fiddes, Ruth Gouldbourne, Glen Marshall, and Peter Shepherd, with David Coffey in attendance at some meetings.

176. This title saw it alongside *5 Core Values for a Gospel People.* In 2002 the union would publish *Evangelism for a Gospel People.*

177. *Covenant 21,* 2.

178. *Covenant 21,* 5.

179. *Covenant 21,* 5.

180. *Covenant 21,* 6.

181. Coffey, "Covenant 21."

182. Coffey, "Covenant 21."

fey spoke of covenant as being about continuity, assurance, and renewal.[183]
Coffey co-opted the concept of covenant to his concern to give the union a
new start. It is a pragmatic use which reflects his view of the union as agency
rather than ecclesial.

During the assembly of 2001, the Doctrine and Worship Committee
and the Baptist Historical Society hosted a joint seminar in relation to *Covenant 21* which Nigel Wright addressed.[184] This is the only place Wright
has said anything substantial on covenant, it being an absent or very muted
theme in his other work.[185] His paper sets *Covenant 21* in the context of the
denominational changes and follows the section in the material of covenant
in Scripture, and Baptist history and practice, albeit with a Wrightian gloss.
With regard to *Covenant 21* he says that "despite a little criticism, it has
been widely well received when people have seen it as a resource to be used
creatively and appropriately."[186]

Wright says that covenant does not mean control and it does not mean
contract. Against those who saw covenant and the changes in the union as a
move to create the Baptist "church," Wright speaks the language of freedom:
"covenant is about relationship freely entered into and freely maintained."[187]
Covenant is also to be differentiated from contract, for belonging to the Baptist Union is theological. It is theological, because it begins with God, who is
communion, and we the church are called to "reflect and mirror" God's own
life.[188] To share in the covenant service is therefore, according to Wright, to
recognize "a wider communion in association with other churches"[189] and
thus reflect to the world the "relatedness" within the triune God. Covenant
is also biblical. It is one of the lenses through which we should read the Old
Testament and also the New Testament.[190] Wright does not attempt here
to argue for a horizontal aspect to covenant and treats it purely in terms
of its vertical aspect. Historically he says covenant is foundational to Baptist churches, and the covenant proposed in terms of a commitment to the

183. *BT*, May 31, 2001, 5.

184. See Minutes of Doctrine and Worship Committee, June 2000, 2.

185. It is referred to briefly in Wright, *Free Church*, 58, 197.

186. Wright, "Covenant and Covenanting," 287.

187. Wright, "Covenant and Covenanting," 288. I have argued elsewhere that freedom is central to Wright's ecclesial understanding. See Goodliff, "Nigel Wright's Radical Baptist Theology," 71–72.

188. Wright, "Covenant and Covenanting," 288. The theology here follows fairly
closely that of Wright's doctoral supervisor Colin Gunton. See Gunton, *Promise of
Trinitarian Theology*, especially ch. 4, which Wright quotes in Wright, *Free Church*, 5.

189. Wright, "Covenant and Covenanting," 289.

190. Wright, "Covenant and Covenanting," 289.

union, is expressing something assumed. The BU has always had a "spirit of covenant" about it, even if we have not spoken in those terms.[191] This spirit of covenant, argues Wright, is to understand that our freedom in Christ also makes us captive to Christ, to enter freely into covenant with one another is to recognize we are bound to one another as we are bound to Christ. Wright's final point is to look at covenant with mission: if the covenant we make is with God, who is triune, then mission follows, because God is one who "overflows, reaches out, sends."[192]

Bound for Glory? God, Church, and World in Covenant

In 2002 a new group of Baptist ministers,[193] following in the footsteps of Fiddes and others, published a collection of essays on covenant picking up some of the threads of the earlier *Bound to Love*. This book and another the group wrote,[194] demonstrate that the theological renewal stream was widening. The essays in *Bound for Glory? God, Church and World in Covenant* were also presented at the 2001 consultation called Baptists Doing Theology in Context, which Fiddes and the other principals had initiated in an earlier consultation in 1999.[195] *Bound for Glory?* marks a new stage in the discussion of covenant. Fiddes wrote an introduction. The essays here assume that covenant has become a broadly accepted notion among Baptists, there is no hint that it is contested.[196] They write in the light of the warm glow of *Covenant 21* and as such are unaware of or content to overlook the contested status the concept of covenant had during the 1990s. The majority of the essays in this collection are not driven by the ecclesial status of the union, but a broader theology of covenant rooted in the triune God[197] and with the whole of creation in view.[198] Other essays explore that a theology of covenant can be used in narrow and restricted ways.[199] *Bound to Glory?* shows that the concept of covenant was one that was still seen as a "rich

191. Wright, "Covenant and Covenanting," 290.

192. Wright, "Covenant and Covenanting," 290.

193. The group were Anthony Clarke, Robert Ellis, Stephen Finamore, Marcus Bull, Graham Sparkes, Tim Carter, and Viv Lassetter.

194. Clarke, *Expecting Justice, But Seeing Bloodshed.*

195. For the story see the preface to Fiddes, *Doing Theology in a Baptist Way,* v–vi.

196. See Clarke, *Bound to Glory,* 9, 20, 59, and 74. Finamore speaks of covenant "becoming increasingly accepted," 84n5.

197. See the chapter by Bull.

198. See the chapter by Ellis.

199. See the chapters by Carter and Sparkes.

seam of investigation"[200] for Baptist theological reflection, at least for those who gave attention to doing theology.

Questioning Covenant

The British Methodist theologian David Carter in his review of *Tracks and Traces* acknowledges Fiddes's attempt to challenge "excessively voluntaristic or isolationist aspects"[201] of Baptist ecclesiology, but ends his review by asking whether Fiddes's covenant theology has any basis among Baptists "*in practice.*"[202] Carter suspects there to be a gap between what might be espoused theologically and the ordinary theology[203] of local churches, between formal and operant theology. A second related question is whether Fiddes's covenant theology, while evident among seventeenth-century Baptists and Separatists, has a firm enough biblical basis.[204]

In his response Fiddes takes the biblical question first, accepting that he has largely assumed it to be "valid exegesis."[205] He begins with the importance of Matt 18:20 and also 2 Cor 6:16–18, which for John Smyth (and others) are understood to be "an echo of covenantal language"[206]—"I will be your God and you will be my people" (Ezek 34:30–21; 36:24–28; Jer 31:33–34). Fiddes also find support in the Pauline epistles where "church" is used both as a reference to the local church and the wider church. Furthermore, he points to how early Baptists looked to the covenants God made with families (so Abraham and David) as well those with Israel as a nation. Fiddes believes that Scripture does not work with one concept of covenant, but it is applied in different ways to different sized groups, including the whole of creation.[207]

Fiddes answers the "practice" question by saying that Baptist ecclesiology has an inherent "danger" to become "merely voluntary," especially in a culture of voluntary societies and the pressure of charity law.[208] He also faces up to the situation that some (perhaps more accurate would be, *many*)

200. The phrase is one used by Fiddes in his introduction, Clarke, *Bound to Glory*, 6.

201. Carter, "Baptist Ecclesiology," 89.

202. Carter, "Baptist Ecclesiology," 92.

203. For a definition of ordinary theology see Astley and Francis, *Exploring Ordinary Theology*.

204. Carter, "Baptist Ecclesiology," 93.

205. Fiddes, "Response to David Carter," 93.

206. Fiddes, "Response to David Carter," 94.

207. For further reflections (written early in his career) see Fiddes, "Covenant—Old and New."

208. Fiddes, "Response to David Carter," 96.

churches have "lost their memory of the Baptist story" and newer churches are joining the Baptist Union with little or no deep understanding of the Baptist tradition.[209] Fiddes goes on to say that there are signs of a recovery of a "covenant theology," seen in the likes of *Covenant 21* and in the renaming of the list of accredited Baptist Union ministers as the "Register of Covenanted Persons Accredited to Ministry."[210] This provides Fiddes with some belief that covenant has more currency and understanding among British Baptists again. Even where it is "a spirit of pragmatism"[211] that drives it, a reference probably to Coffey's co-option, Fiddes (and others) have sought to provide a theology that undergirds these initiatives toward greater catholicity. Darrell Jackson is less convinced that a theology of covenant has been widely adopted or accepted by local Baptist congregations.[212] His research demonstrates that despite the wide-ranging theological work done by the likes of Fiddes, the majority of Baptist Christians do not understand church membership or belonging to the union in covenant terms.[213]

Conclusion

In their report to council in November 1997 the DCRG suggested a guideline interim statement that said,

> We seem to be moving towards a Union of Baptist communities
> of faith bound together in covenant for mission to the world,
> based on mutual trust and commitment.[214]

This suggests that both mission and covenant were seen as equally important concepts. The emphasis on covenant and the language of trust emerging from the principals' *On the Way of Trust*. However, by 1999 covenant is more marginalized, despite the fact that *Covenant 21* was planned. *Covenant 21* had some connections in the direction of stream 2's theology of covenant, partly through the presence of Fiddes on the task group. Yet the council had never embraced the ecclesial (covenantal) nature of the union.

209. Fiddes, "Response to David Carter," 96.

210. This has taken place in 2001. In addition, not noted by Fiddes, are a eucharistic liturgy shaped around "Covenant making" and a whole section of patterns for "Covenanting Together" in Ellis and Blyth, *Gathering For Worship*.

211. Fiddes, "Response to David Carter," 97.

212. Jackson, *Discourse of "Belonging,"* 77, 92.

213. Jackson, *Discourse of "Belonging,"* 172.

214. The Denominational Consultation Reference Group Report to Baptist Union Council—November 1997 in Minutes, Baptist Union Council, November 1997, 33.

This remained unresolved with a strong contingent seeing the union moving in a functional resource direction. The concept of mission continued to dominate but as demonstrated theologically it lacked a thick definition until the middle of the next decade.

What became clear was the union through the council tended to keep theology at arm's length. It was not able to come to quick agreement and therefore did not pursue theological conversations. The goal to develop a distinctive Baptist identity was not reached in any coherent and shared way. The concept of covenant was developed as a means of articulating the sense of interdependent ties in the union, instead the union sought to organize around mission, I suggest, with little consensus about what that meant.

One document that has not been discussed in this chapter is *Five Core Values* that was referred to in the previous chapter in the section on Anabaptism. I refer to *Five Core Values* here because it was a document that had the possibility of bringing both mission and covenant together. The five core values were included as part of the liturgy in *Covenant 21* and so there was some indication that the covenant the union, associations, and churches were encouraged to make included a committed to the "kingdom vision" that the values presented.

The impact of *Five Core Values* was unexpected. No one had imagined it would become such an important report. It was "enthusiastically received by the Council" and considered "sufficiently significant" to be followed by a set of Bible study materials to think through the reports implications.[215] Paul Goodliff would in 2012 describe it as an "attempt to put theological and ethical flesh upon the bones of the 1995–2000 reforms."[216] One of the core values is to be "a missionary community." It could be argued that the description of a missionary community should be renamed "evangelistic community" and that the five values together—prophetic, inclusive, sacrificial, evangelistic, and worshiping—reflect what it is to be a missionary people in a holistic sense. The added strength of the report was that it did not see these core values as having only significance in the local church but also in the denomination and in the society and the world. This was a report that had significance for churches, colleges, associations, and the union. In this way it was something that had covenantal dimensions, although the report did not make this link.[217] In *Gathering for Worship*, two patterns—one for making

---

215. *5 Core Values for a Gospel People Bible Study Pack.*

216. Goodliff, "Networks," a paper for the Baptist Futures Process (2012). It was made available to the council, but never published.

217. Michael Parsons gestures in this direction in "Church as (Covenant) Community—Then and Now," 215.

and renewing covenant and one for a covenant pattern of induction for a minister—name the core values in the context of covenant in the liturgy.[218]

In the work of Fiddes and Holmes on the theology of mission they begin to explore what might be described as the character of mission, the virtues of mission over against the pragmatics of mission. If mission is a participation in the missionary God, it will reflect the mission God makes in Jesus and the Holy Spirit. Holmes argues that the church is sent "in a cruci-form, purposeful and self-sacrificial way" as this reflects who God is.[219] *Five Core Values* made a similar argument, although not in the language of par-ticipation, but in the language of following Jesus. *Five Core Values* described not what the church should do, but who the church should be: "these values are an embodiment of the gospel in communal form."[220] A missionary union then would not mean necessarily one solely involved in church planting and evangelistic and social action projects, but one that enabled the growing of churches in missionary virtues, that is, a union that was focused on growing missionary communities of character, in the terms of *Five Core Values*, com-munities that were prophetic, inclusive, sacrificial, missionary, and worship-ing. *Five Core Values* then had the potential to bring the developing mission theology and covenant theology together. The weakness of *Five Core Values* was it did not root the values in the Baptist tradition as well as the gospel tradition. It made no attempt to say that Baptists have been a people who in the past embodied the five defined core values. This would have seen it not merely as a report reflecting a broad (radical) evangelicalism,[221] but the kind of "marks of a believers' church in the radical evangelical dissenting tradition."[222] Wright has suggested that the core values need two extra values of faithfulness and freedom toward this end.[223] Fiddes and Haymes make no mention of the core values in *Tracks and Traces* or *On Being the Church* or any other subsequent work. Here again it could be said was an opportunity missed. In fact, there has been little to no ongoing mention or engagement

218. Ellis and Blyth, *Gathering for Worship*, 96–99 and 140–43.

219. Holmes, "Trinitarian Missiology," 89.

220. Ellis, "Spirituality in Mission," 180.

221. I use the word "broad" because the call to be inclusive communities was one that troubled the moderate conservatives in the union, most notably Nigel Wright. See Wright, "Inclusively Exclusive," 27, and Wright, "Spirituality as Discipleship," 97. Wright had made this point back in October 1997 in a letter to Tony Peck. DCRG Papers. The task group that wrote the report had been chaired by Bernard Green who was a broad evangelical.

222. *A Ten Year Plan Towards 2000*, 6.

223. Wright, "Inclusively Exclusive," 27, and Wright, "Spirituality as Discipleship," 98–99.

with 5 *Core Values* in any Baptist work post-2000. However, I contend that in this document is the means of holding mission and covenant together in a meaningful way. 5 *Core Values* could have been the clear, coherent, and widely accepted theology Champion had said was required.

Chapter 5

Renewal in Divergence

THE RENEWAL OF BAPTIST life was one that was taking place in the context of the ecumenical movement.[1] One group of Baptists that emerged in the late 1960s and named the Baptist Renewal Group argued that the future of Baptist life was a fully ecumenical one.[2] The BRF in particular had been much more suspicious.[3] When Mainstream emerged there was a basic commitment to ecumenism. This was seen as easier in terms of ecumenism among evangelicals and, as was seen in chapter 3, many involved in Mainstream were involved in the EA. Yet as the Inter-Church Process began in the mid-1980s several Mainstream members were an important part of the argument for saying yes to Baptist involvement in the new ecumenical future, even though this new future was also one which the Roman Catholic Church in Britain was committed to joining.

The Baptist relationship to ecumenism is a complex one. On the one hand several Baptists have played a central part in the ecumenical movement; the contributions made by Ernest Payne,[4] David Russell,[5] Morris

1. For an account of Baptist ecumenical engagement see Jones, "Twentieth Century Baptists." Paper presented to the Baptist Historical Society Summer School, July 2019. Through the twentieth century, Jones contends, that the cautious stance of the union was in tension with the willingness of Shakespeare, Aubrey, Payne, and Russell as general secretaries to active and prominent involvement.

2. An account of the Baptist Renewal Group remains to be written, for a brief mention see Randall, *English Baptists*, 336, 342. Significant people involved were Michael Taylor, Roger Nunn, Alec Gilmore, and Paul Rowntree Clifford. An early publication was Taylor, *Baptists for Unity*.

3. See Hill, *Baptist Revival Fellowship*, 40–44.

4. Payne was chair of the BBC Executive Committee, 1962–1971 and vice chair of the WCC Central Committee, 1954–1975.

5. Russell was a Member of the WCC Centre Committee, 1968–1983. He was also

West,[6] Keith Clements,[7] John Briggs,[8] Myra Blyth,[9] David Goodbourn,[10] and Paul Fiddes,[11] among others, have been significant and prominent. As Anthony R. Cross remarks, "The degree to which Baptists have been involved within the ecumenical movement at all levels has been frequently underestimated, often misrepresented or just simply unknown, but it is a fact that many leading British ecumenists have been and are Baptists."[12] It should be noted that no member of stream 1 has ever held an ecumenical position, outside of Coffey's period as one of the four presidents of CTE between 2003–2007.

On the other hand, while the union was a founding member of the WCC and the BCC, there has been dissension among the churches and individuals within the Baptist Union, especially between the 1960s and 1970s and from the mid-1980s to the mid-1990s (the latter being the years of the Inter-Church Process).[13] As this chapter will tell, in some ways the question of Baptist involvement within the ecumenical movement was settled by the two votes in 1989 and 1995.

---

particularly involved in various ecumenical committees and projects to do with human rights, see Williamson, "The Defence of Human Dignity."

6. West was a member of the WCC Faith & Order Commission from 1964 until 1983.

7. Clements was CCBI Coordinating Secretary for International Affairs, 1990–1997, and general secretary of the Conference of European Churches, 1997–2007.

8. Briggs was a member of the WCC Central Committee, 1983–1998, and the Executive Committee, 1991–1998.

9. Blyth was youth secretary for BCC, 1982–1988, and then held senior roles in the WCC, 1988–1999.

10. Goodbourn was general secretary of CTBI, 1999–2006. He was a lay Baptist who had worked in theological education at Northern Baptist College and for the Church of Scotland. See Simon Oxley, "Dr David Goodbourn 1948–2014," *Baptist Times*, https://www.baptist.org.uk/Articles/422472/Dr_David_Robin.aspx.

11. Fiddes has chaired conversations with both the Anglican Communion (2000–2005) and the Roman Catholic Church (2006–2010), and in the 1992 was chair of the conversations that began with the Church of England in 1992 and a member of the CTE working party on baptism and church membership, 1994–1997.

12. Cross, "Service to the Ecumenical Movement," 107.

13. See the relevant sections of Randall, *English Baptists*.

1985–1989: The Inter-Church Process and the Leicester Assembly

Ecumenism changed in the 1980s with the birth of the Inter-Church Process (ICP).[14] There was a feeling that change was needed in the BCC. There was interest from the Roman Catholics to be more ecumenically involved[15] and in addition there was the increasing number of black churches (many of which were Pentecostal).[16] This had its beginnings in 1984,[17] but the key year was 1986, when all participating Churches in the process took part in a Lent study course called *What on Earth Is the Church For?* This generated a huge response from Christians in local churches, collated as *Views from the Pews*,[18] alongside *Reflections*,[19] which were responses at a national level from the twenty-six partnering churches. *What on Earth Is the Church For?* asked questions about church, salvation, church practices, and mission. Of the responses received only 4.6 percent were Baptist (although some who responded "Christian" or "Ecumenical" might have also been members of a Baptist church). This relatively low percentage reflects that ecumenism, or at least Lent Study courses, were not high on the agenda of Baptists.

The Baptist response to *Reflections* recognizes three tensions.[20] A tension about mission—is mission equated with evangelism or is mission a social engagement with the world, in which evangelism is a part? A tension about unity—for some difficulty with unity with those considered non-evangelical and for many the uniqueness of Baptist congregational polity at odds with other church models. A tension about churchmanship—a tension among Baptists about identity and the varying streams within the union. These tensions might be named part of what Coffey would have called the "ferment" among Baptists.

14. The most in depth account remains Palmer, *Strangers No Longer.*

15. Although the leader of the English Catholic Church, Basil Hume, Archbishop of Westminster, was a late convert. See Howard, *Basil Hume,* 205–9.

16. In the background was of course also the WCC Faith and Order Commission report *Baptism, Eucharist and Ministry,* which was, as the Baptist Union response stated, "a notable milestone in the search for sufficient theological consensus," "Baptist Union Of Great Britain and Ireland," 70–77. Morris West had been part of drafting group of BEM, see Clements, "Larger Context."

17. See *Baptist Union Annual Report 1984,* 31.

18. *Views from the Pews.*

19. *Reflections.*

20. *Reflections,* 10–17.

The following year saw national ecumenical conferences in England,[21] Wales and Scotland and then a joint British and Irish conference in September.[22] Out of the final conference came the Swanwick Declaration.[23] The Declaration spoke of reaching a "common mind," that no longer were the churches strangers, but pilgrims together. The heart of the statement said:

> We now declare together our readiness to commit ourselves to each other under God. Our earnest desire is to become more fully, in his own time, the one Church of Christ, united in faith, communion, pastoral care and mission. Such unity is the gift of God . . . In the unity we seek we recognise that there will not be uniformity but legitimate diversity. It is our conviction that, as a matter of policy at all levels and in all places, our churches must now move from co-operation to clear commitment to each other, in search of the unity for which Christ prayed, and in common evangelism[24] and service of the world. We urge church leaders and representatives to take all necessary steps to present, as soon as possible, to our church authorities, assemblies and congregations, the Report of this Conference together with developed proposals for ecumenical instruments to help the churches of these islands to move ahead together.[25]

The report goes on to include the aims and principles of the new ecumenical instruments that would be created. The aims were: to be a visible sign of commitment; the promotion of theological reflection and continuing discussion about the nature, purpose, and unity of the church; to bring churches together in agreed areas, to enable the churches to arrive at a common mind and make decisions together; and to enable the churches to respond to needs and speak to secular authorities. A crucial moment for many at the conference was the address given by the Roman Catholic Cardinal Basil Hume that stressed the importance of mission and beginning at the local, both of which were essential to Baptists.

---

21. Baptist representatives at the England conference in Nottingham included: Gethin Abraham-Williams, Myra Blyth, Christopher Ellis, Bernard Green, Jane Hassell, Roger Hayden, Roger Nunn, Grenville Overton, Alan Pain, Morris West, and Anne Wilkinson.

22. Baptist representatives at the Britain and Ireland conference in Swanwick included: Paul Beasley-Murray, Christopher Ellis, Bernard Green, Roger Hayden, Douglas Sparkes, and Morris West.

23. To which all the Baptist representatives adopted and personally signed.

24. Watson Moyes records that it was Paul Beasley-Murray who "secured a clear wording on evangelism," Moyes, *Our Place among the Churches*, 75–76.

25. *Not Strangers But Pilgrims*, 3–4.

A subsequent report published in early 1989 set out in detail what potential member churches were being asked to join.[26] It was this on which the decision to become a member would be made. The confessional basis of the new Churches Together in England was to be:

> . . . those churches in England which, acknowledging God's revelation in Christ, confess the Lord Jesus Christ as God and Saviour according to the Scriptures; and, in obedience to God's will and in the power of the Holy Spirit commit themselves to seeking a deepening of their communion with Christ and with one another in the Church, which is his body, and to fulfil their mission to proclaim the Gospel by common witness and service in the world, to the glory of the one God, Father, Son and Holy Spirit.[27]

From January 1989 a debate within the pages of the *Baptist Times* began on whether the Baptist Union should join CTE and the CCBI at the assembly in April. As Derek Tidball remarked, "the involvement of the Catholics was crucial."[28] In March two Baptist ministers—Michael McGill and Michael Bochenski[29]—argued for saying no and for saying yes. McGill, who had trained at Bristol and been in ministry since 1983, was an ex-Catholic. He defined himself as "first and foremost an evangelical."[30] His problem with the proposals were twofold, what he called "ecumenicalism" and "the doctrines of the Roman Catholic Church." He believed that "the Evangelical Gospel is far removed from the Ecumenical Gospel" that he saw underlining Churches Together in Pilgrimage. While he was happy to cooperate with other churches, he was against the move to "clear commitment."[31] This commitment would lead, he argued, to truth being subservient to unity. His view of the "ecumenical gospel" was that it is socio-liberal and not evangelical and would lead to Baptists being asked to compromise.[32] The doctrines of the Roman Catholic Church, he argues, are a move away from New Testament Christianity and as an example he looks at the doctrine of transubstantiation, justification by faith and purgatory. He concludes, "there

26. *Churches Together in Pilgrimage.*

27. *Churches Together in Pilgrimage*, 27–28.

28. *BT*, February 23, 1989, 5.

29. Bochenski was editor of the *Mainstream Magazine* between 1994–1998. He was also a member of the General Superintendency Review Group that produced *Transforming Superintendency*. In 1999 he was president of the Baptist Union.

30. *BT*, March 9, 1989, 10.

31. *BT*, March 9, 1989, 10.

32. *BT*, March 9, 1989, 10–11.

is no way that I can agree to 'hold hands in the dark' with a Church which holds doctrines so divorced from Scripture."[33]

Bochenski's argument for saying yes was that he believed the basis was "thoroughly biblical" and that from his reading of the Bible he saw a "God so much bigger than I have yet realised."[34] Bochenski saw a clear call in Scripture to unity with diversity. Alongside Scripture, he argued that Baptist history was about freedom of conscience and tolerance. He also claimed that there was a review process in five years which meant Baptists could leave if our "worst fears" had been founded.[35] He was an Evangelical and identified with Mainstream. He acknowledged that the issue many had was Roman Catholic involvement, but argued that what Roman Catholicism, historically, had given the church be recognized and so, he says, "I cannot unchurch, de-Christianise or spurn a tradition that has produced a Francis of Assisi or a Francis Macnutt."[36] He finally argued that the proposals would not affect local church autonomy and "each Baptist church will remain free to makes its own local response to the ICP."[37]

Terry Griffith writing in the January 1989 edition of the *Mainstream Newsletter* was critical of the proposals because he claimed they "reflect an 'institutional' agenda" and were disempowering to the local church.[38] His other argument was again a lack of "sufficient theological basis."[39] For Griffith, "it is not denominations that divide us so much as different theologies."[40] He presented the EA as "the best ecumenical scheme at the re-gional/national level" and the "largest ecumenical gathering in this country is Spring Harvest."[41]

The vote which took place at the 1989 Baptist Assembly held in Leicester, saw 74 percent of delegates vote in favor of joining the new ecumenical instruments. John Briggs proposed the motion and it was supported by Douglas McBain. McBain accepted some of the criticism of the ICP, but argued that the positive of saying yes was it secured "the rights of the local

33. *BT*, March 16, 1989, 9. McGill would write a letter to every member of the Baptist Union Council ahead of the March 1989 meeting stating the same argument.

34. *BT*, March 9, 1989, 11.

35. *BT*, March 9, 1989, 11.

36. *BT*, March 16, 1989, 8.

37. *BT*, March 16, 1989, 8.

38. Griffith, "Instruments," 2. Griffith was a Baptist minister in London and editor of the Mainstream newsletter between 1986–1990. He competed a PhD on 1 John from King's College London in 1996.

39. Griffith, "Instruments," 2.

40. Griffith, "Instruments," 3.

41. Griffith, "Instruments," 3.

church," that is, "all major decisions would be referred to the local church," which was not the case with the BCC.[42] McBain had in January addressed the Mainstream conference arguing that Baptists "ought to be there."[43] His conversion to ecumenism had come from a friendship with a Roman Catholic Benedictine monk. Paul Goodliff argues that McBain's support for the resolution played a key role.[44] For those who voted "no" there was an option to register their dissent, while remaining part of the union.

Stream 2 were not that present publically in the ICP.[45] They were though supportive of the ecumenical movement. In *A Question of Identity* Haymes said he believed "that the quest for the Unity Christ wills is a primary sign of an obedient Church on the road to genuine renewal"[46] and in 2000 wrote that "I see no serious Christian future that does not take the ecumenical calling seriously."[47] Fiddes had been involved in the BCC study commission on the doctrine of the Trinity[48] and from 1985 Keith Clements joined the Plenary Commission of the WCC Commission on Faith and Order and in 1990 became coordinating secretary for International Affairs in the CCBI.[49]

1991–1995: F.A.B. and the Plymouth Assembly

The 1990s continued to be full of ecumenical activity. In 1992 informal conversations between the Baptist Union and the Church of England began, which would run into the next decade.[50] These discussions were engaged around the topics of baptism, episcope, and apostolicity. The BU responded to both Pope John Paul II's encyclical *Ut unum sint* (1995) and the CTE report *Called to Be One* (1996). An increasing number of Baptist churches were part of Local Ecumenical Projects and work was done with regard to *Baptism and Church Membership* (1997). Before 1992, outside of the

42. *BT*, April 27, 1989, 8.

43. *BT*, February 2, 1989, 3.

44. "The very direction of the Union has owed much to his leadership," *BT*, October 19, 2006, 14.

45. I'm not aware of anything they wrote with regards the interchurch process between 1985–1989. Haymes would write positively of the 1992 CCBI assembly in *BT*, March 5, 1992, 6.

46. Haymes, *Question of Identity*, 1.

47. Haymes, "Theology and Baptist Identity," 2.

48. *The Forgotten Trinity* 1. *The Report of the BCC Study Commission on Trinitarian Doctrine Today*.

49. Clements, *Look Back in Hope*, 133. Clements was also appointed in 1984 to the BCC Board of Ecumenical Affairs, Clements, *Look Back in Hope*, 148.

50. Eventually published as *Pushing at the Boundaries of Unity*.

departments of mission and ministry there had only been the ACCR, but this was felt not fit for the increasing needs of the union to engage both ecumenically and denominationally with issues of faith and unity and so the Faith and Unity Executive was born. The story though could have been different. Despite the 1989 vote, continuing serious disquiet within the union saw a need to ask the Baptist Assembly six years later to reaffirm their continuing participation.[51]

After 1989 a new group emerged called F.A.B.[52] This group of nearly all evangelicals included those who had resigned from the union because of the vote, those that intended to resign from the union if a vote to continue membership was lost, and those who would never resign from the union. F.A.B were a more conservative evangelical grouping than Mainstream, who were largely supportive of the ecumenical movement. The ACCR had been working on a paper called "An Evangelical Theology of Ecumenism" as part of the follow up to the 1989 vote. This reflected that there was a need to make a stronger case for ecumenism for evangelical reasons.[53] It was felt by the committee that instead of just publishing it, a more productive way forward would be to engage in conversation with those who had voted no. Coffey as the new general secretary from April 1991, organized a gathering of six of those who had voted no in 1989 with six of those who had yes. There was a meeting of the twelve in August 1991 and then again in December 1991 at Fairmile Court, Surrey. In an aide-memoire of the meeting it was noted that there had been "recognition that ecumenical Baptists, although hitherto usually from the liberal 'wing', had not yielded on Baptist principles."[54] The issues were around the meaning of "commitment" and the lack of difficult issues being on the agenda at ecumenical meetings.

From this meeting, the union published a booklet with papers from both views called *Evangelicals and Ecumenism? When Baptists Disagree.* This included the ACCR paper, which offered five principles based on Scripture for ecumenism: the unity of God, the purpose of Jesus, the gift of the Spirit, the authenticity of love and the challenge of society. It then presents ten theses that flow from the five principles which could be a "brief upon

51. This was only meant to be a review of how CTE and CCBI were working, but under pressure became a vote on continuing membership.

52. The name was short for "Fabulous." A young pastor had said that the opposition to the ICP was fabulous and the name stuck, Randall, *English Baptists*, 491–92. Another meaning was "Fellowship of Anxious Baptists."

53. "Such a statement should not merely respond to current pressures within the life of the Union but reflect on our positive involvement in ecumenical structures," Minutes of ACCR, September 17, 1990, 4.

54. Bowers, "Discussion Relating to ICP."

which all of us in the Baptist family might meet to pray, discuss, agree, and also, in love, disagree."

In the book Faith Bowers, Douglas McBain, and Michael Bochenski offered papers in favor of ecumenism and Robert Amess,[55] John Balchin,[56] and Andrew Green[57] offered more tentative and questioning papers. Here again stream 1 were active in arguing that being Baptist was not at odds with being ecumenically committed. What is evident in the papers on the yes side was an openness to ecumenism and at the same time, one which engaged *as* Baptists and in the clear case of McBain and Bochenski as evangelicals. The new ecumenical instruments were seen as an opportunity, but one in which denominational identity would not be given away. In the papers on the no side there was a clear fear that identity, truth, doctrine were being sidelined.

At the beginning of 1995, as the new vote to remain in CTE and the CCBI approached, another round of articles appeared in the *Baptist Times*. Coffey wrote articles for the *Baptist Times*, *Baptist Leader* and *SecCheck*. Here he set the forthcoming vote at the Plymouth Assembly in the context of a 1994 document from North America called *Evangelicals and Catholics Together*.[58] In this way he sought to challenge an anti-Catholic position as the evangelical position and argue for the union's continuing membership. The case Coffey makes is that it is better to be an insider in the ecumenical debate and be "committed, but critical."[59] Coffey points to the fact that Baptists have historically been a part of the ecumenical movement and this is because "we see ourselves as part of the One Holy Universal Apostolic Church."[60] He also sets the argument for staying in in the context of what he calls the "enormous challenges in our changing world" which need "moral and spiritual renewal" and is best done in coalition with other Christians. Picking up his presidential theme from 1986 about building bridges, he ends by saying it is now time to "cross some of those bridges."[61] It is not clear what Coffey believed were the goals of ecumenism, apart from greater cooperation in mission particularly within a post-Christendom context.

---

55. Amess was chairman of the Evangelical Alliance between 1999–2009. He was author of *One in the Truth? The Cancer of Division in the Evangelical Church*.

56. Balchin was minister of Purley Baptist Church, but had been a lecturer at London Bible College and had a PhD in New Testament from the University of London.

57. Both Balchin and Green had links with Mainstream.

58. See Neuhaus and Colson, *Evangelicals and Catholics Together*.

59. Coffey, "Committed, but Critical."

60. Coffey, "It's time to cross some bridges," 7. The word "universal" is substituted for "catholic."

61. Coffey, "It's time to cross some bridges," 11.

David Rushworth-Smith, secretary of FAB, responded to Coffey arguing that the union should only have observer status.[62] While he agreed unity
was a theme in Scripture, he says there is a difference between false and
true unity, the claim being that membership of CTE and the CCBI alongside the Roman Catholics was to engage in false unity. He was concerned
that the union's ongoing membership would continue to create disunity
among Baptists.

At the Plymouth Assembly in May 1995, the resulting vote saw the
assembly vote 90.21 percent in favor of remaining a member of the CTE
and 81.2 percent in favor of remaining a member of the CCBI. The resolution was one that confirmed the union's membership and at the same
time recognized those who dissented from the ICP and the duty of those
who represented the union to express a diversity of views. This was an
attempt to accommodate the "continuing concerns of the Fellowship of
Anxious Baptists."[63] An attempt from FAB to amend the resolution to see
church's having to opt in rather than opt out of the inter-church process was
soundly defeated.

After the vote Alec Gilmore wrote a critical reflection on the current
status of ecumenism.[64] He says the Plymouth vote was good news, as it challenged a view that Baptists were "isolationists." The growth from 74 percent
in 1989 to 91 percent in 1995 could be accounted for because in Coffey Baptists had a leader whose "position" was more reflective of churches within
the union, unlike his predecessors. In other words, Coffey as an Evangelical
could be trusted. Another reason he offers is that Baptists are indifferent,
where "anything to do with Churches Together anywhere is largely irrel-
evant and left to those who want to do it." A third reason, (and Gilmore
says, the "much more likely") is that "ecumenism has lost its cutting edge."
He argues that the new ecumenical instruments meant that "ecumenism no
longer threatens church structures." Ecumenism was now more local, than
national, and amounted to inter-church cooperation. This was precisely the
basis on which the union had argued for it in 1989 and to a lesser extent in
1995, but Gilmore sees this as negative. A vision of greater unity in faith
and order, which Gilmore had argued for in *A Pattern of the Church* was no

62. *BT*, April 20, 1995, 15. Rushworth-Smith was a non-accredited Baptist minister
who had been involved in the charismatic movement, see Hocken, *Streams of Renewal*.

63. Minutes of the March 1995 BU Council, 6.

64. *BT*, June 1, 1995, 5, 13. Gilmore was by then retired, but had been a Baptist
minister in Northampton and Worthing, and then later working for several Christian
literature organizations. A significant Baptist voice in earlier decades and was one of
several high-church, pro-ecumenical Baptists in the union.

longer something talked about or at least not by Baptists. The union position advocated greater unity in mission.

Gilmore goes on to ask the question "what were Baptists voting for at Plymouth?" He suggests that it was about staying in the mainstream of British Christianity, but the reason most likely being that (at that point at least) many churches were involved locally in churches together initiatives. This grassroots ecumenism, Gilmore believes is a good move, they are "what matter." Of course the intention was that local ecumenism would become more regional and national, but Gilmore argues that for Baptists this is "secondary," instead "that it works effectively at the basis is vital."

Across the two streams there was a positive view of ecumenism, (although there was some dissent within Mainstream). However their views on the goals of ecumenism demonstrated some divergence from one another. For those in the stream 1 they could see no argument to not be involved in working with and alongside other churches, especially with regards to mission and evangelism. This was largely the extent of their ecumenical commitment with regards to CTE and the CBBI. Stream 2, as will become evident in the examination of Fiddes's ecumenical vision, were committed to a journey of pilgrimage, open to "what a true Church in visible unity might be like."[65] This view was also shared by both Keith Jones and later Myra Blyth in their respective roles as deputy general secretary, which also entailed being the union's national ecumenical officer.[66]

1995–2000s: Called to Be One, Ut unum sint, and Pushing at the Boundaries of Unity

After the 1995 assembly decision there were perhaps three significant ecumenical moments all of which demonstrated a more confident union with regards ecumenical engagement.[67] Coffey has described these years as "fruitful"[68] and Jones as the "high point" of Baptist ecumenism.[69] The first was the Pope John Paul II's' 1995 encyclical on ecumenism: *Ut unum sint*, the second was the 1996 CTE report *Called to be One* and the third

---

65. Kidd, *On the Way of Trust*, 21.

66. Blyth followed Jones as deputy general secretary, when Jones became rector of the International Theological Baptist Seminary in Prague. Both Jones and Blyth had ecumenical experience which was important for the role and complemented Coffey whose links were more among evangelicals.

67. See also Jones, *From Conflict to Communion*.

68. See Whalley, "Life in Christian Service," 13.

69. Jones, "Baptists and the Ecumenical Endeavour."

was the 2005 Baptist Union and Church of England report *Pushing at the Boundaries of Unity.*

The BU Council responded to *Ut unum sint* in 1997. Wright believes this was the only formal Baptist response.[70] Here the council was able to agree the words that "amongst most (if not yet all) of our people, there is a growing sense of unity with Roman Catholics: a unity based above all on the bond of love."[71] This would have been unthinkable in 1989, but demonstrates again that after 1995, the ecumenical question was settled in terms of commitment to being part of CTE and the CCBI and in particular the involvement of the Roman Catholics. This was highlighted again at the 1998 Baptist Assembly, when Basil Hume was invited to give an address.[72] The role of Hume in British ecumenism was vital during the Inter-church Process and afterward as CCBI and CTE began.[73] In 2005, in the context of the death of Pope John Paul II, Coffey could speak of the "sea change in formal relationships between Roman Catholics and Evangelicals."[74]

The union response to *Ut unum sint* acknowledges areas of agreement and also areas of difficulty. The response welcomes the Pope's commitment to ecumenism and five other elements—the grounding in Scripture, justification by faith through baptism, the sense of repentance, the need for continuing reformation and the importance of doctrine. In a section headed "clarifications," the response asked for explanation and more dialogue with regards to baptism, the Lord's Supper, apostolic succession, tradition, and the role of the Magisterium. A final section responds to the section from *Ut unum sint* on the place of the bishop of Rome as a means of unity, which notes the difficulty but is open to engagement.

Called to Be One was the "first attempt" (and ultimately the only attempt) to address the question of church unity following the Swanwick Declaration and the beginnings of CTE in 1990. *Called to Be One* was part of the "process through which the member churches . . . have agreed to discuss with one another the nature of the visible unity of the church."[75] Every par-

70. Wright, *Free Church*, 261.

71. A Draft Response to the Papal Enyclical *Ut unum sint, FU97/3*. See also *One in Christ* (1999) 460–65.

72. Hume had been invited by McBain, the BU president in 1998. Hume and McBain had become friends, while in London as Archbishop of Westminster and general superintendent of the Metropolitan Area, respectively. A small group did protest outside the venue at Hume's presence.

73. Clements calls Hume "the chief spiritual impetus behind the Inter-Church Process," *Look Back in Hope*, 177.

74. *BT*, April 21, 2005, 9.

75. *Called to Be One*, vi. Baptists Roger Nunn and Hazel Sherman were part of the

ticipating denomination in CTE was asked how they understood the word
church, the word unity and in context the meaning of the word "visible."
Baptist reception of the report was mixed. Gilmore's review was extremely
critical. The strongest criticism he makes is that it is an "establishment"[76]
document and is about "professional ecumenism."[77] In this sense it does
not reflect the issues local churches are facing and is stuck discussing the
same topics, to which he quips, "hardened ecumenists have already read the
book, seen the film and mostly got the T-shirt."[78] In Gilmore's view a more
honest acknowledgment of ecumenism is that "all churches, at all levels,
do mostly what they want, co-operate with whom they will as long as they
want, and strike off on their own when they choose to." Tony Peck suggested
that *Called to Be One* was significant, encouraging, and disappointing. Significant because this kind of report would not have been possible a decade
earlier, encouraging because it placed mission as the context of the search
for unity, but disappointing because it offered no "clear vision" for the future.[79] Michael Cleaves, echoed Gilmore's response in that the report is not
"earthed in the local experience."[80]

The council's official response to *Called to Be One* affirmed a Baptist
position of unity found in reconciled diversity and to the "Lund Principle"
that spoke of doing things ecumenically where possible.[81] The response also
argued that the starting point of visible unity should be a common faith in
Jesus Christ and not baptism. The other note was the importance of mission, which begins with God who is a missionary God. The response suggests a commitment to mission will lead to more visible unity. The 1997
CTE Forum which marked the end of the *Called to Be One* process saw
agreement for the importance of mission for visible unity and called for reconciliation and for visible expression of a common life.[82] On reflection there
is not much evidence that the report and process advanced the ecumenical

---

Working Party which wrote the report and Morris West was responsible for a paper on
Christian Initiation and Church Membership (appendix B to the report).

76. *BT*, April 18, 1996, 10.

77. *BT*, April 25, 1996, 15.

78. *BT*, April 18, 1996, 10.

79. Tony Peck in *SecCheck* 14 (Summer 1996).

80. Michael Cleaves in *SecCheck* 14 (Summer 1996). Cleaves was a Baptist minister
in an LEP in Milton Keynes.

81. Response of the council of the union to the Report Called to Be One of Churches
Together in England Prepared for the Forum CTE in July 1997, March 1997. The Lund
Principle had arisen at the third world conference on Faith and Order in 1952, see West,
"Lund Principle," 714–15.

82. *BT*, July 24, 1997, 4.

journey.[83] Into the 2000s, for Baptists (and arguably other denominations), CTE membership moved increasingly to the margins of concern.[84] Michael Bochenski in 2000 said that he sensed "a lack of momentum since the 'Called to Be One' process" and he put this down in part to "a significant leadership vacuum."[85]

Pushing at the Boundaries of Unity was published in 2005 and was a product of conversations that had been taking place between the union and the Church of England since 1992. Present throughout these conversations was Fiddes, while Wright was present up to 2001. The report provides first a historical and ecumenical setting before engaging in the issues of baptism and apostolicity. It offered the possibility of making some tangible advances toward mutual recognition between the two denominations. It demonstrated a union, or at least the members of the Faith and Unity Executive, more confident in terms of ecumenical engagement. However, the reception of the report by the Union Council in March 2006 reflected that Baptists were resistant to any perceived change to their principles, especially with regard to baptism.[86] Instead of affirming the proposed resolution to "welcome" the report, the council decided only to "receive" it, which amounted to it being ignored and nothing further followed from it. The Anglican Paul Avis, a co-convenor of the bilateral conversations, spoke, in reference to *Pushing at the Boundaries of Unity*, of the "more ecumenically disposed Baptists,"[87] recognizing there was large constituency of Baptists who were not ecumenically disposed. This reflects perhaps also some of his own disappointment at the wider Baptist response to the report's content. David Goodbourn said that while the report is "an immensely valuable resource," it is clearly an Anglican led report responding to Anglican questions and as such "there is not much about mission, or the discernment of the mind of Christ or the other issues that the BU Declaration of Principle might suggest are at the heart of a Baptist understanding of unity."[88]

---

83. David Cornick's account of British ecumenism makes no mention of it. See Cornick, "Story of British Ecumenical Endeavour." Cornick was general secretary of CTE, 2008–2018.

84. It is Keith Clements's view that by 2003 "there was a lack of interest . . . to ecumenism generally," *Look Back in Hope*, 364.

85. Bochenski, *Baptists and Ecumenism—Still Better Together?*, 9.

86. Minutes, Baptist Union Council, March 2006, 9–11.

87. Avis, *Reshaping Ecumenical Theology*, 9.

88. Goodbourn, "Review," 507.

Summary

For Baptists, the new ecumenical instruments were a positive move for many who had been uncomfortable with the BCC. As Haddon Willmer remarked with regard to the transition: "The denominations have brought ecumenism to heel."[89] This, he argues, meant that "ecumenical inter-church institutions are now relatively weaker than they were before 1990."[90] Membership of CTE and CTBI did not mean that many Baptists were any more willing or open to surrender cherished convictions, particularly around baptism. John Briggs suggested toward the end of the 1980s that Baptists "feel the double pull of ecumenical and evangelical demands."[91] This is a helpful observation. Evangelical Baptists have argued that the Baptist Union should develop more evangelical links with the likes of the Evangelical Alliance,[92] and ecumenical engagement should be for the sake of mission. The more ecumenically minded Baptists argued that the Baptist Union should engage with more commitment and openness in the process for greater unity between the different denominations.

Fiddes and Wright on Ecumenism

Fiddes: The Call of Ecumenism

A key exploration of ecumenism from a Baptist perspective has come from Paul Fiddes. In a paper first presented in 2001, and published in *Tracks and Traces*, he begins by recognizing three trends in the search for unity—unity from the roots, unity as full communion and unity in diversity. The first recognizes that unity begins at the local level. This was the aim and purpose of the new ecumenical bodies set up in the 1990s. The second recognizes that full communion has replaced the language of "organic union" or "one world church." Full communion is a unity based on recognition of one another as churches in communion or fellowship. An ecumenical theology of *koinonia* has become the shared language of nearly all churches.[93] Finally, the third

89. Willmer, "Taking Responsibility," 141.

90. Willmer, "Taking Responsibility," 141. This view is shared by Camroux, *Ecumenism in Retreat*, 134.

91. Briggs, "Double Affirmations," 64.

92. In his 1986 presidential address, Coffey argued that Baptists "must engage in dialogue with black churches, leaders of independent evangelical church groupings and leaders of the 'house church' movement," *Build that Bridge*, 2.

93. This has been the case since the WCC Assembly in Canberra in 1991 and the statement "The Church as Koinonia: Gift and Calling," https://www.oikoumene.org/en

trend, linked to the second, is that diversity will be part of a church unity. The questions that raises, as Fiddes points out, is what are the ends of that diversity, or what is legitimate and illegitimate diversity?

Fiddes's ecumenical theology centers around the call to be one body, one fellowship, and one covenant, which emerges from his reading of Eph 4:3–5. Fiddes argues that a "fundamental image of unity"[94] is the body of Christ, as it is found in three of Paul's letters. The call to be one body that is God's call, is a call to visibility, a concrete sign. Fiddes distinguishes between the universal church as the body of Christ and the local church as a manifestation of that one body. If the local church is a manifestation of Christ's body, then so are groups of churches together. Fiddes claims that it is important that the body of Christ becomes visible in "every level of society"—local, regional, national, and international.[95] The call to be one body then is more than a call to the local church on its own, but a call to churches to embody Christ together. So while we can speak of the invisible and the visible church, this does not mean, says Fiddes, that the visible church is only local. The call of ecumenism is to the greater visibility of the body of Christ. Fiddes quotes from a statement of the German Baptist Union: "It cannot be God's will for denominational barriers to hinder the visible fellowship of all believers."[96] And from the response of the Baptist Union to a review of CTE that "the church universal can at present be 'glimpsed imperfectly in the total global reality of churches, denominations and Christian networks."[97] The greater the visibility of the church, the more it is able to serve God's missionary purposes. The body of Christ image as Paul uses it speaks of the different gifts being given for a common purpose, and so "making Christ visible together . . . means the sharing of gifts and resources to make Christ known."[98] In addition, the ecumenical concern is also around making decisions together, so the Canberra Statement of the WCC says for churches to be in full communion this must "be expressed on the local and universal levels through conciliar forms of life and action."[99] Conciliar forms here means a council or assembly. There has to be a place of meeting where decisions are made. For Baptists this means the local church

/resources/documents/commissions/faith-and-order/i-unity-the-church-and-its-mission/the-unity-of-the-church-gift-and-calling-the-canberra-statement.

94. Fiddes, *Tracks and Traces*, 197.
95. Fiddes, *Tracks and Traces*, 200.
96. Fiddes, *Tracks and Traces*, 204.
97. Fiddes, *Tracks and Traces*, 206.
98. Fiddes, *Tracks and Traces*, 209.
99. Fiddes, *Tracks and Traces*, 210.

meeting, but Fiddes also wants to see this go further in the reception by the local church of decisions and advice that come from the association or union, because Christ is as visible in these gatherings as he is in the local church meeting.[100] The Baptist contribution is to say that wider conciliar forms cannot impose upon the local, for the local is able to discern and test what is received. Baptists offer a "dialectic" approach to decision making that recognizes "two processes of discernment together" and it is, says Fiddes, through both "that Christ becomes visible."[101] He suggests Baptists may need to take the conciliar forms more seriously and even be open to the "development of some kind of synodical structure."[102]

Fiddes moves next to say there is a call to one fellowship, which already exists in God, hence the reference in Eph 4:3–5 to one Spirit, one Lord, one Father. This fellowship or *koinonia* is "an existent reality before us."[103] The Church both "bears witness to" and is a "foretaste" of this communion to come.[104] To ignore the call to one fellowship is to fail to bear witness; that is, according to Fiddes, we "cannot witness to *koinonia* unless we *embody* it."[105] This *koinonia* is a witness against nationalism, the claim that one's nationality precedes one's Christian identity. To discover fellowship is to become part of a greater common story that is God's own story. This story is confessed in creeds and Fiddes encourages their use in worship as a narrative of salvation. To make use of creeds would be to answer the call to one fellowship, at least in some measure. For Fiddes, to speak of the story of salvation is also to be reminded of baptism, but instead of speaking of a common baptism, Fiddes prefers the language of common initiation. To speak of common initiation would help again to answer the call to *koinonia*. It is he believes a "way forward."[106] He acknowledges, that for many Baptists this would be a "large step" to take and be persuaded by, especially in choosing to decline baptism to those already baptized as infants.[107]

In turning to the call to one covenant, Fiddes discusses the thorny issue of *episcope*. To speak of covenant, drawing on the phrase the "bond of peace," Fiddes explains that covenant for Baptists means walking together

---

100. This follows the argument of *Nature of the Assembly*.

101. Fiddes, *Tracks and Traces*, 212.

102. Fiddes, *Tracks and Traces*, 212. He cites Gilmore, *Pattern of the Church*, 149–51, as making a similar argument.

103. Fiddes, *Tracks and Traces*, 214.

104. Fiddes, *Tracks and Traces*, 215.

105. Fiddes, *Tracks and Traces*, 215.

106. Fiddes, *Tracks and Traces*, 218.

107. Fiddes, *Tracks and Traces*, 219.

and watching over one another. Watching over is to speak of *episcope*. Fiddes argues that the personal, collegial, and communal dimensions of *episcope* are present in the Baptist understanding of the church, not only locally, but also at the inter-church level. In this way Fiddes claims that Baptists are able to speak the language of episcopacy with other Christian communions and even that there is much that they share.[108]

Where there is a clear difference is the link made by other Churches between episcopacy and apostolicity. For Baptists, and Fiddes says others in the ecumenical scene, apostolic succession is not about the laying on of hands but a "continuing story of the covenant community."[109] That is, what connects each generation with the first apostles is not a line of bishops, but "the succession of the faith and life of the church as a whole."[110] A second aspect of apostolicity centered on the ministry of Word and sacrament is also not a problem for Baptists. The clear area of disagreement is the role of the bishop as necessary in terms of ordination, although Baptists do usually include those who are already ordained, and in most cases a regional minister will be part of the service. Fiddes suggests that whereas regional ministers are not ordained to their role it might be helpful at the induction of a regional minister if there is a clear element of "recalling of their original ordination to *episcope*."[111] This would "affirm" that in this ministry there is a sign of continuity with the apostolic faith[112] and to make it a permanent feature that a regional minister would always be the one who presided over the ordination of new ministers. Fiddes accepts that there is "no real hope of visible unity without agreement on this personal sign of being apostolic" and so he suggests that "all churches will be open to re-thinking, re-visualising in an imaginative way, what this sign might look like."[113] He ends his paper with a reminder that God's church is a pilgrim church, and needs to be ready to move on, when God's calls.

Fiddes is a creative theologian and he looks in this chapter to find ways, on the one hand, of helping other churches to understand that there is a common ground with which they can talk with Baptists over decision-making, the use of creeds, initiation and baptism, and episcopacy.[114] On

---

108. Fiddes, *Tracks and Traces*, 223.

109. Fiddes, *Tracks and Traces*, 223.

110. Fiddes, *Tracks and Traces*, 223.

111. Fiddes, *Tracks and Traces*, 225.

112. In the pattern for inducting a regional minister in *Gathering for Worship* these suggestions were not taken up.

113. Fiddes, *Tracks and Traces*, 225.

114. See also Fiddes, "Learning from Others."

the other, he wants to help his own Baptist community to see that greater visibility and fellowship with other Churches on the issues just mentioned is possible. It is for this reason that Harmon calls Fiddes both the "most prominent constructive theologian identified with the Baptist tradition" and the "tradition's most significant ecumenical theologian."[115]

Wright's Ecumenical Vision

While Fiddes has led Baptists in engagement with the Anglican church, the Roman Catholic Church and the Orthodox, Wright's ecumenical engagement has tended to be more in the direction of those who identify as evangelicals and charismatics and in particular those in the Restoration Movement.[116] Where Wright has spoken of ecumenism, he reflects the perspective shared by others in Mainstream, like McBain and Tidball. At the end of *Challenge to Change*, he writes that "denominational renewal must take place within the context of ecumenical commitment."[117] Although he immediately clarifies that this does not mean, "the exalting of particular and limited institutional forms as all-important."[118] In this he distinguishes between what is often called movement and institution. In the same way that Wright calls "government an ambiguous power,"[119] so he is ambiguous about church institutions and structures.[120] Ecumenism is for the sake of mission: "The New Testament is clear about the potential of Christian unity in forwarding Christ's mission."[121] Wright understands ecumenism as being "about giving and receiving."[122] The Baptist way of being church is something to share with other denominations, as they will share with Baptists. Wright notes here that "spirituality, prayerfulness and fullness of congregational life" as something from which we might receive from others. Wright is positive about the interchurch process in its embrace of diversity in unity. In *New Baptists, New Agenda*, he is in agreement with those who had claimed that the charismatic movement had been the most ecumenical

---

115. Harmon, "Trinitarian Koinonia and Ecclesial Oikoumene," 19.

116. Although Wright has supported the likes of the Anglican Colin Buchanan in arguing for disestablishment of the Church of England, *BT*, April 6, 1995, 6. See also Wright, "Disestablishment."

117. Wright, *Challenge to Change*, 240–41.

118. Wright, *Challenge to Change*, 241.

119. Wright, "Government as an Ambiguous Power."

120. "Denominations are a somewhat ambiguous phenomenon," Wright, *New Baptists*, 47.

121. Wright, *Challenge to Change*, 241.

122. Wright, *Challenge to Change*, 241.

of the twentieth century. He says that the charismatic movement "overcomes the sticking points of formal ecumenism . . . simply by sidestepping them and proceeding directly to shared communion based upon a common experience of a mutually recognizable Christ."[123] Wright's basis for ecumenical engagement and its goal is can Christians recognize Christ in one another.

In *Free Church, Free State*, Wright presents the church as having "twin foci"—catholic and baptist.[124] He argues that "the health and future of the church are in direct proportion to the ability of these two broad models of church to interact and interpenetrate."[125] His ecumenical vision is for the catholic and baptist tendencies "to bring their distinctive offerings into the commonwealth of the church which is yet to be."[126] Wright is alert that for some Baptists his book will be all "too ecumenical." In the final chapter of *Free Church*, he provides a "typology of ecumenical engagement,"[127] that is, based on a conversation between representatives of the catholic and baptist models. The conversation he engages is one between the Roman Catholic Church, prompted by Pope John Paul II's 1995 encyclical *Ut unum sint* and the English and European Baptist responses to it.

Wright's ecumenism goes further than many evangelicals and Baptists might be comfortable with. He says, "There is a case for rapprochement rooted in mutual respect and a commonly confessed apostolic faith, and for seeing where this might take us."[128] Without using the word, there is something of the "pilgrim" idea, picking up the ICP language. He concludes,

> If both the catholic and baptist foci in that ellipse we call Christianity could see the ways in which they could enrich each other, and draw from each other the good things they could bring, without sacrificing what really matters to either side, then it would become possible to imagine a new kind of unity within the body of Christ, the spiritual potential of which would be immense.[129]

There is a development of Wright's thought from *Challenge to Change* to *Free Church, Free State* which sees him moving toward a more catholic

---

123. Wright, *New Baptists*, 47.

124. Wright, *Free Church*, xxiii–xxiv. Wright uses the lower case for both catholic and baptist because he is referring to them as two streams of being church, rather than specifically the Roman Catholic Church of the Baptist World Alliance, or such like.

125. Wright, *Free Church*, xxv.

126. Wright, *Free Church*, xxv.

127. Wright, *Free Church*, 256.

128. Wright, *Free Church*, 268–69.

129. Wright, *Free Church*, 269.

Baptist position represented by the likes of Fiddes. This reflects that the first book was written more specifically for Baptists in Great Britain, while *Free Church, Free State* was intended for a more global Baptist audience (published in the centennial year of the Baptist World Alliance) and an ecumenical one.

Conclusion

In the area of ecumenical involvement the two streams were working alongside one another. It was the likes of McBain who were influential in convincing Baptists to join CTE and the CCBI. Fiddes and others were not leading voices in either 1989 or 1995. Both streams argued for being part of ecumenical bodies. However, there is sense that there was some divergence in the direction of ecumenism. Stream 1 tended to argue for ecumenism on the basis of mission with less willingness to seek ways forward on issues of faith and order.[130] Theirs is a more functional vision of ecumenism. It is not clear from Coffey, McBain, and Tidball what they saw as the goals of ecumenism. I suggest they would have been happy with cooperation between churches, and even commitment, but would have struggled for an attempt at greater communion, outside of that with other evangelicals.[131] Working with other churches in mission was an opportunity for the renewal of Christian mission. In this some were more committed to a closer relationship with other evangelicals and keen to promote a more visible pan-evangelicalism.[132] While stream 2 saw ecumenism as having a more theological basis and as a commitment to Christ.[133] In this they wanted to work for a model of unity in diversity, to keep "open the possibility of discovering through pilgrimage with other Christian people what a true Church in visible unity might look like."[134] They saw theology as ecumenical and catholic in which

130. Coffey would write in 2006 "I share with others a sense of frustration at the lack of progress of all the British churches becoming 'united in mission,'" Coffey, "Missionary Union," 93.

131. I am referring here to what has been called the 5 Cs of ecumenism—competition, coexistence, cooperation, commitment, communion. See Jones, *From Conflict to Communion*, 10–14, which were first developed by John F. V. Nicholson.

132. In 2009 Coffey would write a book on the importance of evangelical unity: *All One in Christ Jesus: A Passionate Appeal for Evangelical Unity*.

133. In his review of *Tracks and Traces*, Sean Winter says that Fiddes's ecumenical Baptist theology "goes far beyond the common view that church unity is simply a matter of missional priority or pastoral condescension," Winter, "*Tracks and Traces*: A Review Article," 444.

134. Kidd, *On the Way of Trust*, 21.

Baptists offered a distinctive witness. In their opinion the life and faith of Baptists would be renewed through ecumenism.[135] Wright moved closer to this position by the time he wrote *Free Church, Free State*.

135. For example see Clements, *Ecumenical Dynamic*.

Chapter 6

Renewal in Dispute

AFTER THE DENOMINATIONAL CONSULTATION the discussions about the renewal of the union, at least in practical terms, were focused on what should happen to the superintendency and to the associations. The two key reports were *Transforming Superintendency* (*TS*) and *Relating and Resourcing* (*RR*). The former was chaired by Brian Haymes and the latter by Nigel Wright and so they can be viewed as reflecting the arguments of the two streams. If there was contention over whether mission or covenant should be the governing theological idea, there was even greater dispute over changes to the superintendency and the associations.

During the twentieth century the union related to the associations via the council and the superintendents. The membership of the council from the late 1960s had become more weighted to representatives from the associations, so that it could be argued that the union in the form of the council was an association of the associations. The superintendents, employed by the union, worked with the associations, being responsible for the spiritual life of the churches, the administration of grants, of settlement, of ministerial recognition, among other things. The union related to the churches via the annual assembly, the superintendents, and to a limited degree the council. The associations related to local churches via their own association assemblies and local systems of oversight and in a limited way through the superintendent (although as stated this was a union appointment rather than an association one). This meant that the union largely bypassed the associations and in effect that there were two parallel structures of relationships between union, associations, and churches which is what needed clarifying or rethinking.

In addition to this was the question of leadership. It has always been a thorny issue for Baptists.[1] While it has been accepted to a degree in terms of the minister of the local church, there has always been suspicion and disagreement over those who might exercise leadership beyond the local church. At the beginnings of the Baptist Union, the general secretary acted more as a administrative secretary and it was not until Shakespeare, from 1898, that there emerged a general secretary who sought to exercise leadership.

What took place during the 1990s was a debate about superintendency, associations, and national leadership. In 1993 Michael Bochenski wrote two pieces for the *Baptist Times*, one headed "Are Associations Dead?"[2] and the other, "Reforming the Superintendency."[3] Bochenski was representative of many others within the union who felt that change was needed. In the same year Coffey addressed the association officers and suggested that a "radical restructuring"[4] including of the superintendency was required. From there followed a discussion that continued through the autumn in the pages of the *Baptist Times*.[5] The discussion moved in a new direction when Rob Warner, at the 1997 Mainstream Conference, argued for the union to have a "National Eldership."[6] Again Warner was not the first to address the question of leadership at a national level, but his address brought it to a wider audience and so became a third strand to the debate over the future shape of the union.

This chapter will first focus on the superintendency before discussing the question of national leadership and that of the associations.

Superintendency

The History of Superintendency

General superintendents were first introduced in 1915. However, there was no dedicated review of the superintendency until 1978 and then subsequently again in 1996 with the report *TS*. That is, following the

1. See Ellis, "Leadership of Some."

2. *BT*, May 5, 1993, 8.

3. *BT*, September 16, 1993, 6.

4. *BT*, September 23, 1993, 2. The comment Coffey makes about the superintendency had come from within the Superintendents' Board itself.

5. *BT*, October 14, 1993, 7, 13; *BT*, October 14, 1993, 12; *BT*, October 21, 1993, 14; *BT*, November 11, 1993, 12. Cf., Hembery, "Superintendents Revisited," 7–8.

6. *BT*, January 23, 1997, 1.

establishment of the ministry of superintendents and its development, there was not much discussion within the union of the theology and practice of superintendency until sixty years later.[7] This is reflected in a comment from Morris West when he wrote in 1981, "The Superintendents have never been defined ecclesiologically and theologically."[8]

The context in which superintendents were created was first, a move to a nationally recognized ministry, and then second, a scheme for ministerial settlement and sustentation. These two moves meant the union was a more robust institutional body and late in the discussions plans appeared for the concept of general superintendents. The drive here for superintendents was at first largely administrative. The creation of a settlement system for ministers and a sustentation scheme that supported churches which could not afford ministry, required a new level of administration that the union and association structures at that point could not undertake. The proposal was for the country to be divided into ten districts (later called areas) with a general superintendent for each one.

The first mention of superintendent appears in January 1915. By February further details were established in terms of who would appoint, and pay them, and what their duties were. In terms of the former they would be appointed and paid nationally by the union. In April the union's council agreed to propose the idea to the forthcoming assembly later that month, where it was accepted. It took under four months for the idea to be suggested and then agreed, meaning there was little consultation or reflection, especially theologically, on what superintendency might mean for the union. The duties of superintendents defined in February were responsibility for the Sustentation Fund in their designated area; being a representative of the union in all matters of settlement; being a point of contact to aid churches where were differences or disputes; and being de facto secretary of the association in all these areas. At the council meeting in April, one further additional duty was included, which stated that the "intention and hope" was that superintendents would not be "unduly absorbed in business and financial cares," but would also carry out a "spiritual ministry in the Churches of the area and promote their closer union and more effective cooperation."[9] The first thought for superintendents was almost purely administrative, only this addition saw a ministry that went further. This is

7. An edition of the *Fraternal* in April 1948 was dedicated to the superintendency, with a set of articles by those who were superintendents, including a foreword by M. E. Aubrey, the then general secretary of the Baptist Union.

8. West, *Church, Ministry and Episcopacy*, 9. This point could be made about much of Baptist practice from infant dedication to arguably even baptism.

9. Shepherd, *Making of a Modern Denomination*, 78.

important because subsequent writings have presented the introduction of superintendents as primarily about spiritual leadership and even that they had an "evangelistic and reconciling ministry."[10] Without the need for the administration of the scheme, there would have been no superintendents, at least not at this point in our history. The emphasis on spiritual leadership developed because all the superintendents were ministers and so naturally they were more than administrators.

When Shakespeare addressed the assembly he argued for the necessity of superintendents for the success of the Sustentation scheme. He said also that this was not an attempt to introduce episcopacy within Baptist life, but reflected an old practice of the old General Baptists. Shepherd questions the claim that there was support in Baptist history for superintendents, which was and has continued to be made in subsequent years, most notably by Payne in his history of the Baptist Union.[11] Payne linked superintendents to the role of messengers among the General Baptists in the seventeenth century. Shepherd, rightly I think, argues that there were considerable differences between the two, most notably that messengers were not national appointments, but local to associations and were focused on evangelism, rather than administration. If the argument is that Baptists have a history of translocal ministry then that is correct, but there is no conscious revival of the messengers in the introduction of superintendents, at least not, as far as can been seen, in Shakespeare's mind.

Shakespeare borrowed the language of "superintendent" from the German Lutheran Church. When he first had the idea for this new ministry is unclear; again it appears it originated with him. Despite Shakespeare's claims that superintendents were not a Baptist episcopate, Shepherd notes, that he had on two occasions in 1914 (a year earlier to the first mention of superintendents) argued for a form of Free Church episcopacy as a means of further church unity.[12] If Shakespeare did see superintendents as a Free Church kind of bishop, it is arguable that another reason he sought their conception was for ecumenical reasons (not shared by other Baptists at the time).

It is unlikely, as Shepherd says, that the creation of superintendents would have happened so quickly and with so little discussion, if at the same time the United Kingdom was not at war. However, when superintendents were appointed at the beginning of 1915, there was support and approval, partly because what came with superintendents was the Sustentation

---

10. Reynolds, "75 Years of the General Superintendency," 231.

11. Payne, *Baptist Union*, 183.

12. Shepherd, *Making of a Modern Denomination*, 80.

Scheme.[13] They were appointed without ceremony and so began their roles without any fanfare. Again this is interesting because this pushes back against those who see that their role was ministerial. The *Baptist Times* reported in March 1916 that the "activities of the General Superintendents will prove the best and most fruitful effort we have ever made."[14] What is also surprising is that there seems no hesitation from some to use the language of "bishop" when describing superintendents. For example, the president of the Western Association, called them, "an ideal Bench of Bishops."[15] How again this language is being used is unclear. There is little to no comparison with Anglican notions of episcopacy.[16] We conclude that the beginnings of the superintendency are shrouded in at least some mystery. They were created to administer the new schemes, but given a spiritual ministry, to the extent that some even were comfortable to call them bishops.

In subsequent decades the role of the superintendent developed, partly through the example of those who began the office. Still early in the history of superintendents, Henry Bonser, writing in 1925 says the work of the superintendent is "concerned with the administration of the [Sustentation] scheme . . . and also with the furthering the purpose for which the scheme was designed, i.e., the spiritual efficiency of Baptist Churches."[17] Administration comes first, spiritual ministry second. He views the superintendency as a ministry and then goes on to state those called to this office are commissioned by the denomination and the local churches:

1. To exercise a spiritual ministry through the area
2. Watch the interests of the denomination thorough the area
3. To cooperate with churches and ministers regarding settlements
4. To organize the simultaneous collection.[18]

Here spiritual ministry comes first, administrative tasks come second. Writing again in 1949, Bonser acknowledges that the early years of the superintendency were not without contention. Bonser says that in 1924 T. R.

---

13. See Shepherd, *Making of a Modern Denomination*, ch. 3.

14. Shepherd, *Making of a Modern Denomination*, 83.

15. Shepherd, *Making of a Modern Denomination*, 80.

16. Both the 1926 reply to the Lambeth Appeal and the 1938 reply to the Federal Council of the Evangelical Free Churches reject Anglican episcopacy, but do not mention superintendency. The 1948 statement The Baptist Doctrine of the Church does mention superintendents as those appointed to "care for the churches."

17. Bonser, "Work of a General Superintendent," 316. Bonser was general superintendent for the North-Eastern Area, 1923–1949.

18. Bonser, "Work of a General Superintendent," 316–18.

Glover saw the office as "a danger . . . to the denomination."[19] And in 1927, in what has become frequently quoted in subsequent work,[20] H. Wheeler Robinson wrote that

> the name [general superintendent] must not be taken to imply more than moral and persuasive authority. It would quite misrepresent their position and work to regard them as "bishops"; but they are more than travelling secretaries. They are encouragers and advisers, and are at the service of the Churches and ministers for all spiritual purposes.[21]

Bonser says it was not until 1926 that the position of the superintendents became more assured, partly because of how those first appointed won over so many and that those who had opposed were eventually challenged first by Aubrey and then others.[22] A report in 1926 wrote, "The General Superintendents as a body are strongly concerned for the spiritual well-being of the Churches, and in view of the heavy administrative tasks laid upon them it is no slight achievement to have accomplished so much."[23] In 1942, another report, supportive of their office, goes on to say "We believe the time has come to take more seriously this view of the office,"[24] by which they meant that of spiritual leadership.

By the late 1940s the position of the superintendents is assured, so that Robert Walton can claim that the appointment of superintendents was an "act of farseeing wisdom and the benefits they have bestowed upon the denomination are incalculable."[25] The importance of them exercising spiritual leadership becomes more emphasized and recommendations are made to alleviate their administrative burdens. Some like Walton felt able to claim that the superintendents were "the man-power committee of the denomination and ought constantly to review the total needs and the total resources of the community."[26] This is to see them as denominational leaders, alongside the general secretary. This is a shift in thought for many of the denominational

---

19. Bonser, "Recollections of a Superintendent," 173. Glover was president of the Baptist Union in 1924. For more on Glover see Clements, *Lovers of Discord*, 109–29.

20. See Underwood, *History of the English Baptists*, 249; Watson, "General Superintendents," 146. Watson was general superintendent for the North-Western Area, 1949–1960.

21. Robinson, *Life and Faith of the Baptists*, 109.

22. Bonser, "First Baptist Union Superintendents," 10.

23. Cited in Bonser, "Recollections of a Superintendent," 173.

24. Also cited in Bonser, "Recollections of a Superintendent," 173.

25. Walton, *Gathered Community*, 153.

26. Walton, *Gathered Community*, 154.

leaders in previous generations were local church pastors who found a wider audience, usually through their preaching;[27] here now leaders are those in roles of oversight. Walton also introduces, as far as I can tell, for the first time, the language that superintendents are "pastors of pastors," which subsequently becomes more common,[28] and in overtly sounding catholic terminology he describes them as "the Fathers in God to the ministers."[29]

In 1948, near the end of M. E. Aubrey's time as general secretary (he retired in 1951), an edition of the Baptist Ministers' Fellowship journal, *The Fraternal*, was dedicated to the superintendency. Aubrey provided a foreword. He makes no mention of Ministerial Settlement or the Sustentation Scheme. Instead in his view they are leaders, advisers to ministers and churches, representatives of the union, administrators, and holders of spiritual gifts. Aubrey mentions that "superintendent" is the Latin word for the Greek *episkopos*, that is bishop, and finds no problem in picking up the description of them as a "good bench of bishops or superintendents."[30] Aubrey provides, again as far as I can tell, the first description of them as evangelists. He ends his supportive and encouraging foreword with a call to "let the Superintendents take the lead in Israel and people give themselves willingly,"[31] revealing the spiritual and denominational leadership the union invested in them.

In November 1978 the working group on the general superintendency presented their report to the Baptist Union Council.[32] This was the first dedicated review, arguably long overdue.[33] The working group had been asked to "consider the purpose and function of the General Superintendency within the context of the Baptist Union, its ministers and churches, recognising the changed denominational, ecumenical and missionary situation since 1916."[34] These changes were a story of growing decline in church mem-

27. E.g., John Clifford, F. B. Meyer, and John Henry Rushbrooke.

28. See Gilmore, *Pattern of the Church*, 43, 147. cf. Fiddes, *Leading Question*, 46.

29. Walton, *Gathered Community*, 154.

30. Aubrey, foreword to *Fraternal*, 4.

31. Aubrey, foreword to *Fraternal*, 5.

32. The working group was chaired by David Harper (association secretary, Suffolk Union), other members included Roger Hayden, Arthur Bonser (East Midlands general superintendent), Harry Mowvley (tutor, Bristol Baptist College) and David Russell (general secretary).

33. In 1953 a report to council had said Baptists "need to give further thought to the function of the General Superintendents and the representative nature of the office to which we have called them," *Church Relations in England*, 10.

34. *Working Group on the General Superintendency to the Baptist Union Council* (November 1978), 2.

bership which reflected a growing missionary situation. In addition was a developing ecumenical scene.[35] By 1978 superintendents were being drawn into a representative role in the various ecumenical bodies and groups. By 1978 the need for missional leaders was also increasingly being heard, and the report reflects this when it says, "We believe there is a need for a person in each Area to encourage and co-ordinate the mission of the churches."[36] In the follow-up 1979 report, the working group recommend that "the Superintendents, in partnership with the associations, give leadership in the development of a 'mission strategy' within the Area."[37] From this point onward, the view that superintendents should be missional leaders becomes a common expression. However the 1978 report emphasizes that pastoral care of pastors and their families should be "the first call upon his time"[38] and in the revised list of responsibilities this is now named and comes first.[39] Following the 1978 report, the requirements for superintendents to administer the Home Mission scheme is removed, one of the tasks which they had been responsible for from their inception.

Prior to the review of the superintendency in 1978, an earlier report on the *Commission on the Associations* (1964) highlighted the tension between the union's designated areas and associations: "There is a need for clear and frank thinking about the Association and the Area and this inevitably includes the General Superintendent."[40] The report argues for an increase in the number of superintendents in order that they might be responsible for around one hundred churches.[41] In 1964 there were ten superintendents, the report recommends increasing this to twenty. This, it is suggested, would bring them closer to the associations and overcome the view that

35. In 1942 the British Council of Churches had been formed, which led to a lot more regular and institutional ecumenism, in which superintendents were seen as similar to bishops in other traditions.

36. *Working Group on the General Superintendency* (November 1978), 3.

37. *Working Group on the Superintendency* (November 1979), 2. By then the Baptist Union report *Signs of Hope* had been published.

38. *Working Group on the General Superintendency* (November 1979), 15.

39. "There shall be appointed a General Superintendent for each Area whose responsibility shall be: to give pastoral care to ministers and their families; to give pastoral oversight to the churches encouraging and advising them in their mission; to provide leadership in the Area taking initiatives for the furtherance of Christian witness and education; to facilitate ministerial settlement; to act as representative of the BU at the appropriate level in ecumenical discussion and action; to act as secretary of the Area Pastoral Committee; generally to promote the objects of the Union." *Baptist Union Directory 1982–83*, 268–69.

40. *Report of the Commission on the Associations 1964*, 29.

41. *Report of the Commission on the Associations 1964*, 34.

they were "once removed"[42] and also provide the means for more effective fellowship and administration.[43] What the report highlights is the desire to see general superintendents as a "servant of both Union *and* Association."[44] This recommendation did not succeed and the question is again asked in the 1978 report. The authors of this report argue against a big increase in the number of superintendents, recommending there should be no more than twelve.[45] They say that this would necessitate a new system of ministerial settlement and that they are not convinced it would make the denomination any more effective in mission. In the 1979 follow-up, another reason is given as the report suggests "it would change the balance away from the local churches towards central organisation."[46] This last point continued to be discussed into the 1990s, as apart of the denominational consultation and subsequent changes.

With regard to the 1978 report, John Nicholson records that it was criticized "for not including any theology of the Superintendents."[47] Nicholson, who would become general superintendent of the North-Eastern Area in 1986 wrote a long article on a theology of *episcope* among Baptists.[48] In his conclusions he offers three models for general superintendency. He understands their ministry as one of episcopacy. The first model, following one of the recommendations of the *Commission on the Associations* report, is that superintendents have pastoral care of no more than a hundred churches, that is, close to one per association, as this would bring the superintendent nearer to the churches. The second model is to hold on to the present situation, but create a team ministry of which the superintendent would be one among others. The third model would see the superintendent as like an area bishop, he would be a leader, and alongside that would be a number of association ministers each responsible for an association or district.

Paul Fiddes, in his study of leadership, published as *A Leading Question*, likewise offered a theological rationale for superintendency. Fiddes

---

42. *Report of the Commission on the Associations 1964*, 29.

43. *Report of the Commission on the Associations 1964*, 35.

44. *Report of the Commission on the Associations 1964*, 30. Italics mine.

45. *Working Group on the General Superintendency to the Baptist Union Council*, 14. In 1981, the number of superintendents increased to eleven and then in 1986 the number increased to twelve.

46. *Working Group on the General Superintendency to the Baptist Union Council* (November 1979), 3.

47. Nicholson, "Towards a Theology of Episcope amongst Baptists," 266.

48. Nicholson had been Ecumenical Officer for England, for the British Council of Churches, 1975–1979.

argues that where there is fellowship there is *episcope*.[49] In the local church, episcope is seen personally in the minister, collegially in the deacons and communally in the church meeting. In the association, the superintendent is one of the forms episcope takes. Fiddes, like Nicholson, discusses the ministry of the superintendent in the context of episcopacy, although he draws a clear distinction between the understanding of Baptists in comparison to that of the wider catholic tradition, which sees the bishop as the source of the unity, that is, the relationship of church to bishop establishes *koinonia*. In contrast, for Baptists, says Fiddes, the *koinonia* comes first—the association exists independently of the superintendent, but that there is *koinonia*, so there must be oversight.[50]

Two final studies are pertinent to our overview. The first comes from Geoffrey Reynolds's review at the seventy-fifth anniversary of the appointment of general superintendents.[51] The article engages with the different examples of translocal ministry: superintendent, messenger, association minister, Baptist bishop, and apostle. In his reading of the creation of superintendents he suggests that from the beginning they were initiated as "an evangelistic and reconciling ministry, rather than a mere administrative necessity."[52] This, as I have argued, overstates the case. With his discussion of the word "apostle" he reflects on the impact of the Restoration Churches upon Baptist life through the late 1970s and 1980s.[53] The ministry of the apostle gets picked up by Mainstream, especially in the 1990s as they became more overtly charismatic.[54] Reynolds concludes that Baptists have a threefold office in superintendent, minister, and deacons. Both superintendent and minister are "first among equals" and this separates a Baptist understanding from that of Anglican or Roman Catholic. This is shared by Fiddes. The difference between superintendent and minister is around function not status. Reynolds argues superintendents are appointed to lead, and this takes priority over administration or pastoral care. Reynolds contends

---

49. Fiddes, *Leading Question*, 43.

50. Fiddes, *Leading Question*, 44–45. Fiddes as a theologian works with and from the catholic tradition, although tracing a particular Baptist understanding from its ecclesiological convictions.

51. Reynolds was general superintendent of the Southern Area between 1981–1999.

52. Reynolds, "75 Years of General Superintendency," 231.

53. Reynolds, "75 Years of General Superintendency," 235.

54. For example, see Virgo, "Apostles Today?," and the entire edition of Mainstream *Talk Magazine* 2.2 (Autumn 2002), with articles by Coffey, Warner, Wright, and also Peter Nodding, Craig Millward, Rob White, and Stephen Ibbotson. In the 1980s McBain, through Manna Ministries, was understood by some to be exercising an apostolic ministry. See his paper to the Mainstream Executive, "Charismatic Apostles and Area Superintendents," dated January 18, 1982. Paul Beasley-Murray papers.

that the "calling" of superintendent must arise from the churches through the association and not only be a union appointment. The superintendent's leadership role within area and association should be acknowledged, mirroring that of a minister to a local church. Finally Reynolds picks up the language of *pastor pastorum* and that this role must be accepted by the ministers within his [sic] pastoral oversight.[55]

The final discussion of superintendency comes from Nigel Wright's *Challenge to Change*, in the chapter that seeks to make what might be considered a surprising case for Baptist bishops. His key argument was for a reform of superintendency in a more apostolic (that is, missional) direction. The seeds of that argument are already present in some form in his earlier book *The Radical Kingdom*.[56] The same argument was then made in a contribution to the Mainstream *Talk* magazine,[57] to a set of Baptist essays published as *Translocal Ministry*[58] and briefly again in his *Free Church, Free State*.[59] He has more recently restated the case, although in new form, in his contribution to a festschrift for Paul Fiddes.[60] As a Baptist and a radical evangelical, it might be expected that Wright would see bishops as too associated with Christendom and the Establishment and so it is perhaps something of a surprise to find Wright making a case for Baptist *bishops*.[61] An argument for translocal ministry would not be unexpected, but he specifically argues for naming this ministry in the language of "bishop." In Wright's words, it has been "an abiding concern."[62] His involvement in the report *RR* means it is appropriate to look more closely at the argument Wright makes.

Nigel Wright's Case for Baptist Bishops

The case Wright presents is one that argues from the New Testament, from history, and from practice. He says that he changed his mind from being against bishops because of his reading of the New Testament, his own need for supervision and oversight and from his experience of the Restoration Movement and its ministry of apostles. This third reason allowed him to

55. Reynolds, "75 Years of General Superintendency," 238.
56. Wright, *Radical Kingdom*.
57. Wright, "Still a Case for Baptist Bishops," 27.
58. Wright, "Case for Translocal Ministry."
59. Wright, *Free Church*, 198–201.
60. Wright, "Three-Fold Order."
61. Wright has been one the most significant Baptist apologists for the disestablishment of the Church of England and the end of Christendom. See Wright, "Disestablishment—Loss for the Church or the Country?"
62. Wright, "Three-fold Order," 146n5.

see that translocal ministry did not have to mean episcopacy in the way the Church of England practiced it. While he rejected some models of apostleship within the Restoration Movement, as smacking of authoritarianism, other models he saw as offering an opportunity to enhance both the freedom of the local church and to serve the local church.[63] In addition to these initial arguments, Wright distinguishes his case for Baptist bishops from any form of historic episcopacy that is found in catholic churches. He argues for a functional episcopacy. While historic episcopacy says the church is where the bishop is, a functional episcopacy says God gives translocal ministry for the health of the church; the church exists independent of it, but such ministry is given for its *bene esse*. This is why it is an abiding concern for Wright. This is not about ecumenism, but about the faithfulness and fruitfulness of the church.[64] Wright endorses the early development of the role of bishops, argued by the likes of Ignatius of Antioch. Where it does go wrong is post-Constantine, as the role of bishops begins to develop a hierarchy and prestige that mirrors the state.[65]

Wright argues that there is no New Testament blueprint to which we can return. The New Testament demonstrates there was flexibility in the early church. Furthermore what words meant with regard to roles is not entirely clear. This is followed by Wright identifying that the New Testament uses two words interchangeably: *episkopos*, meaning one who oversees, and *presbuteros*, meaning an older person, an elder. From these words we get the word bishop. An overseer, or bishop, was "an elder within the church."[66] In the early church they are generally limited to a local sphere. He points out that in chapter 20 of Acts, both words are used to refer to the same people (see Acts 20:17 and 20:28). I will challenge this claim below. In his more recent work he speaks of *presbuteroi, episkopi* and *diakonoi* as a "three-fold order" and "local offices of ministry."[67] It is only in this more recent piece that Wright argues specifically for a threefold order and even uses the language of an "underlying pattern of office"[68] borrowed from Fiddes. Where Fiddes restricts this to a twofold order, Wright uses it to identify a threefold order.

63. For some comments on the Restoration Movement and apostleship see Wright, *Radical Kingdom*, 76–80.

64. In the *Challenge to Change* chapter Wright does not offer any ecumenical reflections, his more recent chapter in *For Sake of the Church* is set in a more ecumenical context.

65. Wright, "Three-Fold Order," 147–48.

66. Wright, *Challenge to Change*, 176.

67. Wright, "Three-Fold Order," 154.

68. Wright, "Three-Fold Order," 157. It is used in the Baptist Union's Doctrine and Worship Committee report *Forms of Ministry among Baptists*, 19, and Wright attributes

For Wright the more important word is apostle, which reflects the impact of the Restoration Movement on his thinking.[69] Wright says the ministry of the apostle post-New Testament is transferred to the ministry of the bishop, a transition from apostleship to episcopacy. Episcopacy becomes translocal like apostles were. Apostle refers to the twelve chosen by Jesus, but also to a broader group (see 1 Cor 15:7; Acts 14:4; 1 Thess 2:7; 1 Thess 2:6; Rom 16:7), who were evangelists and overseers. Wright argues for the continuing need for the ministry of the apostle, which he sees as being translocal and having some equivalence with that of the office of bishop. He believes it made "sense" to use the term "bishop" instead of "apostle" after the original apostles died out.

He notes that some have also argued from the basis of Ephesians for a fivefold ministry, in which apostles are included. This he says is a "key passage" and presents a "recurring pattern" to be found in the church.[70] More recently Wright claims that Ephesians 4 identifies a translocal ministry that is complemented by a local ministry in the form of elders, overseers, and deacons.[71] By "translocal" he means that the ministries are "not limited in service or jurisdiction to one congregation."[72] However, Alistair Campbell has pointed out that in Ephesians 4 (and also 1 Cor 12) Paul is not talking here about church organization, but the growth of the church in Christ-likeness.[73] For Wright this fivefold ministry is still necessary. The five ministries named in Ephesians are gifts of Christ to enable the continuing faithfulness of the church.[74] While Wright seeks to argue for a Baptist version of a threefold order, he thinks more reflection on the fivefold pattern of Ephesians would be valuable, especially with regard to the ministry of apostle and prophet.[75] There are voices in the contemporary church that press a fivefold ministry as some kind of "blue-print ecclesiology."[76] However, most New Testament scholars have been wary in reading this verse in this kind of way. A common point is that the reference to apostles and prophets in 4:11 is linked to Eph 2:20 where Paul speaks of apostles and prophets in the context of the foundation on which the church is built (cf. Eph 3:5). That is

---

it to Fiddes.

69. For one account see Scott, *Apostles Today*.

70. Wright, *Free Church*, 165–66.

71. Wright, "Three-Fold Order," 154.

72. Wright, *Free Church*, 166.

73. Campbell, *Elders*, 109.

74. Wright, "Three-Fold Order," 153; cf. Wright, *Radical Kingdom*, 77.

75. Wright, *New Baptists*, 129.

76. I borrow this term from Healy, *Church, World and the Christian Life*, 25–51.

the apostles and prophets are primary and non-repeatable, so where Christ has given apostles and prophets, they now belong to the past.[77]

Wright's case from the New Testament is brief and at times confusing. He builds a basic picture, without much to support his reading. This may reflect that the case from the New Testament is thin. As Sean Winter says, "There is no one pattern of translocal ministry."[78] Instead what can be gleaned is a more improvised approach. *Episkope* in the New Testament is primarily local, rather than translocal, and it is not entirely clear what is the scope, the character, and authority of translocal ministries. While it is clear that the apostle Paul exercised a translocal ministry over the churches he founded and even with some of those he did not (e.g., Rome), it is not entirely clear what happens post-Paul. Therefore, some caution should be used in terms of claiming Eph 4:11 as a fixed template for ministry, especially in terms of what is meant by apostle and prophet. Furthermore, there should be some caution of seeing a division between, what Wright terms, translocal (Eph 4:11) and local in terms of overseers and deacons. There is a danger Wright pushes a description of ministry to fit his argument. Finally, the ministry of the first apostles cannot straightforwardly translate to the ministry of bishops. While apostles did exercise oversight, they were also evangelists and church planters and it is not clear that this is a role which bishops continued. As Alan Kreider says, while bishops followed apostles, their focus was on "protect[ing] the apostolic truth, not as missionaries who embody and carry out the apostolic task."[79] Being an apostle and being a bishop (as it developed) were not synonymous.

What is surprising is at no point does Wright refer to R. Alastair Campbell's important work *The Elders*.[80] Campbell, a Baptist minister, was Tutor in New Testament at Spurgeon's College between 1989 and 2000 and also a member of Mainstream.[81] Campbell's thesis is a study of the word and role of *presbyteroi*/elders in the New Testament and as such it also engages with the role of overseers and deacons. Campbell argues that in regard to the church in the New Testament we are not dealing with offices. The language of elders was "a way of speaking about leaders, rather than the office

77. This is the view of three major commentaries on Ephesians by Andrew Lincoln, Ernest Best, and John Muddiman: Lincoln, *Ephesians*; Best, *Ephesians*; Muddiman, *Epistle to the Ephesians*.

78. Winter, "Translocal Ministry," 21.

79. Kreider, *Patient Ferment of the Early Church*, 10.

80. Campbell, *Elders*. This was originally a doctoral thesis undertaken at the University of London and completed in 1993.

81. Which is to say he was moving in the same circles as Wright and overlapped with him on the staff at Spurgeon's.

of leadership itself."[82] He challenges the view that overseers and elders were synonymous, and the view that the former was Greek and the latter Jewish. Campbell presents a narrative with regard to the Pauline churches that sees them based in homes and so the head of the household assumes a number of functional responsibilities. Hence, for example, Paul's address to "overseers and deacons" in Phil 1:1. However, theological leadership in the early days resided with Paul and his coworkers, largely being an itinerant team. What is important here is that from the beginning, there was leadership—each house church had a leader, it was not invented post-Paul, *contra* Dunn and others.[83] Campbell argues that as the house churches multiplied, the different "overseers" in each church, were collectively known as "the elders."[84] "Elders" are always spoken of in the plural, rather than the singular, again, in Campbell's view, reflecting their seniority rather than an office. When we move to consider the Pastoral Epistles, written second generation, that is, post-Paul, Campbell contends that we see an argument being made for the appointment of one overseer. The Pastoral Epistles are not written to "effect an amalgamation of overseers and elders, but to legitimate the authority of the new overseer."[85] It is only in the second century that we see the creation of a threefold order, where we see the elders develop into a separate office of ministry subordinate to the overseer/bishop. Prior to that, in the New Testament, we can discern a twofold order of overseers and deacons.

> To put it another way, the words *episkopoi* and *presbuteros* are flexible with changing referents during our period. *Episkopos* first refers to the leader of a house-church, but then to the leader of a town-church.
>
> *Oi presbuteroi* is first a way of referring to the house-church leaders considered together and acting corporately, but then denotes those leaders in the town-church who are precisely *not* the overseer or bishop.[86]

82. Campbell, *Elders*, 140.

83. "The emergence of more formalized leadership was not a development contrary to the Pauline legacy, and . . . it was inherent from the start in the household setting of the earliest congregations," Campbell, *Elders*, 125. Howard Marshall says, "This is the lasting contribution of Campbell's work," *Pastoral Epistles*, 176n78.

84. Campbell, *Elders*, 241.

85. Campbell, *Elders*, 196.

86. Campbell, *Elders*, 204.

Campbell's thesis has been disputed,[87] but has recently found support from a detailed study *The Original Bishops* by Alistair C. Stewart.[88] Stewart argues that a single congregation was led by a single *episkopos* and the language of *presbyters*, similar to Campbell, are those gathered in a city from across congregations. Stewart claims there is evidence that Christian communities "operated some form of loose federation."[89] It was from this federation that monepiscopacy eventually emerged. What began as a loose group eventually moved to a single institution. *Episkopoi* and *presbyteroi* are not synonymous, but they are overlapping.[90] What stands out in Stewart's argument is the case that monepiscopacy develops later than is the more common consensus. He argues against seeing monepiscopacy emerging in the Pastoral Epistles, *contra* Campbell,[91] and raises some important questions in the widely held view that Ignatius was a *monepiskopos*.[92]

What both Campbell and Stewart demonstrate is that the New Testament knows only a twofold order of ministry—*episcope* and *diakonos*, which has been the Baptist position from the earliest of times.[93] Stewart's thesis for how leadership developed finds some connections with how Baptists developed. His description of federation sounds similar to that of the development of associations among Baptists in the seventeenth century. Where eventually the church develops *monepiskopos*, Baptists have historically stopped short.

Wright makes a second case for Baptist bishops from tradition. He points out there is a precedent for a bishop-style ministry in the General Baptist practice of appointing "messengers" in the seventeenth century. In one General Baptist confession of faith it argued for a threefold ministry of "bishops or messengers; and Elders, or Pastors, and Deacons, or Overseers of the Poor."[94] These General Baptists clearly saw the need for a translocal ministry and were not afraid to use the term "bishop," although the language

87. For example see Merkle, *Elder and the Overseer*, but also Campbell's response in his review in *Evangelical Quarterly* 77 (2005) 281–83.

88. Stewart, *Original Bishops*.

89. Stewart, *Original Bishops*, 15.

90. Stewart, *Original Bishops*, 16.

91. Stewart, *Original Bishops*, 155–57.

92. Stewart, *Original Bishops*, 238–68.

93. Although since the 1970s and '80s an alternative threefold pattern has emerged in some Baptist churches of pastor, elders, and deacons. This is a direct result of restorationist influence. See the discussion in Fiddes, *Leading Question*. Cf. Fiddes, *Tracks and Traces*.

94. This was the Orthodox Creed of 1678, which can be found in Lumpkin, *Baptist Confessions of Faith*, 319–20, cited in Wright, "Three-Fold Order," 159.

of "messenger," a translation of apostle, was the more common term. The main role of messengers was evangelism and others duties were subservient to that. Wright, following Nicholson, quotes two Baptist historians Adam Taylor and W. T. Whitley. Taylor argues that these Baptists saw messengers as an "office superior to an elder" and their source was the witness of Acts and the Pastoral Epistles, and particularly the examples of Barnabas, Luke, Timothy, and Titus.[95] Whitley identifies messengers as those commissioned to be evangelists and who were supported by several churches.[96] Having this translocal role meant they also shared in organization and pastoral care of the group of churches they had been sent by. Wright sees the "fullest justification" for this ministry in Thomas Grantham's *A Defence of the Office of the Apostles*. Grantham himself was a General Baptist messenger.[97] Grantham argues that "apostles" still exist, although they are not the same as the original twelve. Apostles are given by God to preach the gospel, teaching, and strengthening pastors and churches and to challenge false apostles and/ or doctrine. For Grantham this is not the same as bishops in the Church of England, because for Baptist messengers "their pre-eminence is only a degree of honour, not of power."[98] Wright acknowledges that not all Baptists accepted the office of messenger and that it disappeared in later generations, but it is a helpful witness in the tradition for the priorities of any similar kind of apostolic or bishoping (episcopal?) ministry. It is also evidence that this kind of ministry is not entirely foreign or a complete anathema to Baptist life.

Ruth Gouldbourne has provided two recent studies of the history and practice of messengers in the seventeenth century.[99] As the title of one of her studies suggests, while Baptists did reject episcopacy, they did not reject episcope, although it developed in ad hoc ways. The history of messengers is more diverse than Wright suggests. Gouldbourne makes a number of observations.[100] First the earliest use refers to travelling evangelists. It is also used for those who were representatives to association or national gatherings and these were not necessarily those who were also evangelists. A further use is in reference to those who had particular role in offering counsel and advice to other churches. What is also apparent is the difference between General and Particular Baptists. Among General Baptists there was a strong

95. Wright, *Challenge to Change*, 179.
96. Wright, *Challenge to Change*, 180.
97. Wright, *Challenge to Change*, 179.
98. Cited in Wright, *Challenge to Change*, 181.
99. Gouldbourne, "Messengers" and "Episcope without Episcopacy."
100. Gouldbourne, "Messengers," 24–32.

suggestion that the role of messengers developed into a more institutional role, in which they carried some form of inter-congregational responsibility. Gouldbourne notes though, that this lasted only three or four generations. A strong theological defence of messengers in this bishop-like role is offered by Thomas Grantham, whom Wright refers to. That Grantham has to argue in this way, Gouldbourne suggests, is evidence that messengers were not entirely or easily accepted and this is further supported by their eventual decline. Where messengers among General Baptists began as evangelists and church planters, by the second half of the eighteenth century they were largely more involved in visiting and caring for existing congregations. In comparison, among Particular Baptists, the role of messengers was mostly evangelistic or representative. They did not exercise the kind of oversight that developed among the General Baptists, which reflected the Particular Baptist stronger emphasis on the authority of the local church and suspicion of anything that challenged that.

Alongside the tradition of messengers in the seventeenth century, Wright also makes reference, more briefly, to the more recent introduction of general superintendents. Wright is less positive about the ministry of superintendents because, unlike messengers, their "primary function" is not evangelism; they oversee too wide a geographical area; and they are appointed centrally by the union and not by local churches acting together.[101] A further problem with superintendents is that from their inception there was no acceptance of what kind of oversight they exercised.[102] As all too common among Baptists, the pragmatic need was recognized, but the theology was left largely unaddressed. The introduction of superintendents was arguably about management, rather than ministry. The positive view of messengers and the more negative view of superintendents, then shapes Wright's argument for Baptist bishops.

Wright's third argument is based on practical arguments. It makes sense to provide translocal ministry if churches are to be both missional and healthy. This is Wright's functional episcopacy. Wright argues that churches need to be more "apostolic and outward looking," that is concerned with church growth. This should see "the most effective and competent ministers . . . encouraged to move into apostolic, missionary roles."[103] Wright shares a vision that can be found also in the Anglican tradition of the "missionary Bishop."[104] While mission must be the priority, he does not dismiss the need

---

101. Wright, *Challenge to Change*, 186.

102. Wright, "Three-Fold Order," 160.

103. Wright, *Challenge to Change*, 182.

104. Goodliff, "Contemporary Models of Translocal Ministry," 58. See also Avis,

for church maintenance or what he also terms keeping churches healthy. Here practically, a bishop's ministry can: help a church avoid insularity; challenge the idea of a local pastor as omnicompetent; provide churches with advice when dealing with questions of vision, disagreement, and doctrine; and lastly provide support and ministerial development for pastors.[105] It is a "resource offering assistance" to those who will receive it or ask for it.[106]

In summary, Wright's case for a functional episcopacy understood ministry in the New Testament as plural and developing organically. Apostolic ministry continued in the emergence of bishops. Historically Baptists recognized the need for an apostolic ministry in the example of messengers. Practically if churches are to grow they need to release missionary-minded leaders to help support them to become more apostolic and outward and with that churches need avoid isolation and insularity. The example from Scripture and history and from practice, also mean that he believed there was a need for a proliferation of ministries (Eph 4:11 again), rather than a model of *area* superintendents. Translocal ministry should be appointed locally. It is the verb form of "bishop"—"bishoping" that should be the focus rather than the noun. The most acceptable language for those who might carry out translocal ministry might be "area or association ministers,"[107] but with the understanding that they fulfil an apostolic function.[108]

Transforming Superintendency

During seventy-five years of superintendents their role went through a number of changes from being administrators, to pastors, to missionary leaders. This reflects the changing context in which they served. The demands upon them also increased as new roles got added and they did not lose the old ones: superintendents continued to hold an administrative role, continued to be *pastor pastorum*, alongside being ecumenical representatives and leading churches in mission. Despite the increase from ten to twelve in the 1980s, there was a strong consensus that the superintendency needed to be reviewed. Emerging from the *Towards 2000* document, a group chaired

---

Ministry Shaped by Mission.

105. Wright, *Challenge*, 183–85. In his later essay he sees bishops as answer to the loneliness of local ministry, 156.

106. Wright, "Three-Fold Order," 157.

107. This is very close to the language of "regional ministers" that the Baptist Union report *Relating and Resourcing* eventually suggested.

108. In "Three-Fold Order," Wright argues for the use of the word "bishop" because of its ecclesial and biblical use.

by Brian Haymes was set up to review the superintendency in 1994.[109] The resulting report was published in 1996 as *Transforming Superintendency* (*TS*). Unlike previous reports, this report was a theological argument, beginning with the doctrine of God.[110] *TS* argued for the ecclesial nature of the union and that superintendents were there to provide unity, to encourage fellowship and to help the church to be the church in the world. Superintendents, according to *TS*, should be "pastoral theologians . . . concentrating on ministering to the ministers."[111] The argument was that by superintendents concentrating on ministry to ministers this would enable the churches to be "more effective in mission."[112] The whole report is framed in the context of the mission of God. That is, the "primary task" the report proposed was for superintendents to be pastors to the pastors, while looking after churches should belong to associations.[113] This indicated that the whole report was a review of superintendency, not just of superintendents, that is, it was a review of oversight among Baptists. Oversight was, said *TS*, invested in both those called superintendents and in associations. This was an argument for the recovery of the importance and significant of associations, which *TS* recognized needed renewal. The emphasis of *TS* was that superintendents should be persons who could teach and pastor and had a "firm grasp of the Faith"[114] much like bishops within the wider catholic tradition whose tasks include being a teacher and defender of the orthodox faith.[115] This was not an emphasis Baptists had made before. *TS* contended that superintendents should remain union appointments, although they recognized they had

109. This had been agreed by Baptist Union Council in November 1993 from a recommendation from the General Purposes and Finances Committee.

110. I suggest that Haymes learned the importance of beginning with God from Leonard Champion, who was principal when he trained at Bristol Baptist College. In an article on the doctrine of the church Champion said: "What I am urging is not simply that we need more thought about a number of questions associated with the doctrine of the church, but also that our thinking must begin from a certain point, namely the gracious will and purpose of God revealed in Christ, and that it must proceed along certain lines, namely, to the pattern of God's saving work in Christ," Champion, "Baptist Doctrine of the Church," 29.

111. *Transforming Superintendency*, 24.

112. *Transforming Superintendency*, 24.

113. *Transforming Superintendency*, 24 and 27. In terms of the latter, the report did see superintendents having a part in oversight of churches. In the discussion at council in March 1997 the language of "primary task" was changed to "primary responsibility," although Haymes stressed that the "task" should not delegated, *BT*, March 27, 1997, 2.

114. *Transforming Superintendency*, 24.

115. As *Baptism, Eucharist and Ministry* says: "They serve the apostolicity and unity of the Church's teaching, worship and sacramental life," *Baptism, Eucharist and Ministry*, 25.

ministry that was both national and regional and as such *TS* proposed that the nominating committee for superintendents should continue in "favour of the Area by two to one."[116] *TS* did not argue for an increase in the number of superintendents, believing that any change in the size of areas, which would affect the number of superintendents should be initiated from the associations and areas themselves.[117]

The report received a mixed reception,[118] perhaps proving not to be bold enough and too cautious in many of its resolutions, in a period that was looking for more radical changes.[119] Brian Nicholls records some of the reception history within the Superintendents Board in his 1997 MTh thesis on "Regional Episcope and Local Church Mission." (This was completed prior to the publication in 1998 of *Relating and Resourcing*.) Nicholls had been appointed general superintendent for the West Midland Area in 1995.[120] Alongside his own critique, Nicholls references also criticisms from Peter Manson[121] and Douglas McBain. Manson was critical of what he called "its failure to be anything other than affirming contemporary theological clichés" and for not giving attention to issues of the kingdom, the gospel, Jesus, holiness, and mission.[122] McBain's criticism was the emphasis in *TS* on oversight of ministers and not churches. McBain argued for the need of apostolic ministry that was called and gifted.[123] Nicholls also references Rob Warner's question, that if superintendents were to pastor pastors, where would the "apostolic dimensions of ministry in terms of vision, direction

116. *Transforming Superintendency*, 44.

117. *Transforming Superintendency*, 25.

118. The March 1998 council did note "that the theological affirmations are foundational in providing clear guidance as we shape the future of our associating together," Minutes, Baptist Union Council, March 1998, 15.

119. The report was completed before September 1996 in which denominational consultation took place, it presented in November 1996, but was not discussed by council until March 1997. This all meant that any discussion of *TS* was now caught in the wider conversation.

120. Derek Tidball mentions Nicholls as "committed to Mainstream," Tidball, "Mainstream," 219.

121. Peter Manson was general superintendent for South Wales.

122. Peter Manson, "Tranforming Superintendency—the Theology." Unpublished paper circulated to the Board of General Superintendents early in 1997, cited in Nicholls, "Regional Episcope," 35.

123. McBain, "Transforming Superintendency—One Superintendent's Response," unpublished paper circulated to the Board of General Superintendents dated January 26, 1997, cited in Nicholls, "Regional Episcope," 37–38.

and inspiration" come from?[124] Warner's alternative vision was to "identify key local leaders" and bring them together as a national team of leaders.

Nicholls's own response makes a number of observations and criticisms. There is what he calls an institutional problem with superintendency, captured in the word itself, and in the way, he argues, it is "wedded to the structures." Following John Finney, he compares the sixth-century Celtic and Roman missions, favoring the former where the "bishop acted as an evangelistic team leader."[125] Nicholls is critical of the *TS* understanding of ministry as too narrow, having equated ministry with those ordained and accredited and argues that the superintendent should operate with a "wider context of ministry at all levels."[126] Another concern of Nicholls is with the meaning of the word mission, while he wants to see mission in a holistic way, he believes that the majority of Baptist churches still equate mission with evangelism. Like McBain and Warner, Nicholls favors a more charismatic model of leadership, which wants to stress the importance of calling and gifting: translocal ministry does "not emerge because God desires to preserve the institution, but because there is a mission imperative to be obeyed."[127] Nicholls's most extended criticism is theological. He is critical of what he sees as a social doctrine of the Trinity operative in *TS* and suggests rather than the Trinity, ministry finds its meaning "in the person and work of Christ."[128] From the person and work of Christ, Nicholls refers to grace, providence, and servanthood. By grace, Nicholls wants to see the ministry of the superintendent extending beyond those "who in some way deserve him, or subscribe to the Home Mission Fund or are seen actively to participate in Association or Union life" and in this way they "model the gracious activity of God."[129] In the incarnation and life of Christ we see providence, and so all ministry is "evidence of the providence of God." Finally, there is servanthood understood as the willingness of Christ to go to the cross. Nicholls argues that "a curiously positive point" of superintendents being a national appointment is that leaves superintendents "not structurally in relationship with the churches he [sic] serves" which he sees as something analogous to the way Christ's being in the world, but not of the world. As such, "Christlike Superintendency will identify with the local, and yet must

124. Warner, "Ageing Structures," 16.

125. Nicholls, "Regional Episcope," 39.

126. Nicholls, "Regional Episcope," 78.

127. Nicholls, "Regional Episcope," 82.

128. Nicholls, "Regional Episcope," 87.

129. Nicholls, "Regional Episcope," 88.

somehow paint the bigger picture of God's purposes regionally, ecumeni-cally and denominationally."[130]

Haymes felt that *TS* did not get the attention it deserved. He gave two reasons, first, the denominational consultation happened and second, the report had faced what he called "serious misrepresentation."[131] When Haymes introduced TS to the council in November 1996 he said, with re-gard to the writing of the report, that "there have been times in our discus-sions when we have known an excitement, a quickening of the spirit, as we have glimpsed new relationships, new possibilities, new visions."[132] The overlooking of the report then was a disappointment to Haymes.

Relating and Resourcing

TS's call for a renewal of associations partly aided the setting up of another group on associating, chaired by Nigel Wright, which published its report in 1998 called *Relating and Resourcing (RR)*. It was this report that provided the framework for the shift from superintendents to regional ministers. *RR* recast the conversation about superintendency in a different direction. It was bolder in its proposals, but much less theological.[133] It argued for a new set of regional associations to replaces the existing twelve areas and Twenty-nine associations. Each regional association would have a leadership team comprising different emphases—vision, pastoral, evangelistic, and other specialist abilities, led by a senior regional minister.[134] This suggestion also fits with Wright's suggestion in *Challenge to Change* for a "proliferation of ministries." In the BU Council debate on *TS*, Tony Peck had expressed con-cern that superintendents "exercised a ministry too 'apart' from others."[135] *RR* goes on to suggest that the title superintendent should be replaced by "regional minister," although without explanation. The choice of title was raised when council came to discuss the report.[136] The shift away from the

130. Nicholls, "Regional Episcope," 89.

131. *People on a Journey* printed as an insert in *BT*, January 23, 1999.

132. Haymes, "Transforming Superintendency—an Introduction," 12. (The article was an adapted version of Haymes speech to the council. Its inclusion in the *Main-stream Magazine* was probably a result of Bochenski who was the editor at that time and who was also a member of the group that wrote *TS*.)

133. It references the key theological claims of *TS* as "very helpful," *Relating and Resourcing*, 3.

134. *Relating and Resourcing*, 11. Theologian or teacher is not included.

135. Minutes, Baptist Union Council, March 1997, 16.

136. Minutes, Baptist Union Council, September 1998, 3–4. Some wanted to re-claim the title messenger, Christopher Ellis hoped it would include pastor and Wright's preference was for bishop.

language of superintendent to regional minister is closer to Fiddes's view that translocal ministry is an extension of the local episcope: "different in scope but not in kind."[137] *RR* shifts the responsibility of these regional ministry teams to "leading the association in mission, for general oversight of the churches, for encouraging inter-church associating and for the pastoral care of ministers."[138]

Mission takes priority and pastoral care comes last. The report says this does not differ from *TS* because regional ministry is plural and therefore pastoral care is not lost. The first priority though is leadership in mission.[139] When the resolution came to council in November 1998, the order had changed to:

> leading the association churches in mission, particularly through the pastoral care of ministers, general oversight of the churches and promoting and encouraging clusters of churches.[140]

Reflecting the concern for the importance of pastoral care, Haymes challenged that a "primary part of the task of the senior regional minister should be the pastoral care of the ministers." In his view, it was not a general responsibility of the team. Wright responded that the proposal was meant to be "liberating rather than restrictive," that is, it would be for the regional ministry team to decide.[141] A frustration with *RR* is that it is a relatively short report and its explanations for each of its proposed resolutions are brief. This means that what is meant by missional leadership of associations is not defined.[142] Criticism of *RR* came from Paul Beasley-Murray who had a meeting with the union's senior management team on his concerns. Beasley-Murray's chief criticism was that it was a shift away from the importance of the local church and its ministry to the creation of what he called "greater bureaucracy."[143] He argued that what was being suggested would "take away Home Mission money from supporting ministry in the local church to supporting ministry beyond the local church." Added to this was his view that more regional ministers were not needed and despite the vision for

137. Fiddes, *Tracks and Traces*, 222.

138. *Relating and Resourcing*, 11.

139. A similar argument had been made by Steven Hembery, "Superintendents Revisited," 7–8. Hembery was a member of the Mainstream Executive during the early 1990s.

140. Minutes, Baptist Union Council, November 1998, 17.

141. Minutes, Baptist Union Council, November 1998, 17.

142. Wright does not give any clearer definition in either *Challenge to Change* or *Free Church*.

143. Beasley-Murray, "Concerns about *Relating and Resourcing*."

something different he feared they would "end up being more concerned with maintenance and pastoral care rather than with leadership and evangelism." The final difference between *TS* and *RR*, is that the latter proposes that "regional ministers should be called, employed and paid locally by the regional association."[144] This again follows the argument made by Wright in *Challenge to Change*. The implication is a shift of power from the union to the association for regional ministers are now answerable to their association rather than the union. At several council meetings this was a key issue of debate. The council minutes record:

> The Rev Dr W M S West warned that since regionalisation was a proposal common to both reports, the totality of the Union must be protected, and the Superintendents provide that link ... The Rev A A Peck observed that the Superintendents were in an ambiguous role as they were Union employees who had line management responsibilities within Associations.[145]

> The Revd Dr B Haymes said that Superintendents had currently a uniting role for all within the Union, and the Superintendency Task Group had wanted to underline and to continue this national aspect, and the Revd M I Bochenski commented that the Superintendents were "the glue" that held the Union together, although an "independent" person might be helpful within a Region. The Rev R E Warner thought that if Associations were to be challenged to give up much to achieve reform, the Union must also be seen to be sacrificing something, otherwise it would be easy to interpret the whole process as "Didcot taking over ..."

> ... The Rev D E Hall said that adoption of R3.6 of the Report would attribute "local ownership" to the Regions, but the Rev D C Sparkes cautioned that the churches themselves wanted the Superintendents to have a national dimension, and the Union was not noticeably being urged to relinquish them.[146]

> The Rev Dr B Haymes reminded Council that TRANSFORM-ING SUPERINTENDENCY was opposed to either the Union or the Region being wholly responsible for the appointment and financing of the Superintendents. The question of how the

144. *Relating and Resourcing*, 12.

145. Minutes, Baptist Union Council, March 1998, 11.

146. Minutes, Baptist Union Council, March 1998, 14–15. The proposition to see regional ministers "called, employed and paid locally" was agreed in principle by 71 votes in favor, 52 against, and 30 abstentions.

Trans-local Leader related nationally still had to be resolved. The Rev Dr N G Wright as Convenor of the Group on RELAT-ING AND RESOURCING replied to the debate . . . In regard to Trans-local Leaders, he could see no reason why they could not be independent even if they were called and paid by the Region, any more than that a local Pastor lost his "independence" by being paid by his church.[147]

The Rev Dr R L Kidd believed that employment by a central body gave security to senior ministers, as well as strengthen-ing their superintendency of the churches, but the Rev Dr N G Wright commented that the pattern of a local church calling ministers and accepting responsibility for them was funda-mental to the theology of Baptists. Nevertheless, the Rev Dr B Haymes thought that it was essential to maintain a national role for such senior ministers.[148]

Here is the clearest evidence of the streams of renewal in dispute. The decision to call, employ, and pay regional ministers locally was carried. This was a key decision because it reflected differing understandings of the union. For those like Haymes and Kidd, there was a desire to hold on to a national body. Whereas Wright and Warner wanted a more decentralized future, which Wright described to the Superintendent's Board as "churches in a powerless structure seeking fellowship."[149] Wright was content to de-scribe the structures of the union as "resource agencies,"[150] while Haymes had said in the November 1996 council meeting that he would "deplore any trend to treat Didcot merely as a 'resource centre.'"[151]

Summary

In 2002, eighty-seven years after they were introduced the office of super-intendent was ended and in its place regional ministers were introduced. Arguably this was a simpler structure: the disconnect between area and association had been overcome, although in reality the size of the new

147. Minutes, Baptist Union Council, September 1998, 4.

148. Minutes, Baptist Union Council, November 1998, 18. The recommendation which included the calling, employing, and paying locally of regional ministers "was approved," with no record of actual votes.

149. Roger Hayden, "Task Group on Associating: Summary of Recommendations" (no date but likely in 1997 when Wright visited the Superintendent's Board). DCRG Papers.

150. Wright, "Time to Associate," 12.

151. Minutes, Baptist Union Council, November 1996, 17.

regional associations[152] meant churches were part of much bigger associations and regional ministers still had many churches to look after and lead, despite there being more of them. Furthermore, despite the intention, the ministry of regional ministers was not that different in kind to that of superintendents before. There was still administration of settlement and home mission, pastoral care of churches in crisis, ecumenical representation, as well a lot of new missional ventures. Perhaps the only fundamental difference was that it was now shared between two or four people (depending on size and finances of the association). The tension between union and association remained for most of the 2000s and an attempt to resolve them in more structural changes was made in 2012.[153] In setting aside *TS* there was a rejection of its call for pastoral theologians, those who might hold a teaching ministry. The decisions made also reflected that there was still not agreement on what a theology of Baptist translocal ministry was. This reflected a wider problem of not being able to agree with what Baptist ministry of any kind is.[154] Baptists have recognized the need for a ministry wider than the local church, but generally this has been of the "resourcing" kind, rather than a more "catholic" type focus on relating and on unifying.

National Leadership

Alongside corporate *episkope* exercised by the council and assembly, the *Nature of Assembly* report argues that there is also a personal form of *episkope* in the persons of general and deputy general secretaries and the president of the union. They are part of a "team ministry" that offer national leadership to the union.[155] The report also sees that the heads of departments (ministry, mission, and administration) and general superintendents might also be said to be part of this national leadership team. The report emphasizes this is not about hierarchy, "only a difference in the area of *koinonia*."[156] The

---

152. The size of the regional associations was largely the same as the areas, although the Northern Area was separated into Yorkshire and Northern.

153. Part of the issue is the regional associations do not have the history of the country associations they replaced. The regional associations are almost solely institutional bodies, with little real associating being possible, because of the geographical distances. This ironic because the intention was to have less institution and more flexible structures.

154. See Goodliff, *Ministry, Sacrament, Representation*, 34–71.

155. *Nature of the Assembly*, 30.

156. *Nature of the Assembly*, 31.

report names the general secretary as the "senior minister in a pastoral team which offers *episcope* at the national level."[157]

In *Forms of Ministry*, the Doctrine and Worship Committee suggested that the "Senior Management Team" at Baptist House be named as "the Pastoral Team which guides the Union."[158] Their personal *episcope* is shared with the corporate *episcope* of council and assembly such that it "flows back and forth" between the two.

TS recommended that the council "consider the creation of a Mission and Ministry Forum."[159] This would act as a "think tank" that would discuss and survey what is happening in the churches and wider society, reporting to council. This forum would be made up of senior union staff, superintendents, and college principals—representing the different constituent parts of the union.

In 1997, Rob Warner made his call for a "National Eldership" which would offer vision to the churches of the union. Warner said, "it seems to me that many local Baptists, particularly pastors, are crying out for a larger sense of vision and direction for the nation."[160] Glen Marshall, cochair of Mainstream, echoed Warner's views, saying that what was needed was "more scope for leadership" nationally. Coffey responded by pointing to *The Nature of Assembly* report.[161] Fiddes resisted the word "eldership" and said it was about wanting "to give weight to the pastoral dimension of the officers' roles in the Baptist Union."[162] Warner, following up his comments, spoke of releasing the general secretary from "administrative and management responsibilities" so that they might function like a five-year president.[163]

A response to Warner was offered in *On the Way of Trust*. The principals interpret Warner's call as a desire to free leadership from the institution, what they call "the committee structures and plethora of relationships which constitute the wider church."[164] They respond that all pastoral leadership must be part of "the texture of relationships" that are covenant communities.[165] They argue, "Strength of leadership rests not on the office persons hold, nor on the gift of personality they have, but on the quality of their

---

157. *Nature of the Assembly*, 33.

158. *Forms of Ministry*, 26.

159. *Transforming Superintendency*, 41.

160. *BT*, January 23, 1997, 1. Cf. Warner, "Ageing Structures," 16.

161. *BT*, February 13, 1997, 1; *BT*, February 20, 1997, 5.

162. *BT*, February 20, 1997, 5.

163. *BT*, February 20, 1997, 5.

164. *On the Way of Trust*, 33–34.

165. *On the Way of Trust*, 34.

service and the levels of trust nurtured and articulated within the community which recognises and respects them."[166]

RR made the recommendation that "the general secretaries, senior regional ministers and heads of Union departments should constitute a national leadership team for the oversight of mission, pastoral care and the encouragement of associating."[167] Where the rest of the report was arguing for a more decentralized union, this national leadership team would offer a balance and provide a means of "binding the Union together." In *Challenge to Change* Wright had argued against seeing the union as the association of associations, but the suggestion of a national leadership team in which regional ministers would be members would be a move in this direction, as regional ministers were now association representatives not union ones. *RR* sees the proposed "Mission and Ministry Forum" recommended by *TS* as coming from a radically reformed council.[168]

In March 1998, the council agreed to establish a National Leadership Team.[169] In November 1998 the council agreed to the creation of a National Pastoral Team (this was favored over the term National Mission Forum), which was a renaming of the National Leadership Team.[170] This pastoral team would "take a strategic overview of the work of the Union." It would include one senior regional minister from each association, the general secretaries and heads of departments, two representatives of the colleges, one representative of BMS and the BUGB president. Its responsibilities were to include being a national "think tank" for the work of the union, to take a strategic overview of mission, to note trends in mission and church life, to monitor reactions and responses of the churches to union-generated reports, to achieve good communication and encourage the overall cohesion of the union, to model the way of trust in relationships between elders, and to act as a bridge between regional and national ecumenical life.[171]

In November 1999 the National Steering Group[172] presented the Terms of Reference for the new National Pastoral Team.[173] This now proposed an "additional membership" of five members from council to ensure there was

166. *On the Way of Trust*, 35.

167. *Relating and Resourcing*, 13.

168. *Relating and Resourcing*, 14.

169. Minutes of the BU Council, March 1998, 15.

170. Minutes of the BU Council, November 1998, 15.

171. Report of the DCRG to BU Council, November 1998, 4.

172. This group was set up in March 1999 "to take on the responsibilities of the DCRG and the Task Group on Implementation."

173. Appendix 4 to the Reports of the National Steering Group, November 1999, 11. See Peck, "National Pastoral Team," 4–6.

broader representation on the team. On the advice of the National Steering Group, the team was renamed the National Strategy Team, which changed once more to the National Strategy Forum.[174]

As the discussion moved from 1994 through to 2002, there was a shift in meaning in what national leadership could entail. *The Nature of Assembly* was an acknowledgment that those in national ministries were pastors and so exercised a ministry of oversight. By the end of the decade this had shifted to a national strategy forum acting like a think tank. This was a move again from a theological vision to a functional one. It also reflected the struggle for the union to come to any shared understanding of national episcopacy.[175]

Associating

The whole of the twentieth century for Baptists might be understood as an attempt by denominational leaders and theological voices to argue for interdependency as a central part of being Baptist. Throughout the century, and especially from the 1940s onward there is a strong rejection of independence as a mark of Baptist ecclesiology. The statement agreed by the 1961 denominational conference (which had been Ernest Payne's idea)[176] began by saying that

> the independency which has characterized the outlook and practice of many, if not all, of our churches in the last 100 years, needs now to be supplemented by a much clearer realization of the necessity of their interdependency.[177]

The default Baptist position, inherited from the nineteenth century, had become one of the independent Baptist church. Toward the end of the twentieth century, this was also true sociologically, as engagement in and attendance of association life became less and less. Associations were struggling to practice associating. This was the view across the two streams and can be found in Haymes, White, and Wright.

Haymes writes of the "disturbing features . . . that Association life is marginal to most congregations."[178] White rejects the view that said Bap-

174. "National Strategy Forum."

175. The debate would continue in the review of the Presidency. See the *Final Report of the Review Group for the Presidency of the Baptist Union of Great Britain*, March 2003.

176. West, *To Be a Pilgrim*, 122.

177. "Statement Agreed by the Denominational Conference," in *Denominational Conference May 1961*, 30.

178. Haymes, *Question of Identity*, 11.

tists have "cherished the principle of 'association'" and says instead Baptists have "tended to put their independence first and their cooperation, in any practical or theological sense, a long way second."[179] In 1991, Wright speaks of "renewing association" in a more relational direction, over against a perceived institutionalism.[180]

One of the four commitments in the 1992 Statement of Intent in *Towards 2000* was with regard to associating and the recognition that reform was needed.[181] It was not though until after the denominational consultation, in which it became apparent that associating was the most important item for which delegates felt change was required, that a group to explore reform was set up. The consultation advice was for "smaller geographical areas/regions," for "structures which are lighter and more flexible" and for resourcing that "may imply devolution from the national/Union level."[182] It was suggested that "areas" might be "between 30 and 50 churches."[183]

The changes made to Baptist life by Shakespeare in many ways bypassed the associations.[184] Some Baptist associations had historic roots,[185] older than the union, but the relationship between union and association was overlooked, especially in the development of the union under Shakespeare. This created a long standing question of how association and union related to one another. The statement of the 1961 denominational conference spoke of "unanimous agreement on the importance of the Associations for the healthy development of our denominational life on the grounds of both history and present experience." From this a commission in 1962 was set up in part to look at the relationship of the associations to the union and its committees and departments.[186] It reported in 1964. It made a large number of recommendations. The key argument was to suggest that the Baptist

179. White, "Practice of Association," 20; he is citing *The Report of the Commission on the Associations, 1964*, vi.

180. Wright, *Challenge to Change*, 133–50.

181. *A Ten Year Plan Towards 2000*, 8. The aim was "to reform the structures of associating at every level."

182. 277 voted in favor of this, with 3 against.

183. 278 voted in favor of this with 2 against.

184. "The development of the Baptist Union over the 150 years of its existence has gone on without a great deal of serious consideration ever being given to its relationship to the Associations," *Report of the Commission on the Associations*, 11.

185. Five of the thirty-one associations were founded between 1640 and 1690, three associations dated back to the later eighteenth century, the rest being founded during the nineteenth century.

186. *Report of the Commission on the Associations*, iii.

Union is the "Associations associating together."[187] The report claimed this would make it clear in the structures of the union the place of associations. Although this was not a unanimous recommendation, for the report says that "*some* of us feel that this really is the way ahead for Associations and Union together."[188]

The focus of the report *The Nature of Assembly* on the union meant it said very little about associations and associating, apart from that they were expressions of covenant relationship. *TS* makes the statement that the renewal of Baptist churches was dependent on "the renewal of Association life."[189] The report sees associations largely staying as they are with their own leadership. This leadership would come from the churches and not through an increase in full or part-time staff, which they say has "had the effect of distancing Association leadership from the Churches" and ask if this has not meant that associations have become organizations in themselves.[190] *TS* says what is needed is a new spirit of associating, rather than more bureaucracy.[191] *TS* argues that the care of the churches lies primarily with the associations.[192] The superintendent would be involved, but the responsibility lies with the association. *TS* claims that "this emphasis is true to our ecclesiology."[193]

RR seeks to live up to its terms of reference and offer a "radical revision of our Associating."[194] *RR* sees the word associating as a synonym for relating. This relating is not one of power but of fellowship, which can be expressed as a covenant. *RR* claims that for the purposes of mission and spiritual growth churches need one another. The report calls for a "rediscovery" of relationships between congregations, which institutional reform can aid, but not establish. This rediscovery is for the sake of the "spiritual health" of Baptist churches and "the proper fulfilment of the mission" of God.[195] Stephen Copson, in an article published in 2000, presented a historical account of associating from the early eighteenth century. In his conclusion he cautions that the *RR* claim that Baptists have "largely lost the reality of associating" needed to be tested against a more historical account

187. *Report of the Commission on the Associations*, 22.

188. *Report of the Commission on the Associations*, 26.

189. *Transforming Superintendency*, 30.

190. *Transforming Superintendency*, 30.

191. *Transforming Superintendency*, 31.

192. *Transforming Superintendency*, 27.

193. *Transforming Superintendency*, 27.

194. *Relating and Resourcing*, 1.

195. *Relating and Resourcing*, 10.

of associating, that is the reality of the past is more complex than was being suggested.[196] He goes on to argue that "the relationship between associating and association awaits a fuller examination."[197] *RR* argues that relationships between congregations may not be purely inter-Baptist, but "reach beyond the boundaries of Baptist churches alone."[198] The report does not see this as a problem, but already a matter of fact, but does argue that there should be more than "nominal ties" to the Baptist Union.[199] This was the argument Wright had made in *Challenge to Change*: "Some Baptist churches will be experimenting as a result of this with new forms of association across the historic denominational divides, and I have no quarrel with this."[200] A line of thought can be traced from *Challenge to Change*, through the development of Mainstream as a Word & Spirit Network, to the proposals in *RR*.

The report saw relating and resourcing moving in two directions. At one level churches would seek to "cluster" with other churches locally as an expression of relating. At another level, the institutional level, churches would be part of regional associations, replacing the county associations, as a means of resourcing. Resourcing which had been mostly done at a national level would move closer to a regional level. The implications were that county associations would be combined with others in new regional association.[201] This latter suggestion was in direct conflict with the consultation statement advocating smaller geographical associations. What clustering might look like or mean is relatively thin in the report. The argument for regional associations is to "streamline" the structures, effectively dissolving the county associations into one association that reflected the already existing areas. *RR* contends that bureaucratic models of working should be replaced by functional and mission-orientated ones. Every church should be directly represented on an association council, enabling a "direct voice in the government of the Association."[202] Where *TS* argued that associations

196. Copson, "Renewing Associations." Copson is secretary of the Baptist Historical Society, a role he has held since 1996.

197. Copson, "Renewing Associations," 271.

198. *Relating and Resourcing*, 5.

199. In an unpublished, but widely shared paper from 2012, Paul Goodliff argues that this proposal from *RR* was "regrettable" and a "pragmatic" one, *Networks*, 22.

200. Wright, *Challenge to Change*, 149.

201. A similar proposal had been explored in the Central Area with its four county associations: Bedfordshire, Buckinghamshire, Hertfordshire, and Northamptonshire between 1992–1995. See *A Single Association for the Central Area? Some Questions and Answers* (no date). Ultimately Northamptonshire said no to the proposal.

202. *Relating and Resourcing*, 13.

should look after churches pastorally, this role is the responsibility of the proposed new team of regional ministers.

RR was a proposal to radically decentralize the union back to associations,[203] albeit associations now much larger than they were before. The key places of power would be in those who had oversight of the associations. The national expression of union: those who worked in national roles were recast as the "national resource." What is apparent in *RR* is that the union moves into the background, the emphasis is on clustering and regional associations. There is little in the report that describes the purpose of the union. This was observed by Faith Bowers at the March 1998 council who could not find "any reference to wider Denominational resourcing."[204]

The outcomes of this dispute about renewal of the structures were that stream 1 was ultimately more convincing. The argument of *RR* found support from the council and its proposals were largely agreed. It has been described as initiating the "most radical changes in Baptist life beyond the local congregation for more than a century."[205] The union that Shakespeare had built, and Payne had tried to strengthen was dismantled in significant ways and in its place were thirteen newly created associations in which their leadership was accountable to them and not the union. The historic county ties were weakened, but the vision was for closer ties to be discovered through local clustering. There was agreement that the purpose was God's mission, but where *TS* saw that in strengthening local ministers, *RR* spoke of leading in mission, without a clear sense of what that meant. In reality it would come to mean individual mission strategies for each of the thirteen associations. Both streams saw the need for a clear sense of national leadership and arguably they were each perhaps dissatisfied with council's decision to set up a think tank.

The dispute at the heart of the issues around superintendency and associating was the place of the union. Wright had argued in *Challenge to Change* that the union was an example of Baptists accommodating themselves "to the pattern of the established church" and that this led to a "wrong turn in a centralising direction."[206] He argued that what was a needed was a "policy of decentralisation."[207] Wright's view was that the Baptist theology of the church was at its strongest at the level of the local church and in

203. *Relating and Resourcing*, 13.
204. Minutes, Baptist Union Council, March 1998, 11.
205. Thompson, *Protestant Nonconformist Texts*, 4:128.
206. Wright, *Challenge to Change*, 158.
207. Wright, *Challenge to Change*, 163.

the concept of association and was its weakest in national structures.[208] Associations could be relational, while the union could only be bureaucratic. The union would become a "national resource agency" accountable to the council, which would be made up of those elected by the associations.[209] The union in Wright's vision would "serve the same function in national terms that the Baptist Missionary Society does internationally."[210] A good amount of this argument is then turned into proposals in *RR*.

While Wright had been part of the Doctrine and Worship Committee that had written *The Nature of Assembly*, it is not clear that he owned the description of the union within it. The report was almost entirely the work of Fiddes and was a clear argument for the union as being ecclesial. Fiddes and Haymes made the argument again with the other principals in *Something to Declare* and *On the Way of Trust*. They shared the view of Payne who argued that the union was a "necessary expression of Christian fellowship" and a "necessary manifestation of the Church visible"[211] and they offer a theology in support.

RR shared with *TS* the tension between the church as a movement of God and as one in which institutional forms were necessary. The use of the word "movement" was to say something theological: the church is primarily grounded in God than in institutional structures. In the words of *TS*: "a movement of God rather than an institution of our making."[212] The difference between the two reports might suggest that *TS*'s proposals remained too committed to the institution. They were not radical enough. Whereas *RR*, with its emphasis on the associating, gave more scope to the church as a movement, more flexible and responsive. However, in *RR*'s proposals for sixteen regional associations that would be responsible for employing a team of regional ministers, the associations, now larger in area, would become more institutional in form and practice. What *RR* inadvertently introduced in regional associations were larger institutions which were further away from the local church than had been the case in the old model. It is difficult to imagine what the church as a movement might look like when in view are two thousand churches, thirteen associations, five colleges, and a national center.

208. Wright, *Challenge to Change*, 162.

209. Wright, *Challenge to Change*, 167.

210. Wright, *Challenge to Change*, 169–70.

211. Payne, *Fellowship of Believers*, 31. Payne includes associations, synods, and assemblies as also necessary expressions and manifestations of the church.

212. *Transforming Superintendency*, 13, referenced in *Relating and Resourcing*, 5.

It could be argued that while associations were more important than union to Wright, the reverse was true for Haymes, Fiddes, and Kidd. They believed it was vital that the superintendents had a national ministry and so a unifying one, while Wright was more concerned that they were appointed and paid for by the region so they might more easily exercise leadership as those within the association and not outside it. It would have been interesting to know if *TS* had, in light of the advice from the denominational consultation, proposed more superintendents, whether this would have given the report more support and momentum. In the model of national superintendents the union was central and the associations secondary, in the model of team regional ministry the associations were central and the union came second, albeit the council was still in place and would resist the "radical reform" called for by *RR* until 2012.

A final comment might be made with regard to the place of the local church in the denominational reforms. A view shared by both streams was that Baptist ecclesiology began with the local church and that any kind of form of associating beyond the local was provisional rather than fixed in some kind of definitive structure. The argument made by some was that the developments in the union through the twentieth century in a centralizing direction were those in which the local church was "press[ed] . . . to adapt to meet the needs of the wider Church."[213] Increasingly, it was claimed, the starting point of Baptist ecclesiology had become the union rather than the local church. In other words, rather than the union enabling the local church in mission, the local church increasingly was aiding the union in mission.[214] The response to this view was to make the case that in the union there was a dynamic understanding in which authority, although resting mostly with the local church, also flowed from and to the association and union. I struggle to recognize the view that the liberty of the local church was under threat from the wider structures, either before or after the denominational reforms. Both *TS* and *RR* are arguments for seeing the local church as the primary place for mission. What Baptist ecclesiology has always required, but not always had in abundance, is trust.[215] Alongside that I suggest is what Champion argued for back in 1979: "a clearer, more coherent, and more widely accepted theology."

213. Shepherd, *Making of a Modern Denomination*, 186.

214. Shepherd, "Renewal of the Union," 24.

215. See *On the Way of Trust*.

Chapter 7

Conclusions

THIS STUDY HAS OFFERED a detailed study of the denominational reforms that took place within the Baptist Union of Great Britain during the 1990s. It has argued that how they should be understood and interpreted is through two streams of thought which developed through the 1980s and came into closer interaction through the appointment of two individuals from each stream to significant roles within the denomination.

As chapter 2 argued, the first stream, Mainstream, originated in the context of church decline and was launched on a manifesto for life and growth. Its vision was to see the denomination renewed, both its churches and structures. The second stream, took up the challenge posed by Leonard Champion to see the union renewed through the development of a new theology of Baptist life and mission.

The first stream gained the most profile and from the mid-1980s onward began to see those from within its numbers take up key appointments in the union. By the early 1990s this included the general secretary of the union, the secretary for Mission and Evangelism and several general superintendents. From this position they were able to initiate a process of reform and renewal within the union led by David Coffey as general secretary.

The second stream, a small group working together on publications were not so influential in the 1980s, but they consistently made the case for the importance of theological thinking. By 1994 three members of the original group were Baptist College principals. From here they became members of council and most importantly of the Doctrine and Worship Committee, a new group tasked with providing theological reports for the union.

Chapter 1 told the story of the key events in the 1990s, central to which was the denominational consultation in 1996. This gave new energy to the reform process and from it emerged the biggest changes to union life in the restructuring of the superintendency and associations. Through the process Coffey was articulating a vision for a union organized for the purposes of mission. Vision for the second stream was centered in a theology of covenant.

Chapter 2 analyzed the development of the two streams and their key thinkers. In stream 1 we saw that Mainstream was an inclusive grouping of evangelicals—some charismatic, others committed to church growth and others more traditional. By the beginning of the decade, the stream's key thinker, Nigel Wright, issued a challenge for Baptists to change at the levels of the local church, the association, and the union. Stream 2 wanted Baptists to take seriously the need for a theological engagement in the context of a society becoming increasing secular and pluralist and in response to a changing church scene. They found in the concept of covenant a treasure from the past to be retrieved for the present. Brian Haymes emerged as the key thinker in the 1980s with a booklet that explored Baptist identity, but it would be Paul Fiddes who would become this stream's most important theological voice.

Chapter 3 examined the sources that Wright and Fiddes were drawing on in their respective theologies of renewal. These sources saw them reach backward, Wright to the Anabaptists and Fiddes to the English Separatists, and reach outward to evangelical (Wright) and Baptist catholic (Fiddes) traditions in which they situated themselves. Added to this they participated in the growing interest taking place ecumenically and academically in a theology of mission.

Chapters 4 to 6 picked up specific areas where the two streams were interacting. In chapter 4 this was around whether the central idea was mission or covenant, tracking how these ideas unfolded and where they ended at the point the reforms were enacted in 2002. Chapter 5 explored the Baptists' engagement in the new British ecumenism of 1990 that followed the Swanwick Declaration. This chapter suggested that the two streams, while both being ecumenically committed, diverged on the goal of ecumenism. Chapter 6 saw the two streams in dispute around the purpose of superintendency and associations. Stream 1 advocated recasting the union in more decentralized structures, arguing that this would reduce bureaucracy and release regional leaders in mission. Stream 2 contended for less change in structures, but rather for a revisioning of superintendents as pastoral theologians whose first priority was the care of local ministers in order that they might be encouraged, supported, and enabled in their role as pastoral carers and leaders of the church. This they argued was the best way to see the churches become more effective in mission.

From the story I have told, I want to now offer some conclusions as we consider the intentions of the two streams and the outcomes for a Baptist denomination renewed for a new millennium. I will suggest that during 1990s there were three key areas of tension: first, with regard to the identity of the union; second, to how the union and association related; and third, between theology and pragmatism. In each area of tension, in the background was, for stream 1, the spectre of church decline. This was a motivating force and highlighted in the extensive framing of everything through the lens of mission. Also in each area of tension, in the background was, for stream 2, a perceived apathy to theological questions. The motivation of stream 2 was the challenge of articulating a theology for the times and highlighted principally in the concept of covenant.

Before reflecting on these tensions, one other conclusion should be acknowledged, that is, the impact of David Coffey. His position gave him the platform to lead and persuade the union, and in particular the council, into renewal. His force of personality and vision kept the union on the journey toward change and in this he achieved far more than his immediate predecessors.[1] This is notable because Coffey was an advocate of the Mainstream agenda.[2] He was an Evangelical and wanted to see the union be a means of encouraging life and growth in the denomination. This meant that the vision of stream 1 through Coffey had a clearer channel to be advanced. Coffey was not indifferent to the theological case of stream 2, as seen in his foreword to *Something to Declare*, but a case can be made that he sought to adapt the argument they advanced for covenant to his broader vision for a missional renewal as evidenced by his foreword to *Covenant 21*. Coffey was committed to his idea of a missionary union.

Tension 1: Conceiving the Union

In the previous chapters I have demonstrated that there was a tension between two different conceptions of the Baptist Union. The first, arising from stream 1 was a missiological concept: the union as an agency for mission. The second, arising from stream 2, was a theological concept: the union as an ecclesial body. Stream 1 identified the union primarily as an agency which existed to help local churches do mission through the resources it provided. The risk here, as Graham Hill has suggested, is that this can too

1. Ian Randall commented that "he has been truly inspirational" ("History's Lessons," 4).

2. At least in the broad sense that it was articulated in Mainstream's first decade. In 1988 he come off the executive and became more of a background supporter.

often become missional pragmatism rather than missional ecclesiology[3] and so always looking for what might work. The thesis in chapters 4 and 6 drew attention to how this had a tendency toward a more functional and pragmatic understanding of the structures and of translocal ministry.

Stream 2 argued for the union being primarily a "living tradition" (see ch. 3), which was a means of having a continuing "conversation about what it means to be Baptist."[4] The union, for stream 2, bore ecclesial marks and this was a difficulty, in their view, for the union's relationship with the BMS and with those who wanted the union to be more like the BMS as was argued in chapter 4. Here then was a key tension: was the union an agency for mission or was it a legitimate expression of being church? In an attempt to describe denominations ecclesiologically, Barry Ensign-George has argued that a "denomination binds congregations together in formal patterns of mutual life" and provides a "space in which to discern" and a "means for living out differing forms of a faithful Christian life."[5] This resonates with stream 2's understanding of covenant and trust in terms of the union, described in chapters 3 and 4. Ensign-George goes on to describe denominations as "contingent, intermediary, interdependent, partial and permeable"[6] which articulates a theological defence of the denomination as an ecclesial category and is supportive of the claims made by Fiddes and others. Stream 2 affirmed the contingency of the union; it is not, they said, a church. The union is an intermediate expression between the church local and church universal and as such a visible sign of the interdependent nature of the church, albeit partial and permeable, that is: the union is a demonstration that Baptists are a pilgrim people.[7] Of course it might be said that denomination is not coterminus with union and that this conflation was one of the consequences of Shakespeare's centralizing moves.[8]

The interaction of the two streams ultimately left the question of the identity of the union unresolved. This was demonstrated by some in the

3. Hill, *Salt, Light, and a City,* 265.

4. I'm drawing here on the argument of Harmon, *Baptist Identity,* 140–41, who is interacting with Ammerman, "On Being a Denomination," 21–31, and in the language of "living tradition" drawing on MacIntyre, *After Virtue,* 222.

5. Ensign-George, "Denomination as Ecclesiological Category," 5–6.

6. Ensign-George, "Denomination as Ecclesiological Category," 6–7.

7. Kidd, *On the Way of Trust,* 26. Harmon says that Baptist churches "at their best being relentlessly pilgrim communities that resist all overly realized eschatologies of the church," *Baptist Identity,* 224.

8. See Shepherd, *Making of a Modern Denomination,* 170–72. Cf. Briggs, "Confessional Identity, Denominational Institutions and Relations with Others," 16–24. See discussion in Jackson, "Discourse of 'Belonging,'" 97–101.

early 2000s calling for *The Nature of Assembly* to be reconsidered.[9] In naming those who worked at a national level at Baptist House as the "National Resource" and in the shift to see associations as regional resources, there was a move to treat the union as more like an agency. To an extent this was balanced by *Covenant 21* and *Five Core Values* (with its invitation to both the local church *and* the denomination to consider each of the values) with some ongoing sense of the union as also being ecclesial.[10]

There was a tension in which the ecclesially-minded thinkers, like Fiddes and Haymes, did seek to join covenant and mission together in *Something to Declare* and *TS* and the mission-minded thinkers, like Coffey, did acknowledge covenant as a helpful idea that could unite the union around mission. It was a tension, however, that pulled in different directions for the language of agency and ecclesia are dissimilar. The mission minded thinkers would have been content to see the union become an organization closer to the BMS, which had a clear purpose, but was a voluntary society. The ecclesial minded thinkers resisted any attempt to down play the churchly character of the union, because this would have been, in their view, a denial of the covenant relationship between the churches, associations, and colleges that made up the union.

The Statement of Intent agreed in 1992 had a fourfold vision: for mission and evangelism; for Baptist identity; for associating; and for sharing resources. It had been reordered in the council discussion to give mission top priority.[11] This reflected stream 1's concern for "life and growth." It indicated both the historic Baptist commitment to mission, as expressed in the third article of the union's Declaration of Principle, and a keen awareness that Britain was increasingly a post-Christian, pluralist society in which the church needed to find ways beyond decline.[12] Mission at the beginning

9. For example, Sean Winter. See his "Some Comments on *The Nature of Assembly and the Council of the Baptist Union of Great Britain*" prepared for the Doctrine and Worship Committee, June 22, 2000. He argued that there were issues arising from the report that "are still with us and warrant further consideration."

10. The Methodist, David Carter says of *Five Core Values* that it "raises interesting ecclesiological issues both for the Baptists and others. The tripartite structuring of the implications of the core values was significant for its consideration of issues for the local Church, denomination and witness in society at large. For the Baptists, it raises again the question of the ecclesial nature and necessity or otherwise of structures beyond those of the local Church. Would Baptists necessarily need tighter structures, with greater authority, in order to make their programme more effectively realizable?" Carter, "Where Are We Ecclesiologically?," 231.

11. The original order had Baptist identity first.

12. Gilbert, *Making of Post-Christian Britain*; Newbigin, *Gospel in a Pluralist Society*; Gill, *Beyond Decline*. I have referenced the titles of these three books because they all are referenced by Tidball in *Catching the Tide*, 63–70.

of the decade was framed as the task of the church given by God and it required "imaginative and effective strategies." As the decade unfolded the focus on mission was embraced by the second stream and in both *Something to Declare* and *TS* they outlined a theology of *missio Dei*. However, the focus on mission, they claimed, arose from the church's doctrine of God rather than any concern for church decline. While stream 1 paid close attention to statistics about church numbers, stream 2 gave it little attention. While there was an urgency for the likes of Coffey and Tidball around the issue of the reform of the union in line with mission, Fiddes and Haymes felt the urgency facing the union was a theological one. Here, the evangelical theology of stream 1 held a stronger church-world separation, whereas, for Fiddes certainly, there was a more positive view of culture.[13]

Tension 2: The Roles of Union and Association

The second area of tension was between the role of union and the role of associations. Stream 1 favored a decentralized model in which associations were strengthened as the more necessary expression of inter-church fellowship and oversight, while stream 2 held a much stronger place for the union and had little to say about associations. Possibly the second stream favored continuing smaller county associations but increasing the number of superintendents.[14] The proposals from *RR* for regional associations did offer a more simple structure, although not as light-weight and flexible as suggested, due to the legal and administrative responsibilities that associations held. One of the key arguments of *RR*, taken in tandem with the recasting of the union's Mission Department as one focused on training and research, was to decentralize mission back toward the local church with the creation of regional ministers as mission enablers. *RR* argued for mission to be the purpose of associations. Stream 2 argued for association and union to be examples of "catholicity." They were the means of relating and expressions of relating that already existed in Christ.

There was an issue in separating associating from associations, that is in suggesting associating (relating) was largely done by clusters and resourcing was done by associations. It was dependent upon local churches actively engaging in clusters. It was a top-down vision (from the council) of new ways of relating, but required bottom-up participation by the churches. In the decade that followed, anecdotally, clustering developed in some areas,

13. For example see, Fiddes, "Story and the Stories," and Fiddes, "Christianity, Culture and Education."

14. This followed the advice given by the denominational consultation.

but elsewhere was absent, and so local churches became even more remote from their association.[15] I suggest what was lacking was a shared identity that bound Baptist congregations together. While Baptists churches had in high numbers identified as evangelical, this did not translate into "build[ing] mutually supportive relationships," even though that had been the call of *RR* to the churches.[16] This was anticipated in *RR* when it suggested that some associating by churches would not necessarily be between Baptist churches. The relationship between association and union was still left unresolved and this was reflected when in 2007 the council issued a task group to look at Roles and Tasks and in particular the "ways in which the National Resource and Associations work together to serve churches."[17]

Tension 3: Theology versus Pragmatism

In both the previous tensions discussed the purpose of the union and the role of associations was the question of theology. In 1996 Haddon Wilmer wrote an article in the *BMJ* called "A Defence of Theology."[18] He argued that the church has to talk theologically because God is "theo-logical."[19] An article defending theology reflected some of the difficulty that stream 2 faced through the 1990s as it sought to give the conversations in the union a serious theological grounding.[20] In the aftermath of *The Nature of Assembly* report, the Doctrine and Worship Committee, still in its infancy, was despondent to its reception. It was said at the committee meeting that "Baptists had not exercised the ability to think doctrinally for a long time, so now it was challenging for all" and that this was reflected in what was

15. Paul Goodliff states that "the reality is that the implementation of the recommendations about more local associating has been fragmentary and lacking in vision and vigour," Goodliff, *Networks*, 3.

16. *Relating and Resourcing*, 10. Haymes has reflected that in a few generations Baptists had moved from singing "Blest be the tie that binds" to "Bind us together," Haymes, "Still Blessing the Ties That Bind," 100–101.

17. *Report of the Roles and Tasks Group*. Presented to the Council of the Baptist Union in November 2008. The proposals of this report failed to find any agreement.

18. Willmer, "Defence of Theology." Willmer, a Baptist, was Professor of Theology at the University of Leeds from the mid-1990s having been lecturer and then senior lecturer from 1966. The article was at the request of the then editor, Gethin Abraham-Williams. He had written to Willmer asking him to write about "the uneasy relation between theological reflection and pragmatic activism" and suggested that "in a survival situation, theology appears to be a luxury we can no longer afford," 15.

19. Willmer, "Defence of Theology," 18.

20. Wright also saw the importance of theology, *Challenge to Change*, 240, and Wright, "Theology in the Service of the Church," 33–38.

termed a "cultural vandalism in the resistance to theological terms."[21] The committee members were left wondering whether they were being asked to provide "theological thinkers" or were they an "educational unit." Both Fiddes and Wright understood theology to be in service of the church, the difficulty was that many of those on council at the key moments did not appear that interested in theology.

Haymes has claimed that for all the restructuring and new ideas in the union, "the heart of the problem has been in our limited understanding of our shared life in God."[22] In his view "contemporary British Baptists . . . are nothing if not pragmatic," which means, he says, that they "have a wariness of 'theology' for we can fear that it is remote, academic, out of touch with the realities of life."[23] This is despite the second stream and its call to mind in 1981 and its argument for a Baptist way of doing theology in 2000. The impact of stream 2 was limited, as they acknowledged.[24] Again context here matters. They were making arguments for greater theological engagement in a period when the church was facing up to church decline and where a large part of evangelicalism had embraced a form of "charismatic entrepreneurialism" that was focused on activism and a tendency, in Stackhouse's terms, to "faddism."

It is my view that the more theologically rich reports written by the Doctrine and Worship Committee, along with *TS*, struggled to get a good hearing. This was for several reasons. First of all there was not enough time given to their consideration. In most cases a section of one council meeting was given to their discussion. While the process engaged in listening, it was undertaken at a pace that left some of the big questions, such as those identified above, unresolved. This might be viewed as the price that was paid to ensure change happened and avoid the inertia of the previous thirty years. The impact of this is the more theological reports which could have been the basis for reaching the kind of theological agreement that Champion had said was needed were passed over. In a similar way to Haymes, John Briggs has named "pragmatism and an easy seduction by the anticipation of short term success" as the "besetting sin of Baptists."[25]

Second, the reports were written as theological arguments in a setting not used to doing theology, or at least not the kind of theology that speaks

21. Minutes, Doctrine & Worship Committee, January 9, 1995, 3.

22. Haymes, "Still Blessing the Ties That Bind," 102.

23. Haymes, "Still Blessing the Ties That Bind," 97.

24. "It would be foolish to suggest that our efforts were ever more than small contributory waves within the immensely broader tide of our denominational history," Fiddes et al., "Doing Theology Together" in *Doing Theology*, 16.

25. Briggs, "Baptists and Higher Education," 111.

in the language of the catholic tradition.[26] The other reflection from within the committee on *The Nature of Assembly* was that while it was good theology, it was poorly communicated. There is then, perhaps, a shared problem of communication and reception that Baptists struggled to overcome and did not adequately attempt to address. In Willmer's article there is a comment made that the key question asked is too often not "Is it true?" but "Does it work?"[27] Recognizing the strong strand among Baptists, present more in stream 1, for the functional and pragmatic over the often complex questions theology throws up.[28] Third there was a lack of clarity within the committee and wider in the council with the purpose of the Doctrine and Worship Committee, which hindered the style of the report and its reception. Fourth, and perhaps most important, the theology of covenant did not find sufficient consensus. Here perhaps it failed to show how its argument was biblical for a denomination that largely still looked for the plain sense of Scripture. Stream 2's argument from Baptist tradition was not one that found support in a denomination that was increasingly defined by a pan-evangelicalism encouraged by stream 1. Here stream 2 did not attempt to address the denomination in an evangelical voice and so missed an opportunity to build some bridges and convince a wider constituency. The concept of covenant did not disappear after 2002. Others have continued to engage with it and argue for it,[29] but it has remained a "minority report."[30]

In 1992 Haymes had asked "where are the scholars?" He was concerned that the denomination was not taking seriously the need for Christian scholars for the renewal of the church. He wrote, "The active encouragement of scholarly reflection is a sign of a lively church."[31] I would argue that Baptists have not really known what to do with the theologian. They have no equivalent to the Anglican position of Canon theologian. Baptists

26. For example, see Fiddes's brief remarks about the response to use of the word "episcope" during the discussion of *Forms of Ministry* in *Tracks and Traces*, 221.

27. Cf. Briggs, "Baptists and Higher Education," 111. Briggs says the same point had been noticed by George Beasley-Murray.

28. This can be seen in Coffey's comment that "those in the BUGB in the ecumenical structures have worked to move the debate from traditional questions like 'who is a true minister?' and 'who presides at the Eucharist?' to more mission-focused questions like 'how do we proclaim the Kingdom of God in a secular society?' and 'how do we engage in God's mission in an alien culture?'" Coffey, "Missionary Union," 93–94.

29. See Winter, *More Light and Truth?*; Dare, *Always on the Way and in the Fray*; and Sutcliffe-Pratt, *Covenant and Church for Rough Sleepers*.

30. Holmes, *Baptist Theology*, 159.

31. *BT*, August 6, 1992, 8.

have valued the pastor[32] and to a certain extent the historian,[33] but have not developed an appreciation for the theologian. Fiddes has made a defence of the "professional Christian scholar," even calling them in catholic language, "doctors of the church" who stand alongside those who hold pastoral office.[34] He sees the Christian scholar standing in the place between church and culture, or Jerusalem and Athens. Stephen Holmes has also reflected on the place of the scholar in Baptist life, arguing that "scholarship is necessary, but the scholar is not possessed of any authority within the church."[35] It is the gathered church who are called to discern the mind of Christ and while this must include "tak[ing] seriously what the best minds that God has given to His church have made of this or that question,"[36] they do not have the final say. Holmes here begins to describe the place of the scholar among Baptists, but it requires those who gather to recognize the place of theology in the act of discernment, which is problematic, as Holmes also says, when theology "has been something of a dirty word."[37] It is not just that theology for some Baptists has been a "dirty word," but as Sean Winter notes in reviewing Fiddes's *Tracks and Traces* that there is an "enormous gap that has to be crossed for theology of this depth and sophistication genuinely to connect with ministers and churches."[38] What this demonstrates, and this thesis has pointed to, is that for Baptists, particularly those on its council, there was a difficultly to engage in the kind of theological conversation that the likes of stream 2 were offering. Theology appeared superfluous in the argument for the priority of mission. Here then is another reason why Wright's more accessible theological treatment in *Challenge to Change* and *RR* and also the Bernard Green–chaired *Five Core Values* found a more favorable response. They were not untheological, but they were geared toward solutions rather than analysis.

Where the theological renewal stream succeeded, as mentioned in chapter 2, was in continuing to create spaces in the union for theology. In 1999 the principals organized a consultation for pastoral theologians and a second one was held in 2001, and further ones followed in 2006 and 2008.

---

32. They have also generally expected the pastor to be theologically educated. See Cross, *"To Communicate Simply."*

33. In the twentieth century see W. T. Whitley, A. C. Underwood, Ernest A. Payne, B. R. White, Roger Hayden, David Bebbington, John H. Y. Briggs, Brian Stanley, and Ian Randall.

34. Fiddes, "Place of the Christian Scholar," 140.

35. Holmes, "Theology in Context?," 8.

36. Holmes, "Theology in Context?," 8.

37. Holmes, "Theology in Context?," 3.

38. Winter, *"Tracks and Traces*: A Review Article," 445.

This encouraged a space for theology to be present in the life of the union, even if it only came from the margins. I suggest theological reflection has been a marginal activity in the life of the union as its leadership has continued to be overwhelmed by existential questions about its future.[39] This was demonstrated by the decline of the Doctrine and Worship Committee from the mid-2000s, already by then it had become more of talking shop than one producing reports. After its first three reports, all written largely by Paul Fiddes between 1992–1996, it produced only one more report based on a survey of Baptist worship in local churches,[40] indicating the specific role Fiddes had played. The Doctrine and Worship Committee became an example of an interesting exercise which failed to find a continuing place in the life of the union, which reflects the argument I've made about theology.[41]

The tension in the union between theology and pragmatism was reflected in the wider ecumenical conversation. As was discussed in chapter 5, the commitment of Baptists to ecumenism was an encouraging sign that most churches and ministers had accepted that there was no longer a need to be suspicious of ecumenism. There was no problem with being Evangelical and being ecumenical. However, the new ecumenism was no longer concerned with unity, at least in terms of faith and order, and was an expression more of shared commitments to mission that were cross-denominational. The endeavor of seeking to find theological solutions to church unity gave way to activity of common mission, which overlooked differences in ecclesiology.[42] Arguably, the evangelical activist mood took over the British ecumenical movement: it was easier to engage in mission together than to be a united church. This was one of the reasons that ecumenism had become even more palatable to Baptists by 1995—there was no suggestion of a united church in England on the horizon. Stream 1 were content with this position, but stream 2, particularly Fiddes, continued to push for the possibility of greater recognition in terms of baptism and ministry, seen in *Pushing at the Boundaries of Unity*. The slow and careful work of bilateral ecumenism was unpalatable to those who felt called to get on with the task of mission and evangelism.[43] Keith Clements wrote in 2007 that

39. Darrell Jackson would ask in 2002, "Does the Future Have a Denomination?"

40. Ellis, *Baptist Worship Today*.

41. By 2004 it had disappeared as a named committee in the Baptist Union Directory.

42. In the UK this had arguably been happening to some degree from the days of the Billy Graham missions in 1950s and onward.

43. Evident most clearly in the response of the council to *Pushing at the Boundaries of the Unity*.

the Free Churches need to ask if they have been accomplices in their own marginalisation, which cannot be accounted for by their numerical decline. Where have all the prophets gone, who could alarm people with a new nonconformist conscience? Or why is there now so little talk of actual visible unity except on Anglican or Roman Catholic terms?[44]

He went on to say that, "yes, we are 'together' but so what? At the end of the day, it is still the entrenched denominational structures that call the tune, protecting their mutually recognised no-go areas." Ecumenism dropped down the agenda of Baptist life, as arguably it did in other denominations and no significant attempts at greater unity have been made.

What Happened Next

The decade following 2002 saw the union undergo further discussions around reforms. Major reports on the role of the union president, the roles and tasks of the national resource and associations and a finance review were all undertaken, although without resolution. The union would appoint trustees in 2006 as demanded by the Charity Commission, although challenged by Fiddes and others,[45] and this added another layer to how the union made decisions. The National Strategy Forum organized, but led by Coffey, what was called The Dream Tour in 2003 to encourage local churches to think missionally.[46] The forum itself was discontinued in 2006. Coffey retired as general secretary in 2006 after fifteen years in post and was followed by Jonathan Edwards.[47] Through his tenure Coffey had been influential in holding the union together, through his ability to form good relationships and the wide respect in which he was held. After Coffey, this became harder as the regional associations had gained more power through the decisions made in 1999 and initiated in 2002. By 2012 a further financial crisis saw the union begin what was called the Futures Process and further changes in the union were made, some of which were arguably the completion of some of the proposals in *RR*. The union rebranded itself in 2013 as Baptists

44. *BT*, March 15, 2007, 13.

45. See Fiddes and Sparkes, "Trusteeship." This paper was present to council for discussion at the November 2005 meeting and had been prepared by Paul Fiddes and Graham Sparkes.

46. Coffey, "Sharing the Dream," 1–2.

47. Edwards had been the regional minister team leader in the South West Baptist Association.

Together.[48] The impact is arguably that the union is now weaker than it was during the 1990s and that this is a result, at least partly, although unintentionally, from the decisions that were taken in this decade. It might be claimed that the emphasis on mission over identity has meant that Baptists in the twenty-first century are even more uncertain on what it means to be Baptist. That is, Baptists still await "the clearer, more coherent and more widely accepted theology" that Champion had called for in 1979.

The 1980s and 1990s were an exciting time to be a Baptist. Mainstream and the wider evangelical and charismatic movements did bring life to Baptist churches, at least in terms of worship. At the beginning of 1991 there was an anticipation about what the decade would bring and this bore fruit in the creativity of thinking, both theologically and structurally, that took place in these years. The "Champion" group gave new energy to the theological thinking of the union and some of the reports and booklets during this period have had a continuing legacy of sorts, twenty years on.[49] It must be recognized that the task of renewing the union that Coffey and others undertook was immense. Stuart Murray called it an "attempt to recalibrate the denomination for mission."[50] The need for renewal was one that was rightly discerned and the commitment to see it through should, I suggest, be applauded.

When compared to the United Reformed Church, the Baptist Union largely held their numbers between 1980 and 2002. Between 1980 and 2000, the number of members in churches in membership with the Baptist Union fell by 11,918 (7.7 percent) to 142,058.[51] In the same period in the United Reformed Church, the numbers of members fell by 60,087 (40.7 percent) to 87,250.[52] By 2009 the Baptist Union had dropped to 136,808 and the United Reformed to 68,616.[53] This might be an argument that the denominational reforms got something right, that despite not generating church growth, Baptists had not witnessed serious decline. What made the Baptists different from the URC? Martin Camroux's assessment of the URC is it is "a church largely dying by its roots."[54]

48. See Andy Goodliff, "BUGB and Baptists Together: Reflections on a Baptist Rebranding," *Baptist Times*, https://www.baptist.org.uk/Articles/375533/BUGB_and_ Baptists.aspx.

49. They are referenced every now and again in council minutes and reports, although arguably not with any sustained engagement.

50. Murray, *Church After Christendom*, 142.

51. Table 9.2.2 in Brierley, *Religious Trends 1998/1999*.

52. Table 8.11.4 in Brierley, *Religious Trends 1998/1999*.

53. See Brierley, *UK Church Statistics 2005–2015*.

54. Camroux, *Ecumenism in Retreat*, 190.

Historically the Congregationalists had been the Baptists' closest neighbors.[55] They moved in 1967 from being a Congregational Union to a Congregational Church, which paved the way for the creation of the United Reformed Church with the Presbyterians in 1972. This suggested that there was greater openness ecumenically in contrast to the Baptists who have been much more wary and guarded. In addition, there was also a shift in theology, while Baptists became more evangelical, the Congregationalists became more theologically liberal.[56] The result being that the two denominations became increasingly "distinct organizationally and theologically"[57] from each other. They moved from being neighbors, with hopes of greater union in the late nineteenth century, to charting quite different paths.

It was evangelical churches in England that were growing[58] and the Baptist Union was much more an evangelical denomination.[59] Baptists through the 1990s responded to the challenge to change by undergoing "a blending of Baptist identity into a broader charismatic-evangelicalism" which articulated the importance of relevant mission.[60] Camroux's analysis argues that the big problem within the URC has been the task of articulating a shared identity in a Church that has emerged from three traditions in the mix of wider markers of identity and the creation of new structures.[61] It might also be noted that for financial reasons the URC have had to consolidate ministry, with many congregations having to share ministry, where the majority of Baptist churches have been able to continue with ministry in each local congregation,[62] with some churches able to invest in also appointing youth workers and other specific ministries.[63]

55. Ernest Payne argued that "the history of Baptists and Congregationalists is, I believe, one and indivisible . . . Only by ignoring the facts of history, or by special pleading, can the two denominations be regarded as entirely separate Christian traditions," *Free Churchmen*, 93.

56. See Briggs, *Two Congregational Denominations*, 26–46. This was despite the attempts of the "Genevan" movement described in ch. 3.

57. Camroux, *Ecumenism in Retreat*, 143.

58. According to Brierley between 1990–2000 the only groups of Christians growing were Charismatic Evangelicals and Mainstream Evangelicals, table 2.17.2, Brierley *Religious Trends 1998/1999*.

59. The URC had a similar evangelical group like Mainstream called GEAR (standing for Group for Evangelism and Renewal), which had been set up in 1974, but they were smaller in numbers, more conservative and never had the impact that Mainstream had.

60. Randall, "Baptist Growth in Britain," 76.

61. Camroux, *Ecumenism in Retreat*, 166–67. Cf. Orchard, "Case Study 1," 82.

62. Briggs, *Two Congregational Denominations*, 40.

63. The growth of paid youth workers among Baptists was recognized by the

Therefore while Camroux's recent study of the URC tells the story of a denomination in decline, this study has not given an account of a Baptist Union in decline.[64] It has argued that the renewal of the union left much unresolved and as such was not as successful as had been hoped, and that this in part reflected, I have argued, a theological malaise in which doing (at least in terms of mission) was elevated above a shared story and sense of belonging, which means that the conversation about what it means to be Baptist, and also evangelical, and ecumenical, must go on.

---

creation in the union of the office of "Youth Specialist" as a recognized accredited ministry in the late 1990s.

64. While the number of churches in membership with the Baptist Union and the number of church members did fall (see appendix 3), it was a slow decline and this was offset by an increase in regular attendance to Sunday services. See Jackson, "Attenders, Members, and Candlestick Makers in an LCF Age." Cf. Randall, "Baptist Growth in Britain."

Appendix 1

Timeline of Key Events between 1991–2002

1991   Appointment of David Coffey and Keith Jones as General and Deputy General Secretary

Listening Days in each of the 12 Areas of the Union

1992   March: Council agree *Towards 2000* document with Statement of Intent

Creation of Faith & Unity Executive, including the Doctrine & Worship Committee

1993   March: Council agree National Mission Strategy

1994   *The Nature of Assembly and the Council of the Baptist Union of Great Britain*

1995   Assembly reaffirms Coffey and Jones for another 5 years.

Assembly agrees to continue membership of CCBI & CTE

Listening Days across the Union.

1996   *Transforming Superintendency; Something to Declare*

September: Denominational Consultation

November: Council agrees to set up Denominational Consultation Report Group (DCRG)

1997   March: Council agrees to the creation of the Department of Research and Training

in Mission

November: Council receives report on Translocal Leadership

1998   *Relating and Resourcing; 5 Core Values for a Gospel People*

Area Focus Days

1999   March Council: Final Report from DCRG

13 March: National Baptists Leaders Day

November: Council receives reports from National Steering Group
& Covenant Task Group

2000   March: Council agrees to establish a National Strategy Forum and a
National Settlement Team

Assembly affirms Coffey for a third term as General Secretary

2001   *Covenant 21*

2002   January: 13 New Regional Associations created with Regional Ministers

Appendix 2

Mainstream Members of Baptist Union Council

1979: Douglas McBain, Paul Beasley-Murray, Raymond Brown, David Coffey, and Barrie White.

1985: David Coffey, Douglas McBain, Jack Ramsbottom, Raymond Brown, Barrie White, Paul Beasley-Murray, Pat Goodland, and David Staple.

1990: David Coffey, Derek Tidball, Peter Grange, Stephen Ibbotson, Pat Goodland, Michael Bochenski, Terry Griffith, Paul Beasley-Murray, Brian Nicholls, and Douglas McBain.

1994: David Coffey, Stephen Gaukroger, Derek Tidball, Terry Griffith, Michael Bochenski, Douglas McBain, Peter Grange, Stephen Ibbotson, and Nigel Wright.

1998: Douglas McBain, David Coffey, Michael Bochenski, Nigel Wright, Steven Hembrey, John Weaver, Lynn Green, Stephen Gaukroger, Peter Grange, and Brian Nicholls.

Mainstream People and Baptist Union Appointments

1986 David Coffey was President of the Baptist Union.

1988 David Coffey was appointed the Baptist Union Secretary for Evangelism.

1989 Douglas McBain was appointed General Superintendent for the Metropolitan Area.

1990 Derek Tidball was President of the Baptist Union.

1991 David Coffey became General Secretary of the Baptist Union and Derek Tidball was appointed the Secretary for Evangelism.

1994 Peter Grange was appointed General Superintendent for the East Midland Area and Stephen Gaukroger was President of the Baptist Union.

1995 Brian Nicholls was appointed General Superintendent for the West Midland Area.

1998 Douglas McBain was President of the Baptist Union.

1999 Michael Bochenski was President of the Baptist Union.

2002 Nigel Wright was President of the Baptist Union.

Appendix 3

Baptist Union of Great Britain Church Statistics[1]

Year	No. of churches in membership with the BU	No. of church members	No. of baptisms
1968	2,189	216,190	
1969	2,200	210,495	
1970	2,194	207,017	
1971	2,179	201,646	
1972	2,179	198,324	
1973	2,197	190,565	5,295
1974	2,182	187,144	5,323
1975	2,191	187,066	5,215
1976	2,137	181,798	5,090
1977	2,086	178,461	5,575
1978	2,091	174,578	5,711
1979	2,100	170,999	5,782
1980	2,058	170,338	6,516
1982	2,052	168,582	6,455
1983	2,070	166,688	6,472
1984	2,064	168,300	8,383
1985	2,064	170,318	7,940
1986	2,132	170,160	7,408

1. These numbers have been taken from the figures found in the annual *The Baptist Union Directory*.

1987	2,111	167,466	6,079
1988	2,155	164,095	5,781
1989	2,151	161,377	6,124
1990	2,150	159,945	5,554
1991	2,118	160,143	5,443
1992	2,113	158,207	5,204
1993	2,130	156,939	4,830
1994	2,130	154,916	4,662
1995	2,130	152,603	3,950
1996	2,131	150,289	4,029
1997	2,114	147,089	4,062
1998		144,932	3,736
1999		144,056	3,976
2000		144,636	4,036
2002	2,028	138,089	3,951

Between 1971 and 1977 a total of 52 churches left the Union, largely as a result of the Michael Taylor controversy.

In 1983, the Union changed how it recorded the number of churches. From this point the returns made in the January were taken as a record of the previous year's statistics.

The increase in membership and baptisms in the mid–1980s correlates with the Billy Graham Mission England events. See Randall, "Baptist Growth in England," 59–60.

There is without doubt a steady drop in membership from 1968 to 2002, although actual church attendance through the 1990s increased. People were involving themselves in church life and attending worship, but were not becoming formal church members. There was a membership problem.

Bibliography

Angus Library, Oxford

Baptist Union Council, Minutes and Supporting Documents
Also including Doctrine and Worship Committee, Mission Committee, Advisory
   Committee for Church Relations
Fellowship of British Baptists, Minutes and Supporting Documents
Paul Beasley-Murray Papers
Barrie White Papers, including minutes of Mainstream Executive
1992 Listening Days
Denominational Consultation
Denominational Consultation Review Group

Baptist Union Reports

Listed Chronologically

The Baptist Doctrine of the Church. London: Baptist Union, 1948.
Church Relations in England. London: Carey Kingsgate, 1953.
The Report of the Commission on the Associations. London: Baptist Union, 1964.
Call to Obedience: A Study in Evangelism. London: Baptist Union, 1969.
Visible Unity in Life and Mission. London: Baptist Union, 1977.
Working Group on the General Superintendency to the Baptist Union Council. London:
   Baptist Union, 1978, 1979.
Signs of Hope. London: Baptist Union, 1979.
A Call to Commitment. London: Baptist Union, 1980.
The Structures Report. N.d.: Listening Day Process, 1992.
Towards 2000: Notes from the Special Interest Groups March 1992 Council. N.d.: Listening
   Day Process, 1992.
A Ten Year Plan towards 2000 Incorporating the National Mission Strategy. Listening
   Day Process. Didcot: Baptist Union, 1993.
A "Green Paper" on Council Restructuring. Listening Day Process. Didcot: Baptist
   Union, 1994.
The Nature of the Assembly and the Council of Baptist Union of Great Britain. Didcot:
   Baptist Union, 1994.

Forms of Ministry amongst Baptists: Towards an Understanding of Spiritual Leadership. Didcot: Baptist Union, 1994.

Believing and Being Baptized: Baptism, So-Called Re-baptism, and Children in the Church. Didcot: Baptist Union, 1996.

Transforming Superintendency: The Report of the General Superintendency Review Group. Didcot: Baptist Union, 1996.

Beginning with God: A Guide to Prayer, Study and Reflection in Preparation for the Denominational Consultation. Didcot: Baptist Union, 1996.

Responses: Denominational Consultation. Didcot: Baptist Union, 1996.

Summary of Response: Denominational Consultation. Didcot: Baptist Union, 1996.

Relating and Resourcing: The Report of the Task Group on Associating. Didcot: Baptist Union, 1998.

Five Core Values for a Gospel People. Didcot: Baptist Union, 1998.

Five Core Values for a Gospel People: Bible Study Pack. Didcot: Baptist Union, 1999.

National Baptist Leaders' Day. Wembley, March 13, 1999. Didcot: Baptist Union, 1999.

Continuing the Journey: The Final Report of the Denominational Consultation Reference Group. Didcot: Baptist Union, 1999.

Clustering: A Dynamic for Mission. Didcot: Baptist Union, 1999.

Covenant 21: Covenant for a Gospel People. Didcot: Baptist Union, 2000.

Making Moral Choices in Our Relationships. Didcot: Baptist Union, 2000.

Evangelism for a Gospel People. Didcot: Baptist Union 2002.

Baptist Union Directory. London/Didcot: Baptist Union, 1970–2013.

Baptist Union Annual Report. London/Didcot: Baptist Union, 1970–1995.

Baptist Leader. A Baptist Union magazine for ministers, theological students, and those in leadership, 1–28. Didcot: Baptist Union, 1992–2002.

SecCheck. A Baptist Union magazine for church secretaries, treasurers, and administrators, 1–28. Didcot: Baptist Union, 1992–2002.

InfoMission. Didcot: Baptist Union, 1992–2002.

Home Mission News. Didcot: Baptist Union, 1996–2002.

Transform. Didcot: Baptist Union, 2002–2006.

Ecumenical Reports and Documents

Listed Chronologically

Baptist, Eucharist and Ministry. Faith and Order Paper no. 111. Geneva: World Council of Churches, 1982.

What on Earth Is the Church For? London: British Council of Churches, 1986.

Views from the Pews: Lent '86 and Local Ecumenism. London: British Council of Churches, 1986.

Reflections: How Churches View Their Life and Mission. London: British Council of Churches, 1986.

Not Strangers but Pilgrims. Report of the Swanwick Conference, August 31 to September 4, 1987. London: British Council of Churches and Catholic Truth Society, 1988.

Churches Together in Pilgrimage. London: British Council of Churches and Catholic Truth Society, 1989.

The Forgotten Trinity 1: The Report of the BCC Study Commission on Trinitarian Doctrine Today. London: British Council of Churches, 1989.

Called to Be One. London: Churches Together in England, 1996.

General Bibliography

Amess, Robert. *One in the Truth? The Cancer of Division in the Evangelical Church.* Eastbourne: Kingsway, 1988.

Ammerman, Nancy. "On Being a Denomination." In *Findings: A Report of the Special Study Commission to the Study the Question; "Should the Cooperative Baptist Fellowship Become a Separate Convention?,"* edited by W. Randall Lolley et al., 21–31. Atlanta: Cooperative Baptist Fellowship, 1996.

Atherstone, Andrew. "*Reinventing English Evangelicalism*: Reviews and Responses." *Anvil* 26 (2009) 201–5.

Astley, Jeff, and Leslie J. Francis, eds. *Exploring Ordinary Theology.* Aldershot: Ashgate, 2013.

Aubrey, M. E. Foreword to *Fraternal* 68 (1948) 3–5.

Avis, Paul. *A Ministry Shaped by Mission.* London: Continuum, 2004.

———. *Reshaping Ecumenical Theology.* London: T. & T. Clark, 2010.

"Baptist Union of Great Britain." In *Churches Respond to BEM*, edited by Max Thurian, 1:70–77. Faith and Order Paper 129. Geneva: World Council of Churches, 1986.

Beasley-Murray, George. "Confessing Baptist Identity." In *A Perspective on Baptist Identity*, edited by David Slater, 75–85. Ilkley: Mainstream, 1987.

———. *Renewed for Mission.* The Presidential Address delivered at the Annual Assembly of the Baptist Union of Great Britain and Ireland, London, April 29, 1968. London: Baptist Union, 1968.

Beasley-Murray, Paul. "Assembly—a Deliberative Body?" *Fraternal* 180 (June 1977) 19–23.

———. *A Call to Excellence.* London: Hodder & Stoughton, 1995.

———. "Concerns about *Relating and Resourcing*." Unpublished paper presented to Senior Management Team of BUGB, April 1999.

———. *Dynamic Leadership.* Eastbourne: MARC, 1990.

———. "Evangelism—a National Priority." *Fraternal* 215 (1986) 17–23.

———. *Fearless for Truth: A Personal Portrait of the Life of George Beasley-Murray.* Carlisle: Paternoster, 2002.

———. "Mainstream—the Fountain Trust in Another Guise?" *Mainstream Newsletter* 7 (1981) 1.

———. "A Mainstream Retrospective." *Mainstream Magazine* 63 (1998) 10–12.

———. *Radical Believers: A Baptist Way of Being Church.* Didcot: Baptist Union, 1992.

———. "Renewal in Baptist Churches." *Renewal* 130 (1987) 27–28.

———. *This Is My Story.* Eugene, OR: Wipf & Stock, 2018.

———. "Toward a Biblical/Theological Framework for Evangelism." *Fraternal* 232 (1990) 18–23.

———. *Turning the Tide: An Assessment of Baptist Church Growth in England.* London: Bible Society, 1981.

Beaumont, Mike. "Growing Together in Committed Covenant Relationships." *Mainstream Newsletter* 13 (1983) 2–4.

Bebbington, David. *Baptists through the Centuries*. Waco, TX: Baylor, 2012.

―――. "Evangelical Trends, 1959–2009." *Anvil* 26 (2009) 93–122.

―――. *Evangelicalism in Modern Britain*. London: Unwin Hyman, 1989.

Best, Ernest. *Ephesians*. Edinburgh: T. & T. Clark, 2001.

Birch, Ian. *To Follow the Lambe Wheresover He Goeth: The Ecclesial Polity of the English Calvinistic Baptists, 1640–1660*. Eugene, OR: Pickwick, 2017.

Blyth, Myra. *Pilgrim People—Inclusive Community?* London: London Preachers' Association, 2003.

―――. "A Visible Unity." In *Gathering Disciples: Essays in Honor of Christopher J. Ellis*, edited by Myra Blyth and Andy Goodliff, 128–51. Eugene, OR: Pickwick, 2017.

Bochenski, Michael. *Baptists and Ecumenism—Still Better Together?* Signposts for a New Century: Exploring Baptist Distinctives. Hertfordshire: Hertfordshire Baptist Association, 2000.

―――. "Churches Together in Pilgrimage." *Mainstream Newsletter* 32 (1989) 2–4.

―――, ed. *Evangelicals and Ecumenism*. Didcot: Baptist Union, 1993.

Bonser, Henry. "The First Baptist Union Superintendents." *Fraternal* 68 (1948) 8–10.

―――. "Recollections of a Superintendent." *Baptist Quarterly* 13 (1949) 172–79.

―――. "The Work of a General Superintendent." *Baptist Quarterly* 2 (1925) 315–18.

Bosch, David. *Transforming Mission*. Maryknoll, NY: Orbis, 1991.

Bowers, Faith. "Baptists and Other Christians: An Historical Perspective." In *Evangelicals and Ecumenism*, edited by Michael Bochenski, 13–18. Didcot: Baptist Union, 1993.

―――. "Discussion Relating to ICP." December 17, 1991. ACCR 1992 Papers.

―――. "Prophets and Pietists." In *Questions of Identity*, edited by Anthony R. Cross and Ruth Gouldbourne, 189–206. Oxford: Centre for Baptist History and Heritage, 2011.

―――. "Unity in Legitimate Diversity: A Baptist Perspective." *One in Christ* 37 (2002) 55–64.

Brackney, William H. *A Genetic History of Baptist Thought*. Macon, GA: Mercer, 2004.

Brackney, William, et al., eds. *Pilgrim Pathways: Essays in Baptist History in Honour of B. R. White*. Macon, GA: Mercer, 1999.

Brierley, Peter, ed. *Religious Trends 1998/1999*. Christian Research, 1999.

―――. *UK Church Statistics* 2005–2015. Tonbridge, 2011.

Briggs, John H. Y. "Baptists and Higher Education in England." In *Faith, Life and Witness*, edited by William Brackney, 92–115. Birmingham, AL: Samford, 1990.

―――. "Confessional Identity, Denominational Institutions and Relations with Others." In *Recycling the Past or Researching History?*, edited by Anthony R. Cross and Philip E. Thompson, 1–24. Milton Keynes: Paternoster, 2005.

―――. "Double Affirmations: Baptists Since 1945." In *Faith, Heritage and Witness*, edited by John H. Y. Briggs, 60–64. London: Baptist Historical Society, 1987.

―――. *The English Baptists of the Nineteenth Century*. Didcot: Baptist Historical Society, 1994.

―――. "Evangelical Ecumenism: The Amalgamation of General and Particular Baptists in 1891." *Baptist Quarterly* 34 (July and October 1991) 99–115, 160–79.

―――. *Two Congregational Denominations: Baptists and Paedobaptist*. Congregational Lecture 2010. London: Congregational Memorial Hall Trust, 2010.

Brown, Callum. *The Death of Christian Britain*. London: Routledge, 2001.

Burnard, Clive. "Transformational Servant Leadership as Exemplified in the Ministry of the Reverend Doctor David R. Coffey." DMin thesis, University of Wales, 2014.

Cameron, Helen, et al. *Talking about God in Practice*. London: SCM, 2010.

Campbell, R. Alistair. *The Elders: Seniority within Earliest Christianity*. London: T. & T. Clark 2004.

———. "The Grounds of Association." In *A Perspective on Baptist Identity*, edited by David Slater, 31–39. Ilkley, UK: Mainstream, 1987.

———. "An Open Letter to Paul Fiddes on 'Charismatic Renewal.'" *Mainstream Newsletter* 6 (1981) 3–5.

———. "Review: *Bound to Love*." *Mainstream Newsletter* 20 (1985) 14–15

———. "Scratching the Surface." Editorial. *Mainstream Newsletter* 13 (April 1983) 1.

Camroux, Martin. *Ecumenism in Retreat: How the United Reformed Church Failed to Break the Mould*. Eugene, OR: Wipf & Stock, 2016.

Carter, David. "Baptist Ecclesiology." *Ecclesiology* 1 (2005) 87–93.

———. "Where Are We Ecclesiologically?" *One in Christ* 35 (1999).

Champion, Leonard G. "Baptist Church Life in the Twentieth Century—Some Personal Reflections." In *Baptists in the Twentieth Century*, edited by K. W. Clements, 4–14. London: Baptist Historical Society, 1983.

———. "The Baptist Doctrine of the Church in Relation to Scripture, Tradition and the Holy Spirit."*Foundations* 2 (1959) 27–39.

———. "Evangelical Calvinism and the Structures of Baptist Church Life." *Baptist Quarterly* 28 (1980) 196–208.

———. "The Statement of the Denomination." In *The Denominational Conference*, 25–26. London: Baptist Union, 1961.

———. "Whither the Baptists?" In *Bible, Church and the World*, edited by John Briggs, 64–68. London: Baptist Historical Society, 1989.

Chapman, Alister. *Godly Ambition: John Stott and the Evangelical Movement*. Oxford: Oxford University Press, 2012.

Child, R. L. *Expecting Justice, but Seeing Bloodshed: Some Baptist Contributions to Following Jesus in a Violent World*. Oxford: Whitley, 2004.

———, ed. *For the Sake of the Church: Essays to Honour Paul S. Fiddes*. Oxford: Regent's Park College, 2014.

———, ed. *The General Superintendency 1915-1965*. London: Baptist Union, 1965.

Clarke, Anthony, ed. *Bound for Glory? God, Church and World in Covenant*. Oxford: Whitley, 2002.

Clarke, Anthony J., and Paul S. Fiddes. *Dissenting Spirit: A History of Regent's Park College, 1752-2017*. Oxford: Regent's Park College, 2017.

Clements, Keith. "Covenant and Community." In *Bound to Love: The Covenant Basis of Baptist Life and Mission*, edited by Paul Fiddes, 50–62. London: Baptist Union, 1985.

———. *Ecumenical Dynamic*. Geneva: WCC, 2013.

———. "Facing Secularism." In *A Call to Mind: Baptist Essays towards a Theology of Commitment*, 9–21. London: Baptist Union, 1981.

———. "Free Church, National Church: Dropping Pretences for Unity." *Theology* 113 (2010) 421–28.

———. "The Larger Context: Morris West, Servant of World Ecumenism." In *Baptists Together*, 19–29. Didcot: Baptist Historical Society, 2000.

———. *Look Back In Hope: An Ecumenical Life*. Eugene, OR: Resource, 2017.

————. *Lovers of Discord: Twentieth Century Theological Controversies in England.* London: SPCK, 1988.

————. "Moltmann on the Congregation." *Baptist Quarterly* 28 (1979) 101–9.

————. *A Patriotism for Today: Dialogue with Dietrich Bonhoeffer.* Bristol: Bristol Baptist College, 1984.

————. "Profile: David Russell." *Epworth Review* 23 (1996) 21–33.

————. Review of *Making a Denomination. Baptist Quarterly* 40 (2003) 124–28.

————. *What Freedom? The Persistent Challenge of Dietrich Bonhoeffer.* Bristol: Bristol Baptist College, 1990.

Coffey, David. *All One in Christ Jesus: A Passionate Appeal for Evangelical Unity.* Milton Keynes: Authentic, 2009.

————. "Apostolic Ministry for Today?" *Talk: The Mainstream Magazine* (2002) 4–6.

————."Apostolic Ministry within Our Circles: A Baptist Union perspective." Address given to Mainstream Consultation, Gorsley, November 2003. Unpublished.

————. "Beyond the Fringe." *Baptist Leader* 22 (Winter 1999/2000).

————. *Build That Bridge: The Presidential Address Delivered at the Baptist Assembly 28th April 1986, Westminster Chapel, London.* London: Baptist Union, 1986.

————. *Build That Bridge.* Eastbourne: Kingsway, 1986.

————. "Comments from General Secretary at Final Baptist Union Council meeting, Swanwick, 22 March, 2006." Unpublished.

————. "Committed, but Critical." *SecCheck* (Spring 1995).

————. "Continuing Journey of Reform." Address to BU Council, November 2002. Unpublished.

————. "Clear Choices." *Baptist Leader* 19 (Spring 1998).

————. "Covenant 21." *Baptist Leader* 24 (Winter 2000).

————. "Creating the Future." *Baptist Leader* 16 (Spring 1997).

————. "The Denominational Consultation." *Baptist Leader* 13 (Winter 1995).

————."The Evangelistic Task for the 1990s." Address to Mainstream Conference, January 1989. Unpublished.

————. Foreword to *Challenge to Change: A Radical Agenda for Baptists*, by Nigel Wright, 9–10. Eastbourne: Kingsway, 1991.

————. Foreword to *The Home Mission Story*, by Douglas C. Sparkes, 7–10. Didcot: Baptist Union, 1995.

————. Foreword to *Mission in the New Millennium*, edited by Clive Doubleday, 5–6. London: London Baptist Association, 1998.

————. Foreword to *Radical Believers*, by Paul Beasley-Murray, 4. Didcot: Baptist Union, 1992.

————. Foreword to *Something to Declare: A Study of the Declaration of Principle*, edited by Richard Kidd, 6–7. Didcot: Baptist Union, 1996.

————. Foreword to *Translocal Ministry*, edited by Stuart Murray, iii–iv. Didcot: Baptist Union, 2004.

————. "Guard the Vision." *Baptist Leader* 15 (Winter 1996).

————."In the Unshakeable Kingdom—All Structures Are Provisional." Address to Association Officers Weekend, September 1993. Unpublished.

————. Introduction to *Challenging to Change: Dialogues with a Radical Baptist Theologian*, edited by Pieter J. Lalleman, 1–3. London: Spurgeon's College, 2009.

————. Introduction to *Covenant 21*, i. Didcot: Baptist Union, 2001.

————. "It's Time to Cross Some Bridges." *BT* (March 30, 1995) 7–11.

———. "The Journey Thus Far." *Baptist Ministers' Journal* 240 (1992) 3–6.

———. "Listening Day Questions." *Baptist Leader* 12 (Autumn 1995).

———. "Mainstream 20th Anniversary Edition." *Mainstream Magazine* 63 (1998) 3–6.

———. "A Missionary Union: Past, Present and Future Perspectives." In *Truth That Never Dies: The Dr. G. R. Beasley-Murray Memorial Lectures*, edited by Nigel Wright, 87–113. Eugene, OR: Pickwick, 2014.

———. "Misunderstandings and Disagreements." *Baptist Leader* 11 (Spring 1995).

———. "Much Loved throughout Our Churches." *Spurgeon's College Record* 82 (Summer 1986) 5.

———. "National Baptist Leaders Day Wembley, 13 March 1999." Unpublished.

———. "No Reform without Consent." *Baptist Leader* 20 (1998).

———. "The Outsider, the Insider and the Young." *Baptist Leader* 9 (Summer 1994).

———. "Post 2000—What Kind of Union?" *Baptist Ministers' Journal* 255 (1996) 7–11.

———. "Sharing the Dream." *Transform* (Spring 2003) 1–2.

———. "So You Want to Build a Ship?" *Talk: The Mainstream Magazine* 4 (2004) 4–5.

———. "Towards 2000." *Baptist Leader* 3 (1992).

———. "When the Spirit Comes." *Baptist Leader* 10 (Winter 1994/1995).

Colwell, John. "Catholicity and Confessionalism." *Baptist Quarterly* 43 (2009) 4–23.

———. "The Church as Sacrament." In *Baptist Sacramentalism* 2, edited by Anthony R. Cross and Philip E. Thompson, 48–60. Milton Keynes: Paternoster, 2008.

———. "'In the Beginning Was the Word . . .': On Language and Presence." In *Within the Love of God: Essays on the Doctrine of God in Honour of Paul S. Fiddes*, edited by Anthony Clarke and Andrew Moore, 47–60. Oxford: Oxford University Press, 2014.

———. "Integrity and Relatedness: Some Critical Reflections on Congregationalism and Connexionalism." *Baptist Quarterly* 48 (2017) 11–22.

———. *Living the Christian Story*. Edinburgh: T. & T. Clark, 2001.

———. "Mission as Ontology: A Question of Theological Grammar." *Baptist Ministers' Journal* (2006) 7–12.

———. *Promise and Presence*. Milton Keynes: Paternoster, 2005.

Cook, Henry. *What Baptists Stand For*. 3rd ed. London: Carey Kingsgate, 1958.

Copson, Stephen. "General Baptists in the Eighteenth Century." In *Challenge and Change: English Baptist Life in the Eighteenth Century*, edited by Stephen Copson and Peter J. Morden, 29–56. Didcot: Baptist Historical Society, 2017.

———. "Renewing Associations: An Early-Eighteenth-Century Example." *Baptist Quarterly* 38 (2000) 264–76.

Cornick, David. "The Story of the English Ecumenical Endeavour." In *Unity in Process: Reflections on Ecumenism*, edited by Clive Barrett, 60–78. London: DLT, 2012.

Cross, Anthony R. *Baptism and the Baptists. Theology and Practice in Twentieth Century Britain*. Carlisle: Paternoster, 2000.

———. "Service to the Ecumenical Movement: The Contribution of British Baptists." *Baptist Quarterly* 38 (1999) 107–22.

———. "To Communicate Simply You Must Understand Profoundly": Preparation for Ministry among British Baptists. Didcot: Baptist Historical Society, 2016.

Dare, Helen. *Always On the Way and In the Fray: Reading the Bible as Baptists*. 2014 Whitley Lecture. Oxford: Whitley, 2014.

Davie, Grace. *Religion in Britain: A Persistent Paradox*. Oxford: Wiley, 2015.

Doel, Graham. "Church Planting in the Baptist Union of Great Britain, 1980–2010: A Critical Study." MPhil diss., University of Manchester, 2010.

Dudley-Smith, Timothy. *John Stott: A Global Ministry.* Leicester: InterVarsity, 2001.

Edwards, Joel. "The Evangelical Alliance: A National Phenomenon." In *For Such a Time as This,* edited by Steve Brady and Harold Rowdon, 49–59. Milton Keynes: Scripture Union, 1996.

Ellis, Christopher J. *Baptist Worship Today.* Didcot: Baptist Union, 1999.

———. "Spirituality in Mission." In *Under the Rule of Christ,* edited by Paul S. Fiddes, 169–87. Macon, GA: Smyth & Helwys, 2008.

———. *Together on the Way: A Theology of Ecumenism.* London: BCC, 1990.

Ellis, Christopher J., and Myra Blyth, eds. *Gathering for Worship: Patterns and Prayers for the Community of Disciples.* Norwich: Canterbury, 2005.

Ellis, Robert. "'The Leadership of Some . . .': Baptist Ministers as Leaders?" In *Challenging to Change,* edited by Pieter Lalleman, 71–86. London: Spurgeon's College, 2009.

Ensign-George, Barry. "Denomination as Ecclesiological Category: Sketching an Assessment." In *Denomination: Assessing an Ecclesiological Category,* edited by Paul M. Collins and Barry Ensign-George, 1–21. London: T. & T. Clark, 2011.

Fiddes, Paul S. "The Atonement and the Trinity." In *The Forgotten Trinity 3: A Selection of Papers Presented to the BCC Study Commission on Trinitarian Doctrine Today,* 103–22. London: BCC, 1990.

———. "Baptist Ecclesiology: A Response to David Carter's Article Review of *Tracks and Traces.*" *Ecclesiology* 1 (2005) 93–100.

———. *Bound to Love: The Covenant Basis of Baptist Life and Mission,* 50–62. London: Baptist Union, 1985.

———. *A Call to Mind: Baptist Essays towards a Theology of Commitment.* London: Baptist Union, 1981.

———. *Charismatic Renewal: A Baptist View.* London: Baptist Union, 1980.

———. "Christianity, Culture and Education: A Baptist Perspective." In *The Scholarly Vocation and the Baptist Academy: Essays on the Future of Baptist Higher Education,* edited by Roger Ward and David Gushee, 1–25. Macon, GA: Mercer, 2008.

———. "Church and Sect: Cross-Currents in Early Baptist Life." In *Exploring Baptist Origins,* edited by Anthony R. Cross and Nicholas J. Wood, 33–57. Oxford: Centre for Baptist History and Heritage Studies, 2010.

———. "The Church Local and Universal: Catholic and Baptist Perspectives on *Koinonia* Ecclesiology." In *Revisioning, Renewing, Rediscovering the Triune Center: Essays in Honor of Stanley J. Grenz,* edited by Derek J. Tidball et al., 97–120. Eugene, OR: Cascade, 2014.

———. "Covenant—Old and New." In *Bound to Love: The Covenant Basis of Baptist Life and Mission,* edited by Paul Fiddes, 9–23. London: Baptist Union, 1985.

———. "Covenant and the Inheritance of Separatism." In *The Fourth Strand of the Reformation,* edited by Paul S. Fiddes, 63–91. Oxford: Centre for Baptist History and Heritage Studies, 2018.

———. *The Creative Suffering of God.* Oxford: Oxford University Press, 1988.

———, ed. *Doing Theology in a Baptist Way.* Oxford: Whitley, 2000.

———. "Koinonia: The Church In and For the World." In *Baptists Faith and Witness Book,* edited by Eron Henry, 5:37–49. Falls Church, Virginia: Baptist World Alliance, 2015.

———. *A Leading Question.* London: Baptist Union, 1984.

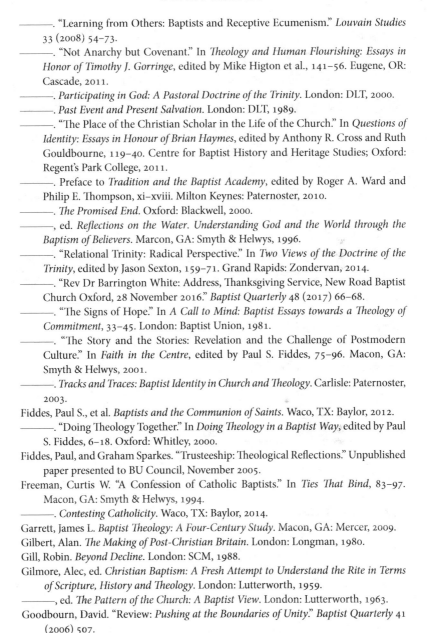

———. "Learning from Others: Baptists and Receptive Ecumenism." *Louvain Studies* 33 (2008) 54–73.

———. "Not Anarchy but Covenant." In *Theology and Human Flourishing: Essays in Honor of Timothy J. Gorringe*, edited by Mike Higton et al., 141–56. Eugene, OR: Cascade, 2011.

———. *Participating in God: A Pastoral Doctrine of the Trinity*. London: DLT, 2000.

———. *Past Event and Present Salvation*. London: DLT, 1989.

———. "The Place of the Christian Scholar in the Life of the Church." In *Questions of Identity: Essays in Honour of Brian Haymes*, edited by Anthony R. Cross and Ruth Gouldbourne, 119–40. Centre for Baptist History and Heritage Studies; Oxford: Regent's Park College, 2011.

———. Preface to *Tradition and the Baptist Academy*, edited by Roger A. Ward and Philip E. Thompson, xi–xviii. Milton Keynes: Paternoster, 2010.

———. *The Promised End*. Oxford: Blackwell, 2000.

———, ed. *Reflections on the Water. Understanding God and the World through the Baptism of Believers*. Marcon, GA: Smyth & Helwys, 1996.

———. "Relational Trinity: Radical Perspective." In *Two Views of the Doctrine of the Trinity*, edited by Jason Sexton, 159–71. Grand Rapids: Zondervan, 2014.

———. "Rev Dr Barrington White: Address, Thanksgiving Service, New Road Baptist Church Oxford, 28 November 2016." *Baptist Quarterly* 48 (2017) 66–68.

———. "The Signs of Hope." In *A Call to Mind: Baptist Essays towards a Theology of Commitment*, 33–45. London: Baptist Union, 1981.

———. "The Story and the Stories: Revelation and the Challenge of Postmodern Culture." In *Faith in the Centre*, edited by Paul S. Fiddes, 75–96. Macon, GA: Smyth & Helwys, 2001.

———. *Tracks and Traces: Baptist Identity in Church and Theology*. Carlisle: Paternoster, 2003.

Fiddes, Paul S., et al. *Baptists and the Communion of Saints*. Waco, TX: Baylor, 2012.

———. "Doing Theology Together." In *Doing Theology in a Baptist Way*, edited by Paul S. Fiddes, 6–18. Oxford: Whitley, 2000.

Fiddes, Paul, and Graham Sparkes. "Trusteeship: Theological Reflections." Unpublished paper presented to BU Council, November 2005.

Freeman, Curtis W. "A Confession of Catholic Baptists." In *Ties That Bind*, 83–97. Macon, GA: Smyth & Helwys, 1994.

———. *Contesting Catholicity*. Waco, TX: Baylor, 2014.

Garrett, James L. *Baptist Theology: A Four-Century Study*. Macon, GA: Mercer, 2009.

Gilbert, Alan. *The Making of Post-Christian Britain*. London: Longman, 1980.

Gill, Robin. *Beyond Decline*. London: SCM, 1988.

Gilmore, Alec, ed. *Christian Baptism: A Fresh Attempt to Understand the Rite in Terms of Scripture, History and Theology*. London: Lutterworth, 1959.

———, ed. *The Pattern of the Church: A Baptist View*. London: Lutterworth, 1963.

Goodbourn, David. "Review: *Pushing at the Boundaries of Unity*." *Baptist Quarterly* 41 (2006) 507.

Goodhew, David, ed. *Church Growth in Britain 1980 to the Present*. Farnham: Ashgate, 2010.

Goodland, Patrick. "Mainstream Reflections: The First Decade." *Mainstream Magazine* 63 (1998) 16–18.

Goodliff, Andy. "Brian Haymes: Doing Theology for the Church." *Baptist Quarterly* 50 (2019) 30–38.

——. "Keith Clements—a Baptist Ecumenist." *Pacific Journal of Baptist Research* 13 (2018) 44–49.

——. "Nigel Wright's Radical Baptist Theology." *Baptist Quarterly* 48 (2017) 69–77.

——. "Women and the Institution: The Struggle for Women to Be Involved in the Baptist Union at the End of the Twentieth Century." *Journal of Baptist Theology in Context* 1 (2020) 21–36.

Goodliff, Paul W. "Contemporary Models of Translocal Ministry: A Critical Appraisal." In *Translocal Ministry*, edited by Stuart Murray, 55–63. Didcot: Baptist Union, 2004.

——. *Ministry, Sacrament and Representation: Ministry and Ordination in Contemporary Baptist Theology, and the Rise of Sacramentalism.* Oxford: Regent's Park College, 2010.

——. "Networks." Unpublished paper written for the Futures Process, 2012.

——. *Shaped for Service.* Eugene, OR: Pickwick, 2017.

Gouldbourne, Ruth. "Episcope without Episcopacy: Baptist Attitudes to the Bishops in Seventeenth-Century England." In *Interfaces, Baptist and Others*, edited by David Bebbington, 29–46. Milton Keynes: Paternoster, 2013.

——. "Messengers: Do They Have a Message for Us?" In *Translocal Ministry*, edited by Stuart Murray, 24–32. Didcot: Baptist Union, 2004).

Grant, John W. *Free Churchmanship in England, 1870–1940.* London: Independent, 1955.

Griffith, Terry. "Instruments, Processes and the Gospel." Editorial. *Mainstream Newsletter* 31 (1989) 2.

Gunton, Colin. *The Promise of Trinitarian Theology.* 2nd ed. Edinburgh: T. & T. Clark, 1997.

Harmon, Steven R. *Baptist Identity and the Ecumenical Future: Story, Tradition and the Recovery of Community.* Waco, TX: Baylor, 2016.

——. *Towards Baptist Catholicity.* Milton Keynes: Paternoster, 2006.

——. "Trinitarian Koinonia and Ecclesial Oikoumene: Paul Fiddes as Ecumenical Theology." *Perspectives in Religious Studies* 44 (2017) 19–37.

Hastings, Adrian. *A History of English Christianity 1920–2000.* 4th ed. London: SCM, 2001.

Hauerwas, Stanley. *A Better Hope.* Grand Rapids: Brazos, 2000.

Hayden, Roger, ed. *Baptist Union Documents, 1948–1977.* London: Baptist Historical Society, 1980.

——. "Baptists, Covenants and Confessions." In *Bound to Love: The Covenant Basis of Baptist Life and Mission*, edited by Paul Fiddes, 24–36. London: Baptist Union, 1985.

——. *English Baptist History and Heritage.* Didcot: Baptist Union, 2006.

——. "The Faith and Other Faiths." In *A Call to Mind: Baptist Essays towards a Theology of Commitment*, 46–54. London: Baptist Union, 1981.

——. "Leonard George Champion, 1907–1997." *Baptist Quarterly* 37 (1998) 211–12.

——, ed. *The Records of a Church of Christ in Bristol, 1640–1687.* Bristol: Bristol Record Society, 1974.

——. "The Stillness and the Dancing: An Appreciation of Leonard G. Champion." In *Bible, History, and Ministry: Essays for L. G. Champion on His Ninetieth Birthday,* edited by Roger Hayden and Brian Haymes, 1–8. Bristol: Bristol Baptist College, 1997.

Haymes, Brian. "The Baptist and Pentecostal Churches." In *The Christian Church: An Introduction to the Major Traditions*, edited by Paul Avis, 107–31. London: SPCK, 2002.

———. *The Concept of the Knowledge of God*. Basingstoke: Macmillian, 1988.

———. "Covenant and the Church's Mission." In *Bound to Love: The Covenant Basis of Baptist Life and Mission*, edited by Paul Fiddes, 63–75. London: Baptist Union, 1985.

———. "Formation, Conviction and Gratitude." In *Why I Am a Baptist*, edited by Cecil P. Staton Jr., 63–69. Macon, GA: Smyth & Helwys, 1999.

———. "Longing for Authentic Christian Belonging and Discipleship." In *Coming Home: Stories of Anabaptists in Britain and Ireland*, edited by Alan Kreider and Stuart Murray, 63–64. Scottdale, PA: Pandora, 2000.

———. "On Being the Church." In *A Call to Mind: Baptist Essays towards a Theology of Commitment*, 55–67. London: Baptist Union, 1981.

———. *A Question of Identity*. Leeds: Yorkshire Baptist Association, 1986.

———. "Still Blessing the Ties That Bind." In *For the Sake of the Church: Essays to Honour Paul S. Fiddes*, edited by Anthony Clarke, 91–102. Oxford: Regent's Park College, 2014.

———. "Theology and Baptist Identity." In *Doing Theology in a Baptist Way*, edited by Paul S. Fiddes, 1–5. Oxford: Whitley, 2000.

———. "Towards a Classic Baptist Ecclesiology." Unpublished paper presented at the Baptist Union Denominational Conference September 6–8, 1996.

———. "Trinity and Participation: A Brief Introduction to the Theology of Paul S. Fiddes." *Perspectives in Religious Studies* 44 (2017) 7–18.

Haymes, Brian, et al. *On Being the Church: Revisioning Baptist Identity*. Milton Keynes: Paternoster, 2008.

Haymes, Brian, and Kyle Gingerich Hiebert. *God After Christendom*. Milton Keynes, Paternoster, 2015.

Healy, Nicholas M. *Church, World and the Christian Life*. Cambridge: Cambridge University Press, 2000.

Hembery, Steven. "Superintendents Revisited." *Mainstream Newsletter* 46 (1992) 7–8.

Hill, Graham. *Salt, Light, and a City: Introducing Missional Ecclesiology*. Eugene, OR: Wipf & Stock, 2012.

Hill, Phil. *The Baptist Revival Fellowship (1938–1972): A Study in Baptist Conservative Evangelicalism*. London: Apostolos, 2017.

———. *The Church of the Third Millennium*. Carlisle: Paternoster, 1999.

Hocken, Peter. *Streams of Renewal*. Carlisle: Paternoster, 1986.

———. *Streams of Renewal: Origins and Early Development of the Charismatic Movement in Great Britain*. 2nd ed. Carlisle: Paternoster, 1997.

Holmes, Stephen R. *Baptist Theology*. London: T. & T. Clark, 2012.

———. "The Dangers of Just Reading the Bible: Orthodoxy and Christology." In *Exploring Baptist Origins*, edited by Anthony R. Cross and Nicholas J. Wood, 123–37. Oxford: Regent's Park College, 2010.

———. *The Holy Trinity*. Milton Keynes: Paternoster, 2012.

———. *Listening to the Past*. Carlisle: Paternoster, 2002.

————. "Theology in Context?" Introduction to *Theology in Context*, 1–11. Oxford: Whitley, 2000.

————. "Three Versus One? Some Problems with Social Trinitarianism." *Journal of Reformed Theology* 3 (2009) 77–89.

————. "Trinitarian Missiology: Towards a Theology of God as Missionary." *International Journal for Systematic Theology* 8 (2006) 72–90.

Hopkins, Mark. "The Downgrade Controversy." In *Truth That Never Dies*, edited by Nigel Wright, 114–30. Eugene, OR: Pickwick, 2014.

————. *Nonconformity's Romantic Generation: Evangelical and Liberal Theologies in Victorian England*. Carlisle: Paternoster, 2004.

Houston, Tom. "The Church Growth Movement." *Fraternal* 179 (1977) 20–26.

————. "An Overview of the Context for Mission in Society." Unpublished paper presented at the Baptist Union Denominational Conference September 6–8, 1996.

Howard, Anthony. *Basil Hume: The Monk Cardinal*. London: Headline, 2005.

Ibbotson, Stephen. "Apostles amongst Fragments." *Talk: The Mainstream Magazine* 2 (2002) 15.

————. "The Variety of Worship." In *A Perspective on Baptist Identity*, edited by David Slater, 61–72. Ilkley: Mainstream, 1987.

Jackson, Darrell. "Attenders, Members, and Candlestick Makers in an LCF Age." In *Membership*, edited by Myra Blyth. Didcot: Baptist Union, 2004.

————. "The Discourse of 'Belonging' and Baptist Church Membership in Contemporary Britain: Historical, Theological and Demotic Elements of a Post-Foundational Theological Proposal." ThD diss., University of Birmingham, 2009.

————. "Does the Future Have a Denomination?" *Baptist Ministers' Journal* 277 (2002) 18–23.

Jones, Keith. "Baptists and Anabaptists Revisited." In *Exploring Baptist Origins*, edited by Anthony R. Cross and Nicholas Wood, 139–55. Oxford: Regent's Park College, 2010.

————. "The Believers' Church Needs to Act Radically." In *Coming Home: Stories of Anabaptists in Britain and Ireland*, edited by Alan Kreider and Stuart Murray, 72–74. Scottdale, PA: Pandora, 2000.

————. *A Believing Church*. Didcot: Baptist Union, 1998.

————. "Called to Be One." *SecCheck* 14 (1996).

————, ed. *Fellowship in the Gospel: Baptist Principles and Practice*. Leeds: Yorkshire Baptist Association, 1989.

————. *From Conflict to Communion*. Didcot: Baptist Union, 1997.

————. "Towards 2000: Progress to Date." *SecCheck* 9 (Summer 1994).

————. "Twentieth Century Baptists: People, Places and Principles; An Ecumenical Highpoint?" *Baptist Quarterly* (forthcoming).

Jones, Norman. *Preparation for Mission*. Living Issues. London: Baptist Union, 1965.

Kidd, Richard. "The Call to Be." In *A Call to Mind: Baptist Essays towards a Theology of Commitment*, 22–32. London: Baptist Union, 1981.

————. "The Documents of Covenant Love." In *Bound to Love: The Covenant Basis of Baptist Life and Mission*, edited by Paul Fiddes, 37–49. London: Baptist Union, 1985.

————, ed. *On the Way of Trust*. Oxford: Whitley, 1997.

————, ed. *Something to Declare. A Study of the Declaration of Principle*. Oxford: Whitley, 1996.

————. "Why 'Covenant' Remains a Crucial Word for Baptists." *Theology Themes* (1995) 13–15.

Kreider, Alan. *The Patient Ferment of the Early Church*. Grand Rapids: Baker, 2016.

Kreider, Alan, and Stuart Murray. *Coming Home: Stories of Anabaptists in Britain and Ireland*. Kitchener, Ontario: Pandora, 2000.

Lampard, Judith, ed. *Such a Feast: Spiritual Nourishment and the Churches*. London: Churches Together in England, 2001.

Lincoln, Andrew. *Ephesians*. Word Bible Commentary. Waco, TX: Word, 1990.

Lumpkin, W. L. *Baptist Confessions of Faith*. Valley Forge: Judson, 1959.

MacIntyre, Alasdair. *After Virtue*. 3rd ed. Duckworth, 2007.

Marchant, Colin. *Signs in the City*. London: Hodder & Stoughton, 1985.

Marshall, Glen. "After All It's Only the BU!" *Mainstream Magazine* 58 (1997) 17–21.

Marshall, I. Howard. *The Pastoral Epistles*. ICC. Edinburgh: T. & T. Clark, 1999.

Mason, Rex. "The End of an Outstanding Principalship." *Regent's Now* (Autumn 1989) 2.

McBain, Douglas. "Charismatic Apostles and Area Superintendents." January 18, 1982. Paul Beasley-Murray Papers.

————. *Eyes That See: The Spiritual Gift of Discernment*. London: Pickering, 1986.

————. *Fire over the Waters: Renewal among Baptists and Others from the 1960s to the 1990s*. London: DLT, 1997.

————. *No Gentle Breeze: Baptist Churchmanship and the Winds of Change*. N.d.: Mainstream, 1981.

————. "Responses to Signs of Hope." *Fraternal* 189 (1979) 14–21.

————. "Survival or Growth?" *Fraternal* 180 (1977) 11–18.

McClendon, James. *Ethics. Systematic Theology Volume 1*. Rev. ed. Nashville: Abingdon, 2002.

Medley, Mark S. "Stewards, Interrogators, and Inventors: Towards the Practice of Tradition." In *Tradition and the Baptist Academy*, edited by Roger A. Ward and Philip E. Thompson, 67–89. Milton Keynes: Paternoster, 2011.

Merkle, Benjamin L. *The Elder and the Overseer: One Office in the Early Church*. SBL 57. New York: Lang, 2003.

Migliore, Daniel. *Faith Seeking Understanding*. Grand Rapids: Eerdmans, 1991.

Millward, Craig. "Chalk and Cheese? An Account of the Impact of Restorationist Ecclesiology upon the Baptist Union." PhD diss., Brunel University, 2003.

Moon, Norman. *Education for Ministry*. Bristol: Bristol Baptist College, 1978.

Morden, Peter J. "Continuity and Change." In *Challenge and Change: English Baptist Life in the Eighteenth Century*, edited by Stephen Copson and Peter J. Morden, 1–28. Didcot: Baptist Historical Society, 2017.

————. *The Life and Thought of Andrew Fuller*. Milton Keynes: Paternoster, 2015.

Morgan, D. Densil. *Barth Reception in Britain*. London: T. & T. Clark, 2010.

Moyes, T. Watson. *Our Place among the Churches*. Scottish Baptist History Project, 2013.

Muddiman, John. *The Epistle to the Ephesians*. Black's New Testament Commentaries. London: Continuum, 2004.

Murray, Stuart. *Church After Christendom*. Milton Keynes: Paternoster, 2004.

————. "Church Planting, Peace and the Ecclesial Minimum." In *Challenging to Change: Dialogues with a Radical Baptist Theologian*, edited by Pieter J. Lalleman, 129–42. London: Spurgeon's College, 2009.

————. *Post Christendom*. Milton Keynes: Paternoster, 2004.

————, ed. *Translocal Ministry*. Didcot: Baptist Union, 2004.

"National Strategy Forum." *Baptist Leader* 28 (Winter 2001–2002).

Neuhaus, Richard, and Charles W. Colson, eds. *Evangelicals and Catholics Together: Toward a Common Mission*. Nashville: Nelson, 1995.

Newbigin, Lesslie. *The Gospel in a Pluralist Society*. London: SPCK, 1989.

Nicholls, Brian. "Regional Episcope and Local Church Mission." MTh diss., Oxford, 1997.

Nicholson, John F. V. "The Office of 'Messenger' amongst British Baptists in the 17th and 18th Centuries." *Baptist Quarterly* 27 (1957–1958) 206–25.

————. "Towards a Theology of Episcope." *Baptist Quarterly* 30.6 and 30.7 (1984) 265–81 and 319–31.

Orchard, Stephen. "Case Study 1: The formation of the United Reformed Church." In *Religion and Change in Modern Britain*, edited by Linda Woodhead and Rebecca Catto, 79–84. Abingdon: Routledge, 2012.

Palmer, Derek. *Strangers No Longer*. London: Hodder & Stoughton, 1990.

Parsons, Michael. "The Church as (Covenant) Community—Then and Now." In *Beyond 400: Exploring Baptist Futures*, edited by David J. Cohen and Michael Parsons, 207–21. Eugene, OR: Pickwick, 2011.

Payne, Ernest A. *The Baptist Union: A Short History*. London: Carey Kingsgate, 1959.

————. *Between Yesterday and Tomorrow: The Church Facing the Future*. 1970 Diamond Jubilee Lecture. London: London Preacher's Association, 1970.

————. *The Fellowship of Believers: Baptist Thought and Practice Yesterday and Today*. London: Carey, 1952.

————. *Free Churchmen: Unrepentant and Repentant*. London: Carey Kingsgate, 1965.

————. *Thirty Years of British Council of Churches 1942–1972*. London: British Council of Churches, 1972.

Payne, Ernest, and Stephen Winward. *Orders and Prayers for Christian Worship*. London: Carey Kingsgate, 1960.

Peck, Tony. "A National Pastoral Team." *Mainstream Magazine* 64 (1999) 4–6.

Pollard, Richard T. *Dan Taylor (1738–1816), Baptist Leader and Pioneer*. Eugene, OR: Pickwick, 2018.

Pushing at the Boundaries of Unity: Anglicans and Baptists in Conversation. London: Church House, 2005.

Ramsbottom, Jack. "Mainstream Memories." *Mainstream* 63 (1998) 21–22.

Randall, Ian. "Anabaptism and Mission: The British Experience 1980–2005." In *Anabaptism and Mission*, edited by Wilbert R. Shenk and Peter F. Penner, 145–65. Schwarzenfeld: Neufeld Verlag, 2007.

————. "Baptist-Anabaptist Identity among European Baptists since 1950." In *Baptists and the World*, edited by John H. Y. Briggs and Anthony R. Cross, 133–51. Oxford: Centre for Baptist History & Heritage, 2011.

————. "Baptist Growth in Britain." In *Church Growth in Britain: 1980 to the Present*, edited by David Goodhew, 59–76. Aldershot: Ashgate, 2012.

————. "A Believing Church: Baptist Perspectives on Anabaptism." *Baptistic Theologies* 5 (2013) 16–34.

————. *Communities of Conviction*. Schwarzenfeld: Neufeld Verlag, 2009.

————. *The English Baptists in the 20th Century*. Didcot: Baptist Historical Society, 2005.

————. *Evangelical Experiences: A Study in Spirituality of English Evangelicalism 1918–1939.* Carlisle: Paternoster, 1999.

————. "History's Lessons for the Great Leap Forward." Interview by Simon Jones. *Talk: The Mainstream Magazine* 5 (2005) 4–7.

————. "Mission in Post-Christendom: Anabaptist and Free Church Perspectives." *Evangelical Quarterly* 79 (2007) 227–40.

————. "Part of a Movement: Nigel Wright and Baptist Life." In *Challenging to Change: Dialogues with a Radical Baptist Theologian,* edited by Pieter J. Lalleman, 143–62. London: Spurgeon's College, 2009.

————. *A School of Prophets: 150 years of Spurgeon's College.* London: Spurgeon's College, 2005.

Randall, Ian, and David Hilborn. *One Body in Christ.* Carlisle: Paternoster, 2001.

Rees, Frank. "Trinity and the Church." *Pacifica* 17 (2004) 251–67.

Reynolds, Geoffrey. "75 Years of the General Superintendency—What Next?" *Baptist Quarterly* 34 (1992) 229–39.

————. *First among Equals: A Study of the Basis of Association and Oversight among Baptist Churches.* Bath: Berkshire, Southern and Oxfordshire and East Gloucestershire Baptist Associations, 1993.

Rinaldi, Frank. *"The Tribe of Dan": The New Connexion of General Baptists, 1770–1891.* Milton Keynes: Paternoster, 2008.

Robinson, Henry Wheeler. *The Life and Faith of the Baptists.* London: Methuen, 1927.

Rowlandson, Maurice L. *Life at the Keswick Convention: A Personal Recollection.* N.d.: OM, 1997.

Rusling, Geoffrey W. "David Syme Russell: A Life of Service." In *Bible, Church and World,* edited by John H. Y. Briggs, 4–20. London: Baptist Historical Society, 1989.

Russell, David. *In Journeyings Often.* London: Baptist House, 1981.

Sarisky, Darren. "Tradition II: Thinking with Historical Texts—Reflections on Theologies of Retrieval." In *Theologies of Retrieval,* edited by Darren Sarisky, 193–209. London: T. & T. Clark, 2017.

Scott, Benjamin G. McNair. *Apostles Today: Making Sense of Contemporary Charismatic Apostolates; A Historical and Theological Appraisal.* Cambridge: Lutterworth, 2014.

Shepherd, Peter. "The Baptist Union's Ministerial Settlement and Sustentation Scheme: The End of Congregational Church Polity." *Baptist Quarterly* 38 (2000) 277–89.

————. "Denominational Renewal: A Study in English Baptist Church Life and Growth 1901–1906." *Baptist Quarterly* 37 (1998) 336–50.

————. *The Making of a Modern Denomination: John Howard Shakespeare and the English Baptists 1898–1924.* Carlisle: Paternoster, 2001.

————. "The Renewal of the Union." *Baptist Minsters' Journal* 256 (1996) 21–24.

Slater, David. *A Perspective on Baptist Identity.* Ilkley: Mainstream, 1987.

Smail, Tom. *Reflected Glory.* London: Hodder & Stoughton, 1975.

Sparkes, Douglas C. *The Constitutions of the Baptist Union of Great Britain.* Didcot: Baptist Historical Society, 1996.

————. *The Offices of the Baptist Union of Great Britain.* Didcot: Baptist Historical Society, 1996.

Stackhouse, Ian. *The Gospel-Driven Church.* Milton Keynes: Paternoster, 2004.

Standing, Roger, ed. *As a Fire by Burning: Mission as Life of the Local Congregation.* London: SCM, 2013.

Stanley, Brian. "The BMS, Baptist Associations, and the Churches: An Historical Perspective." Unpublished paper for the Fellowship of British Baptist Working Group, April 1995.

———. *Christianity in the Twentieth Century: A World History*. Princeton: Princeton University Press, 2018.

———. *The Global Diffusion of Evangelicalism: The Age of Billy Graham and John Stott*. Leicester: InterVarsity, 2013.

———. *The History of the Baptist Missionary Society, 1792–1992*. Edinburgh: T. & T. Clark, 1992.

———. "Looking towards the Future: Which Way Forward for British Baptists in Mission." Unpublished paper for the Fellowship of British Baptist Working Group, November 1996.

———. "Renewing a Vision for Mission among British Baptists." In *Truth That Never Dies*, edited by Nigel Wright, 185–202. Eugene, OR: Pickwick, 2014.

Stewart, Alistair C. *The Original Bishops: Office and Order in the First Christian Communities*. Grand Rapids: Baker, 2014.

Stott, John. *Christian Mission in the Modern World*. Leicester: InterVarsity, 2008.

———. *The Contemporary Christian*. Leicester: InterVarsity, 1992.

———. "The Living God Is a Missionary God." In *Perspectives on the World Christian Movement*, edited by Ralph Winter and Steven Hawthorne, 10–18. William Carey Library, 1981.

Sutcliffe-Pratt, Daniel. *Covenant and Church for Rough Sleepers*. Oxford: Centre for Baptist History and Heritage, 2017.

Synder, Harold A. *Signs of the Spirit*. Grand Rapids: Zondervan, 1989.

Taylor, Michael H. *Baptists for Unity*. Coventry: Reynolds, 1968.

Thompson, Arthur. "An Open Letter to Dr. David Russell." *Mainstream Newsletter* 3 (1979) 2–4.

Thompson, David M., ed. *Protestant Nonconformist Texts*. Vol. 4, *The Twentieth Century*. With John H. Y. Briggs and John Munsey Turner. Aldershot: Ashgate, 2007.

Tidball, Derek. *Catching the Tide: The Church and the Challenge of Today's Society*. Didcot: Baptist Union, 1989.

———. "Mainstream: 'Far Greater Ambitions'—an Evaluation of Mainstream's Contribution to the Renewal of Denominational Life, 1979–1994." In *Grounded in Grace: Essays to Honour Ian M. Randall*, edited by Pieter J. Lalleman et al., 202–22. London: Spurgeon's College, 2013.

———. "Presidential Address: Church Growth; Has it Failed? Reflections on 25 Years of British Church Growth Advocacy." *Church Growth Digest* 22 (2001) 1–3.

———. "A Response to *A Question of Identity*." In *A Perspective on Baptist Identity*, edited by D. Slater, 7–16. Ilkley: Mainstream, 1987.

———. "What's Right with Evangelicalism?" In *British Evangelical Identities Past and Present*, edited by Mark Smith, 253–69. Milton Keynes: Paternoster, 2008.

———. *Who Are the Evangelicals?* London: Marshall Pickering, 1994.

Underwood, A. C. *A History of the English Baptists*. London: Carey Kingsgate, 1947.

Virgo, Terry. "Apostles Today?" *Mainstream Magazine* 64 (1999) 12–17.

———. *No Well Worn Paths*. Eastbourne: Kingsway, 2001.

Voas, David. "The Church of England." In *Growth and Decline in the Anglican Communion: 1980 to the Present*, edited by David Goodhew, 269–91. London: Routledge, 2016.

Volf, Miroslav. *After Our Likeness: The Church as the Image of the Trinity*. Grand Rapids: Eerdmans, 1998.

———. "Kirche als Gemeinschaft." *Evangelische Theologie* 49 (1989) 52–76.

Wainwright, Geoffrey. *Lesslie Newbigin: A Theology Life*. Oxford: Oxford University Press, 2000.

Walton, Robert C. *The Gathered Community*. London: Carey, 1946.

Ward, Pete. *Selling Worship*. Milton Keynes: Paternoster, 2005.

———. "The Tribes of Evangelicalism." In *The Post-Evangelical Debate*, 19–34. Oxford: Triangle, 1997.

Warner, Rob. *21st Century Church*. Eastbourne: Kingsway, 1993.

———. "Ageing Structures and Undying Convictions." *Mainstream Magazine* 58 (1997) 12–17.

———. "Baptist Evangelicals and Evangelical Baptists." Editorial. *Mainstream Newsletter* 45 (1992) 1.

———. "Baptists in Renewal—a New Mainstream Network?" Editorial. *Mainstream Magazine* 46 (1992) 1.

———. "British Baptists—a New Wave of Growth." *Alpha* (1991) 18–20.

———. "The Charter for the Charismatic Baptist Network." Unpublished paper, February 1993. Paul Beasley-Murray papers.

———. "Mainstream—a Troublesome Irritant?" *Mainstream Magazine* 63 (1998) 28–31.

———. *Prepare for Revival*. London: Hodder & Stoughton, 1995.

———. *Reinventing English Evangelicalism, 1966–2001*. Milton Keynes: Paternoster, 2007.

———. "Transformations of English Evangelicalism." *Anvil* 26.3 and 4 (2009) 209–17.

Warner, Rob, and Cliver Calver. *Together We Stand: Evangelical Convictions, Unity and Vision*. London: Hodder & Stoughton, 1996.

Warren, Robert. *Building Missionary Congregations*. London: CHP, 1995.

Watson, Hubert L. "The General Superintendents." *Baptist Quarterly* 25 (1973) 146–50.

West, W. Morris. *Baptist Principles*. London: Baptist Union, 1960.

———. *Baptists Together*. Prepared by J. H. Y. Briggs and Faith Bowers. Didcot: Baptist Historical Society, 2000.

———. *Church, Ministry and Baptism: Two Essays on Current Questions*. London: Baptist Union, 1981.

———. "Lund Principle." In *Dictionary of the Ecumenical Movement*, edited by Nicholas Lossky et al., 714–15. 2nd ed. Geneva: World Council of Churches, 2002.

———. *To Be a Pilgrim: A Memoir of Earnest A. Payne*. Guildford: Lutterworth, 1983.

Whalley, Ernie. "Life in Christian Service." *Baptistic Theologies* 5 (2013) 1–15.

"What Is a Missionary Congregation?" *Baptist Leader* 18 (Winter 1997–1998).

White, B. R. "The Denominational Enquiry and the Local Church." *Mainstream Newsletter* 2 (1979) 2–3.

———. *The English Baptists of the Seventeenth Century*. Rev. ed. Didcot: Baptist Historical Society, 1996.

———. *The English Separatist Tradition*. Oxford: Oxford University Press, 1971.

———. "Inter-congregational Authority among the Baptists." Unpublished paper presented at Mainstream Conference, 1983.

———. *Opening Doors to God*. Mainstream, 1980.

————. "The Practice of Association." In *A Perspective on Baptist Identity*, edited by David Slater, 19–29. Ilkley: Mainstream, 1987.

————. "The Task of a Baptist Historian." *Baptist Quarterly* 22 (1968) 398–408.

White, Barrie. "The Beginning of an Exciting New Era." *Regent's Now* (Autumn 1989) 132–33.

Wilkinson-Hayes, Anne. "Lending Greater Integrity to Being Church." In *Coming Home: Stories of Anabaptists in Britain and Ireland*, edited by Alan Kreider and Stuart Murray, 132–33. Scottdale, PA: Pandora, 2000.

Williamson, Roger. "The Defence of Human Dignity: Dr David Russell and the Ecumenical Commitment to Human Rights." In *Bible, Church and World*, edited by John H. Y. Briggs, 35–45. London: Baptist Historical Society, 1989.

Willmer, Haddon. "A Defence of Theology." *Baptist Ministers' Journal* 256 (1996) 15–19.

————. "Taking Responsibility." In *20/20 Visions: The Futures of Christianity in Britain*, edited by Haddon Willmer, 136–54. London: SPCK, 1992.

Winter, Sean. *"More Light and Truth?" Biblical Interpretation in Covenantal Perspective.* Whitley Lecture 2007. Oxford: Whitley, 2007.

————. *"Tracks and Traces*: A Review Article." *Baptist Quarterly* 41 (2006) 439–46.

————. "Translocal Ministry: New Testament Perspectives." In *Translocal Ministry* edited by Stuart Murray, 14–23. Didcot: Baptist Union, 2004.

————. "Reflections on a Baptist Theology of Mission: A Discussion Starter for the Doctrine and Worship Committee." Unpublished paper, September, 2003.

Woodhead, Linda, and Rebecca Catto, eds. *Religion and Change in Modern Britain.* Abingdon: Routledge, 2012.

Wright, Nigel. "An Agenda for Baptist Christians." *Mainstream Newsletter* 35 (1990) 2–4.

————. "A Baptist Evaluation." In *John Wimber: His Influence and Legacy*, edited by David Pytches, 244–56. Guilford: Eagle, 1998.

————. "The Baptist Way of Being Church." In *A Perspective on Baptist Identity*, edited by David Slater, 41–45. Ilkley, UK: Mainstream, 1987.

————. "Becoming a Denomination Worth Joining." *Talk: The Mainstream Magazine* 1 (2001) 18.

————. "Book Review: *Past Event and Present Salvation.*" *Mainstream Newsletter* 35 (1990) 13.

————. "The Case for Translocal Ministry." In *Translocal Ministry*, edited by Stuart Murray, 4–23. Didcot: Baptist Union, 2004.

————. "Catching the Bell Rope." *Anabaptism Today* 1 (1992) 17–20.

————. "The Challenge of the 'House Church' Movement." *Mainstream Newsletter* 5 (1980) 5–7.

————. *Challenge to Change: A Radical Agenda for Baptists.* Eastbourne: Kingsway, 1991.

————. "The Charismata and the Second Naïveté." In *The Wisdom of the Spirit: Gospel, Church and Culture*, edited by Martyn Percy and Pete Ward, 127–38. Farnham: Ashgate, 2014.

————. "Covenant and Covenanting." *Baptist Quarterly* 39 (2002) 287–90.

————. *Disavowing Constantine: Mission, Church and the Social Order in the Theologies of John Howard Yoder and Jürgen Moltmann.* Carlisle: Paternoster, 2000.

————. "Disestablishment: A Contemporary View from the Free Churches." *Anvil* 12 (1995) 121–35.

———. "Disestablishment—Loss for the Church or the Country? A Dissenting Perspective." *Journal of European Baptist Studies* 4 (2004) 22–32.

———. "Does Revival Quicken or Deaden the Church? A Comparison of the 1904 Welsh Revival and John Wimber in the 1980s and 1990s." In *On Revival: A Critical Examination*, edited by Andrew Walker and Kristin Aune, 121–35. Carlisle: Paternoster, 2003.

———. *The Fair Face of Evil: Putting the Powers of Darkness in their Place*. London: Marshall Pickering, 1989.

———. *Free Church, Free State: A Positive Baptist Vision*. Milton Keynes: Paternoster, 2005.

———. "From Poacher to President." *Talk: The Mainstream Magazine* 2 (2002) 18.

———. "Gleanings from the North West." *Mainstream Newsletter* 9 (1982) 4–6.

———. *God on the Inside: The Holy Spirit in Holy Scripture*. Oxford: Bible Reading Fellowship, 2006.

———. "Government as an Ambiguous Power." In *God and Government*, edited by Nick Spencer and Jonathan Chaplin, 16–39. London: SPCK, 2009.

———. "Inclusively Exclusive." *Talk: The Mainstream Magazine* 6 (2006) 27.

———. "'Koinonia' and Baptist Ecclesiology: Self-Critical Reflections from Historical and Systematic Perspectives." *Baptist Quarterly* 35 (1994) 365–75.

———. "My Life with Mainstream." *Mainstream Magazine* 63 (1998) 33–35.

———. *New Baptists, New Agenda*. Carlisle: Paternoster, 2002.

———. "The Petrine Ministry: Baptist Reflections." *Pro Ecclesia* 13 (2004) 451–65.

———. "A Pilgrimage in Renewal." In *Charismatic Renewal: The Search for a Theology*, edited by Thomas Smail et al., 22–32. London: SPCK, 1995.

———. *The Radical Evangelical: Seeking a Place to Stand*. London: SPCK, 1996.

———. *The Radical Kingdom*. Eastbourne: Kingsway, 1986.

———. "Still a Case for Baptist Bishops." *Talk: The Mainstream Magazine* 2 (2002) 26.

———. "Spirituality as Discipleship." In *Under the Rule of Christ: Dimensions of Baptists Spirituality*, edited by Paul S. Fiddes, 79–101. Macon, GA: Smyth & Helwys, 2008.

———. "Sustaining Evangelical Identity: Faithfulness and Freedom in Denominational Life." In *Truth Never Dies*, edited by Nigel Wright, 203–22. Eugene, OR: Pickwick, 2014.

———. "Theology in the Service of the Church." *Journal of European Baptist Studies* 2 (2001) 33–38.

———. *A Theology of Mission*. Didcot: Baptist Union, 1990.

———. "The 'Three-Fold Order' in a Radical Protestant Perspective." In *For the Sake of the Church: Essays in Honour of Paul S. Fiddes*, edited by Anthony Clarke, 145–62. Oxford: Regent's Park College, 2014.

———. "Time to Associate." *Mainstream Magazine* 62 (1998) 9–12.

———, ed. *Truth Never Dies: The Dr. G. R. Beasley-Murray Memorial Lectures 2002–2012*. Eugene, OR: Pickwick, 2014.

Wright, Nigel. *Charismatic Renewal: The Search for a Theology*. With Tom Smail and Andrew Walker. London: SPCK, 1995.

Zizioulas, John. *Being as Communion*. Crestwood, NY: St Vladimir's Seminary Press, 1985.

Index

af

n
s
o